Alternative Realities is a travelogue, a memoir, a satire and a feminist critique of Muslim women's lives, interwoven with the author's own ongoing struggles as a Muslim woman.

Each chapter presents personal stories of women living in cities, small towns and villages in India, Pakistan and Bangladesh—the three lands to which Nighat Gandhi belongs. In writing their stories, she attempts to break the silence enshrouding Muslim women's sexuality, and the ways in which they negotiate the restrictions placed on their freedoms within the framework of their culture. Women like Ghazala, who prefers the life of a second wife, 'living like a married single woman', to being bound within the ties of a conventional marriage; Nusrat and QT who believe theirs is a normal marriage, except that they are both women; Nisho, who refuses to accept that her transsexuality should deny her the right to love, and Firdaus, writer and feminist, who can walk out of a loveless marriage but not give up on love, with or without marriage.

Nighat also explores her own story as a woman who dared to make choices that pitted her against her family and cultures. *Alternative Realities* is her jihad or struggle to deconstruct the demeaning stereotypes that prevail about all Muslim women. It is a reflection of the myriad ways in which, despite these misogynistic forces, they continue to weave webs of love and peace in their own lives and in the lives of those they live with.

~

Nighat Gandhi is a writer, mother, Sufi wanderer, and mental health counsellor. She spent her formative years in Dhaka and Karachi, and has subsequently spent many years in India and the United States. She consciously identifies as a citizen of South Asia to transcend limitations imposed by narrow nationalisms. She is the author of *Ghalib at Dusk and Other Stories* (Tranquebar, 2009) and *What I am Today, I Won't Remain Tomorrow: Conversations With Survivors of Abuse* (Yoda Press, 2010).

ALTERNATIVE REALITIES

Love in the Lives of Muslim Women

Nighat M. Gandhi

TRANQUEBAR

TRANQUEBAR PRESS
An imprint of westland ltd
61, Silverline Building, Alapakkam Main Road, Maduravoyal, Chennai 600 095
No. 38/10 (New No.5), Raghava Nagar, New Timber Yard Layout, Bangalore 560 026
93, 1st Floor, Sham Lal Road, Daryaganj, New Delhi 110 002

First published in India by Tranquebar, an imprint of westland ltd, 2013

The chapter 'Siraat-e-Mustaqeem—The Straight Path' (p. 139) first appeared in the October 2012 issue of the *Journal of Lesbian Sexuality*.

10 9 8 7 6 5 4 3 2 1

ISBN: 978-93-83260-32-4

Typeset in Aldine401 BT by SÜRYA, New Delhi
Printed at Thomson Press (India) Limited

Afreen texted me on a day I was feeling particularly despondent about completing this book: 'Say what you feel emphatically, or you may stagnate the growth of something beautiful and regret it later.'

This book is dedicated to all who love and live emphatically.

Contents

Acknowledgements

I owe my deepest gratitude to all who shared their life stories with me. Some did not become a part of this book, but continue to enrich my heart, and perhaps belong to another book. Thanks to relatives and friends, and friends' relatives who threw open their homes for me. Without their open-hearted hospitality it wouldn't be possible to find safe and comfortable places to stay as a woman travelling alone, especially in places with no hotels or hostels. Without the unwavering support and encouragement of my daughters, I wouldn't have been able to leave them as often as I did to go off on my journeys. And without the chequered life lived in my three homelands, this book would be inconceivable. So, shukriya India, Pakistan, and Bangladesh.

Preface

What is this book about? A travelogue, a memoir, biography? A book about Muslim women? Why women? Why only Muslim? Let me tell you how I came to write this book. In telling you of the hows, the whys and whats might emerge.

Some of the hows: How I chafed at the tiresome image propagated by the media of the Muslim woman as oppressed, veiled, victimized, with no voice of her own. How I wanted to weave my loves into my writing. How those loves transformed me and eventually turned into the writing of this book. When I started thinking about— travelling, writing, meeting people—I realized how any unearthing of me was also about the revelations carried in things, places and people. Disclosures about me were about me to the extent that they were about my impressions and interactions with things, places and people. I wandered for three years in my three homelands collecting these impressions. In towns and villages of India, Pakistan, Bangladesh, meeting women in these villages and towns, and in their kitchens, courtyards and workplaces, we spoke of their loves and mine.

Al-Ghazali, the eleventh-century Sufi psychologist and philosopher, valued travel as an indispensable tool for spiritual growth. True travel, or safar, according to Ghazali was not just the physical movement of a traveller from one place to another. Safar was about the inner journey of the heart and mind that revealed the truth of one to oneself, and took one closer to that state known variously as enlightenment, self-realization, self-knowledge, *satori*, *fana*— the sort of intimacy with ourselves of which we are all seekers in some measure. My safar to places of my past led me to intimacy with myself. Revealed who I am to me.

Every so often during my journeys I met people, or arrived at places that seemed so perfect in their tininess and caring that the heart ached to settle down, not move on. I tore myself away though the desire to tarry was great, the invitations many! Rent a cottage in the mountains, shack up at the edge of some village, or reside in a Buddhist nunnery? The eighteenth-century Sufi poet of Sind, Shah Abdul Latif Bhitai wandered the forests in the company of yogis before building his abode in the wilderness outside his hometown, where he lived in exile and composed exquisite poetry about seekers and lovers who journeyed for union with Truth. Bhitai had warned about the human tendency to confuse campgrounds with permanence, and only the determined could hope to steer clear:[1]

---

[1] *Shah jo Risalo*: Collection of Shah Abdul Latif Bhitai's verse, translated into Urdu from Sindhi by Shaikh Ayaz.

jis se guzre hain beniyazana
Raah aisi bhi ek nikali hai

that which can be traversed unattached;
such a singular path the seeker carves

Another how: How do I justify writing this book in an over-booked world, with far more books than readers? Is artistic creation always an act of self-cherishing? And my answer is yes, the ego is definitely involved in the production of art. Who in the world cares about me writing this book more than I do? But then what artist can make art without passionate desire? Egotistical striving is only a partial explanation because the inspiration for making art seems to come from somewhere deep inside or beyond the self. Whenever I want to give up, something urges me on. And whenever I write under the influence of that something, unburdened by questions of value or worth, whatever I write in those hours is devoid of the scathing criticism, inertia, judgment and insecurities of my ego.

How do I overcome the ego's admonitions?

Another mysterious how. The rain had been coming down for the third day in a row. Incessant, soft rain, which increased its pace at times, then slowed down to a whimper. Like a lover constantly murmuring of the caprices of an unfaithful beloved, it never stopped completely. I went out into the garden of the Buddhist mountain nunnery, and walked over the wet gravelly path with a strange, quiet pleasure. There was a lovely little snail, sprawled out on the wire fence. There was just a single branch of a rose bush with a profusion of loud, red roses. And beyond the fence lay the field. And in the field, a massive boulder. And on the boulder, a solitary singing bird. The water was making its way down the terraced fields to the river, and in its gurgle, in the lonely melody of the bird, and in the stillness of the snail on the fence, was the answer to all the depression and self-questioning about the value of my writing. Doubts and fears were nothing but mental projections. For where were they this morning? Just as it is said in Buddhism, they were fleeting mental states. If they were real, where had they vanished to? As I gazed up at the mountains beyond the fields, I saw the silver-grey mist covering them. The creative self is like the mountains hidden behind the mist of doubts and fears.

Now I want to tell you how I actually wrote this book. Where did I sit down to write? Writer's retreats in our part of the world are rare. I dreamed of such lonely corners in which I could be left alone to write without worries about personal security, food and laundry. I wrote some chapters during a one-month retreat at the nunnery in Himachal Pradesh. Some were composed sitting on the balcony of Dollar Villa in Dhaka, some in the verandah of a bamboo cottage in Sylhet, some in a cottage overlooking the Ganges in Varanasi. One chapter I wrote during a four-day solitary retreat at my in-laws' flat, another in a friend's apartment who left me her keys when she went to work. Hardly any were written in the family home. Most women who have tried writing seriously while living interruption-filled lives would understand why. Whether or not this book becomes a success, whatever success means, may the writing of it in bits and pieces spur me on to establish a writer's retreat. Failed fantasies fuel revolutions—to give women a room of their own gift-wrapped in solitude, uninterrupted by worries about laundry, meals and ceaseless availability. And may I find the means to offer such a room to writers free of cost, especially to those unsupported by plump wallets or lavish publisher's advances.

1

The Works

Photo: Suroor Seher

A temple and a mausoleum minaret side by side

Masjid dha de, mandir dha de
Dha de jo kuch dhainda
Par kisayda dil na dhaeen
Rab dilan wich rehnda

Demolish mosques, demolish temples
Demolish everything in sight
But never demolish a heart
For the heart is God's abode

    —Bulleh Shah, 18th century Sufi poet of Punjab

'The true focus of revolutionary change is never
merely the oppressive situations which we seek to
escape, but that piece of the oppressor which is planted
deep within each of us, and which knows only the
oppressors' tactics, the oppressor's relationships.'

    —Audre Lourde, *Sister Outsider*

June 1999, USA

Abba came to the table later than all of us. We were into our second and third slices of pizza by then. Juju removed a slice of the mushroom and onion pizza for him.

'Didn't you order anything with meat?' he asked. 'What's in that box?' he pointed at the other carton.

'Oh, that's all mixed things,' said Juju. I could sense the edginess in her voice.

'Mixed? What do you mean—mixed?' He pulled the carton towards himself, lifted the flap and stared at the glistening pink discs of pepperoni and chunks of sausage. 'What's all this?'

'It's all mixed,' Juju said in a begging voice.

'Mixed? You mean pork? You mean pig meat?' he snarled.

We stared at our plates as if we needed some words of deliverance to rent the stillness in the room.

'Is it pork?' Abba repeated in a voice that used to make my stomach heave as a child. Nobody answered.

'Who ordered it?'

Nobody looked up from their plates.

'How could you bring this haraam thing into my house?' he thundered. 'Who ordered it?'.

None of us said a word. None of us could. None of us had the courage to meet his eye. We stopped eating. Prayers of deliverance were still beating in our hearts but hopes were abandoned. The silence in the room expanded like an evil spirit. I wished for the world as we had known it to end—I prayed for some calamity, a crashing noise, a child's cry, an earthquake, anything, but nothing broke the intolerable silence.

'I ordered it,' I found myself saying, blood rushing to my twisted guts, some deep barrier giving way. Finally something was conquering the silence. I had waded through a thick gravy-like dread to break it.

'How could you do such a thing?' my father said, going redder, and becoming once more the man whose fury I feared most. My childhood had never really ended.

'I didn't know there'd be pork in it,' I said, almost stuttering on the forbidden word. I didn't tell him I went ahead and ordered it because I reasoned one could always remove those offending pieces of meat. We were adults after all. Nobody was compelled to eat what they found morally reprehensible. Besides, it was a good deal—the 'Works'— two large pizzas for just 17.99 dollars. He could have the mushroom and onion pizza. There was a deeper motive for ordering it, for inviting his wrath, though it wasn't apparent to my conscious mind, the one that seemed to have made the decision to order a pork pizza.

'I'm not a hypocrite, I'm not the one who prays five times a day and is filled with arrogance. And I don't care if a pizza has pork on it. That's not what it means to be a Muslim.' It was easier to proclaim this with an un-Islamic pizza than to say it in words.

'We are Muslims. Muslims don't eat pork. Don't you know that it's haraam, have you forgotten everything about your religion?' Abba's voice boomed like a maulvi's delivering the Friday sermon. It seemed as if the lamp shade over the table swayed with his voice. 'You all may have become Americans, but I'm still a Muslim who lives by Allah's rules and I haven't forgotten that eating pork is forbidden to Muslims.'

'You can remove the pork. You don't have to eat it,' I found the courage to say.

'Eat what's been contaminated by haraam meat? Is that what your advice is?'

Ammi got up alarmed, ever at his behest, and I looked at her: Are you going to let us down again? Let us down for him, like you always have? Why do I have to feel disappointed at her compliance still? She continues to disappoint, I continue to get disappointed. We've never been inconsistent in that way. But it wasn't the adult in me, it was the child who was disappointed. It was the child who wished she would once, just once, take a stand for her daughter's sake.

'Throw it away!' he ordered and my mother dutifully got up, whisking the forbidden pizza that threatened to undo our Muslimhood from the table. I heard the slices of the 'Works' slide into the garbage can, and the soft thud of the lid.

'When you go to a restaurant, do they fry your steak in a no-pork pan?' I persisted in using logic. I didn't know what was coming over me. 'They use the same pan for cooking all kinds of meat. So even your beef steak might be contaminated.' I needed to make my point, let everything out, let us drown. My stifled rage begged me to. Somebody had to needle the giant even if it unleashed a cyclone.

'I don't want your arguments!' he glared. 'What I've said is final.' Rational arguments were out of place with my father when you were trying to prove him wrong. But his own views on religious matters could never be called irrational or wrong—hadn't we learned that? Then why was I testing it?

'It's not as if I love pork.' I went on stubbornly, trembling with the weight of all that stored up resentment that was threatening to overflow if not allowed passage. 'Why couldn't you just eat the mushroom and onion pizza?'

'I will not listen to such obscenity from my own children.'

'There's nothing obscene or indecent in what I said. Maybe you can tell us why you never listen to what we have to say to you.' I blurted and walked out before my rage turned into tears and shamed me before him.

~

My sisters and I were independent women in our twenties and thirties when the sausage and pepperoni pizza incident took place. We were graduates from well-known American universities. And our father was visiting us that summer in the US, and yelling at us for ordering an offending pizza. And we allowed him to get away with it. Why? For the same reasons that the weak let the powerful get away. We had learnt to perceive ourselves powerless from the way we had seen our mother act around him. From her we had learnt to feel beholden to him for keeping us alive. In the end it boiled down to survival, to pure economics. Though we couldn't have articulated our helplessness in those two words in those days—survival and economics.

The rewriting of the pizza incident is a rare revisiting of old sorrows that have burrowed into my soul-soil over the years. A vague vestigial rage pushes up its soft head through that burial ground. Many meditations and supplications later, complete detachment is still an inaccessible goal—from entrenched traumas that can't be torn out from the walls of the heart; traumas that refuse to float away as specks from a previous life. More than two decades have passed, and the pain is not blunted enough to let me write this chapter disinterestedly. I stopped for months after writing the first page. My father's reddened face in the trembling yellow light over the dining table was staring at me. The words refused to flow, I couldn't go on.

The head still feels heavy and the gut even more twisted. Only something beyond conscious comprehension goads me on. You have to, you have to write it, is the call from the coiled guts. You have to heal yourself. The bloodletting has to begin.

~

My sisters had seen what Abba was capable of. When I married a Hindu, he completely cut off the economic umbilical cord connecting me to him. He ran his family as a dictatorship and I became a ready victim of his tyranny for committing the most heinous sin I could as a Muslim. I had run away from home and married a Hindu. No good Muslim woman does that. She can marry outside her faith, says Islam, but there's a rider to this rule: she can marry if her partner forsakes his faith and converts to Islam. My husband had no faith to forsake to begin with. So he agreed to undergo this conversion to Islam but a paper conversion wasn't enough to make a real Muslim out of him, said my father. Not until he adopted a Muslim name and started observing the five pillars of Islam,[1] could he think of my husband as a proper Muslim. He was right. My husband had agreed to the conversion but not to his name change: 'My name appears on my research papers, my passport, my degree. How can I change it to something else all of a sudden?'

In my father's eyes, he was born a Hindu, a non-believer, and Hindu he would remain all his life. A mere conversion ceremony wouldn't change his Hinduness.

When my sisters finally came upstairs later that night, they related how both of them had been separately interrogated, first by Abba, and then by Ammi about ordering the haraam pizza. Ammi could never condone such shocking misdemeanours. She could not defy her pious husband's injunctions about their shared faith. God, she could defy, but husband, no. My sisters were asked if they were regular

---

[1] The five pillars are the five duties incumbent upon all Muslims. They are: faith in One God and Mohammad, his last prophet; praying, fasting, giving of alms, and hajj—the pilgrimage to holy Kaba. This last pillar is an optional duty, to be performed only by those who can afford it.

consumers of pork, and God forbid, had they also started using that other haraam substance—alcohol?

My sisters, our mother and I, the four loyal subjects of my father's kingdom, had learned to preen and fine-tune our servility to please him. But, by the time I turned twenty-four, this fine-tuning, though it had become a part of my consciousness, started to rankle. I didn't need to think what would or wouldn't please my father: it had become part of my genetic code, wired into my neurons. I learned to keep my views to myself. But even repressed beliefs needed to come up for air sometimes. A father who always said he loved his daughters, believed in his daughters' education and freedom to pursue careers, believed in allowing his daughters to choose their husbands, provided they chose Muslim husbands who met his approval—such a father could be called principled, not narrow-minded. When it came to principles, I had absorbed some of my father's pluck.

Love was one such principle for which I was willing to take principled risks.

'Isn't a Hindu capable of loving a Muslim?' I asked my father.

'Love is not as important as doing the right thing,' he said. 'What's not right in the eyes of Allah, is not right for a Muslim.'

My father was a modern father. He never openly expressed any grief over the fact that Allah hadn't given him a male heir. My mother did. My father believed in women's education. It was he, who against my mother's wishes, sent all three of his daughters abroad for higher education. I felt crushed by his unfailing generosity—his allowances left me speechless, they mired me in indecision. He had been my ally—he had overruled my mother's objections and silenced wagging tongues of relatives to send me to England when I was barely seventeen, and later to the United States. My sisters followed after me. We were the only girls among my cousins to be educated abroad. Women my mother met at weddings expressed doubts and envy about her daughters.

There were other potent memories woven into the fabric of my rebellion. These were images from childhood, more powerful rebellion-stoppers than all the material comforts he later heaped upon us. Sitting next to him on the sofa after dinner, listening to his records—Begum Akhtar singing Ghalib. In a soft voice, he would explain the meaning of the Ghalib couplets. I would listen, not understanding much, but absorbing the extraordinariness of the moment. Knowing in my little seven-year old heart that this listening together to Urdu poetry was weaving a chain of life-long love. Unaware that this chain would later turn into my shackles. The love of music and literature he would infuse into me at seven would become fetters of love in adulthood. How does one break away from them?

Or this: we are in our Chittagong house in Bangladesh. His arms are steadying me over a basin of water on the floor. I've risen from bed after a long illness. I'm too weak to walk to the bathroom at the other end of the house, across the courtyard, past the slippery kitchen floor. 'Ma, *theek hai, theek hai*, Ma, you can brush your teeth and rinse your mouth in this basin. I'm holding you,' says his strong gentle voice, his soothing voice.

~

After the 1971 war of independence in Bangladesh, my family moved from what used to be East Pakistan, to what used to be West Pakistan and was now just Pakistan.

In the summer of 1986, Zia-ul-Haq's military dictatorship was in full swing in Pakistan. My twenty-fourth birthday was approaching and the dictatorship I was imprisoned under was my father's. It was a drunken time for upper-class Muslim males in Pakistan. Zia-ul-Haq's brand of reactionary Islam had strengthened my father's sense of self-righteousness, and he had lost his earlier tenderness, his literary sensibilities. In my childhood, he read romantic and mystical poetry. Now he read exegesis of the Quran by intolerant Wahabi maulvis, and clipped out magazine articles written by the same right-wing maulvis. His daughters had become his liabilities whom he had to keep under his watch until we could be disposed of in marriage. Zia's anti-women stance had added legitimacy to my father's incipient despotism.

The previous summer just before I was to start graduate school in Chicago, I stuttered to my parents about my Hindu boyfriend over the phone. My father thought I had lost my mind. Two years before this, I had confessed about a breakup with an old high school sweetheart. My father was still upset about that. A Muslim boyfriend was bad enough, but a Hindu one? Unthinkable. To make things kosher, my father had met my first boyfriend's family. And approved of each other's social and economic standing. We were almost engaged but my boyfriend who was attending college in the US, got busy with American girlfriends in the time it took me to transfer colleges from England to America.

When I told my father about my plans to marry my second boyfriend, he said in his calm, cajoling voice: 'Why don't you come to Karachi for the Christmas break and we'll discuss the whole thing? There's no need to get married in a hurry. We have to see about your dowry and other arrangements.' I didn't care about a dowry, but at that moment it seemed like a small price to pay to let him do things his way. He convinced me my wishes were uppermost in his heart. His was a voice I could not *not* trust. I've often wondered at my naiveté. How could you trust him, my friends asked me later. But I know how: it was those evenings of listening to ghazals with him when I was seven.

I came to Karachi for three weeks. But I couldn't return after the three weeks were over. My father had no plans for getting me married. He wasn't sending me back to the US until I gave up the preposterous idea of marrying a Hindu. He felt sure he could thwart my madness with time, and when I had come to my senses, he'd marry me off into some sensible, respectable Muslim family.

Thus began my solitary confinement in my parents' home. They wanted me to pretend life was normal. I could go out of the house, but couldn't return to my studies in the US. I adopted aloofness as my mode of non-violent resistance. I refused to leave my room and refused to tell them what they wanted to hear. I gave up going out with my mother to weddings and milaad.[2] My mother was tacitly cooperating with my father in keeping me under constant surveillance though she didn't need to: I never tried to leave my room. In those days I hated my mother passionately. Even more than I hated my father. I wondered if she had any maternal instincts. Was there any part of her heart that was not reserved for her husband? Did that part ever hurt for me? I tried to imagine her coming into my room at night, when my father was asleep: she would tell me how her hands were tied. How she too was a victim of his oppression. She would run her hand through my hair and we would weep. It took me years to realize that she was never going to run her fingers through my hair. She had no capacity to console me. She was affection-starved herself—she had never received this precious gift of love in generous measure from my father or her own father. Her father died when she was a child.

My mother lived in her kitchen. She cooked and shopped for groceries and supervised her servants. She seldom came to my room except to tell me how I was wrecking the peace and honour of the family. She never asked me if I was eating or sleeping enough. I lost weight during those four months but it never bothered her. I never ate any of my meals with them. I reduced my dependence on their food. I was adamant, I could survive on very little. I ate one meal a day and I ate it alone in my room.

---

[2]Milaad: Religious gatherings to celebrate the birth and life of Prophet Mohammed.

It was still the early days of captivity, and I was determined to leave and return to the US. So I asked whoever I could think of for help. My two closest friends were resourceless young women like me. Neither of them was earning any money and both lived with their parents. They had nothing against my love for a Hindu, but how could they help me get out of the country? 'Why didn't you get married before coming here,' they asked. Why had I had acted like a fool and come home unarmed with legal marital status? Raj had suggested we get married before I left the US. But that would mean I was deceiving my father. He had said, come home, let's talk it over, don't get married in a hurry.

If I could rewind my life to that time, I would still do the same—I would still come home to honour those stubborn, clingy memories of a very different Abba I remembered from my childhood.

I went to a well-known social worker for whose organization I had worked as a volunteer. He said he was an atheist but even he had to pray five times a day. 'Who in Pakistan would offer me donations if I said there's no God?' he asked me. 'But, yes, I can loan you money to buy a plane ticket.'

But would he speak to my father? No, he couldn't risk getting involved in such risky ventures. I learnt that even social reformers and activists could believe in one thing and practise another. And that there was no contradiction in this. I didn't have the means to make exit arrangements on my own without my father finding out and putting an end to all plans of escape. My ticket and passport had been confiscated by him.

I went to see an old school teacher. She listened, she even offered empathy. She shook her head sadly and said what most enlightened people said: 'What's wrong with being a Hindu?' But other than sharing my perplexity over this question, she couldn't do much else to help me.

Teachers, social workers—those pillars of society had refused to become my pillars of support in my hour of need. I was close to giving up. Gradually as the months passed, I found resignation a better analgesic than frozen action. Resignation wins approval. So I became resigned—exactly what my father wanted to see. I hardly ever left my room. I read dark dank novels by Dostoyevsky. And I prayed. I stayed up late and wrote dejected notes to Raj in reply to his inspiring, hopeful ones which he sent to my friend's address, and she passed on to me. I had no hopes of ever getting out. Only on some nights, when I lay with eyes closed under the madly whirring fan, I felt a strange strength stirring inside me. Then I knew instinctively I was going to get out but I couldn't have said how or when.

In the nightly vigils I kept in my room, I recalled what had drawn me to Raj. We had met in the common kitchen of the student apartment building in Madison, Wisconsin. I had never met anybody from India and he had never met anybody from Pakistan. We found common ground immediately: food, music, literature, broken hearts. He had broken up with a girlfriend. I had been dumped by my Muslim boyfriend. One snowy December evening, I burst into tears in the library just before my exams. I repeated the painful story of my boyfriend's betrayal. He listened intently. It was late and I thought we were alone in the library. Very gently, and much later, he revealed that the library staff on the lower floor were also listening to the saga of my broken heart, but he felt it was important that he not interrupt me. They, along with him, had heard me tell the tale of my love.

'You should've stopped me! I didn't want the whole world to listen to my idiotic story!'

'I didn't want to stop you just then,' he said affectionately. 'You were too upset. And the librarian didn't mind. She's on your side!'

~

Those months in my parents' house were some of the longest and most devastating of my life. Precious wealth bled out of me: self-confidence, faith, trust, belief, love for the family. It isn't easy to live as a shunned being in one's own home, especially when you've grown up thinking you were loved.

On my twenty-fourth birthday, I asked my mother's permission to meet my friends at a restaurant. She seemed pleased that I was finally returning to normalcy after months of living like a hermit. After some questioning she allowed me to take the car. I left home around 4 p.m. And drove straight to the airport, stopping only to pick up my friend on the way. Let me call her Naila. She wasn't a close friend, at least not until I shared my dilemma with her. 'If you want to leave, I'll get you a passport,' she said. I didn't believe her at first, but this woman had an insane, humane streak in her. She liked taking risks for what she believed in and she believed that I shouldn't be forced to stay against my will. I had never met anybody like her. Perhaps because she didn't belong to the respectable upper crust of Karachi society, she was the only one who was willing to walk her talk. Naila managed to get me a new passport within a few weeks of my confiding in her. I have no idea how she did it, and she also received my plane ticket to London that Raj had sent her.

I remember driving on Sharah-e-Faisal, in the hot, dry afternoon. In those days it wasn't named after a Saudi king, and was known as Drigh Road, the main thoroughfare that connected the south side of Karachi to the airport. The traffic was not as unendurably suffocating then. I was trying to focus my attention on manoeuvring my car through the unruly lines of cars and buses and motorcycles. The sun was beating down through the windshield. The hot breeze flapped my dupatta and blew my hair into my eyes. I had covered my head with my dupatta, so nobody I knew would recognize me. My hands trembled. At each red light, my heart pounded in my throat, my stomach squirmed. I felt nauseous. Naila was watching me sweat.

'Relax, I haven't seen your father yet!' she tried to make light of things.

I couldn't smile at her joke. 'Don't say such things. Do you want my heart to stop before I reach the airport?' My eyes were fixed on the amber light. Why was it taking so long to turn green?

At the airport I parked the car, and before locking it, shook out the crumpled note from my purse and placed it with the car key in the glove compartment. I had written and rewritten it many times during the night, trying to keep it short and devoid of all traces of pain or shame.

Dear Ammi and Abba: Asalamalaikum.
I wish I didn't have to tell you this. But you have left me no choice. I have tried and failed to make you understand that the person I want to marry is a good human being even though he's not a Muslim. I am leaving because I can no longer stay in your house, as I feel I no longer belong to this family. I respect both of you for all the sacrifices you have made for my excellent education and upbringing. And I hope some day I can repay you for all you have done for me. Please don't blame any of my friends. It has been entirely my own decision to leave.

I must confess that I removed a fifty pound note from Abba's closet. I didn't take anything else from the house. I hope you will forgive me in time.

Your daughter,
Nighat

I didn't know then if I would ever be able to come back to Karachi. There should have been a formal leave-taking. This was the loneliest of send-offs. Why did it feel so funereal? I was going to get married but there was no joy, eagerness, no starry flutterings of the heart a bride-to-be feels. I wanted my dadima who was perhaps the only one who would understand, who would give me her blessings. I hadn't told her anything. She was powerless to change my father's views but it was her powerlessness which made her heart so expansive. I remembered the first time I was leaving for boarding school in England, it was dadima who had cried the most. She had come to the airport with garlands to put around my neck.

I hugged Naila at the departure gate. We were careful to hide our tears. We didn't want to attract attention. I still had enough belief in what I was doing. Though my head felt laden enough with guilt I had refused to lower it in shame. Respectable woman from respectable family—could I call myself that? I hadn't even said goodbye to my baby sister whom I loved like a mother. Since her infancy, I had fed, bathed and made her do her homework whenever I came home for the holidays. The day before I was to leave, I held her and hugged her repeatedly. She seemed puzzled but what could I tell her?

'They'll come to your house and ask you a hundred questions. Will you be okay?' I asked Naila.

'I'm going to be at my evening class tonight,' Naila said. 'Even if they come to my house, they won't see me. But I'll handle them later. You just get back to America safely. And send me a ticket later. Don't forget. I want to get out of here too!'

The man at the airline counter leafed through the pages of my passport suspiciously. It was brand new. No visa stamps. England was one of the few countries that didn't require a visa to allow Pakistanis to enter in those days.

'You travelling alone? Nobody's going with you?' he frowned.

'Yes, I'm travelling alone, but my parents are outside. They came to see me off,' I lied calmly.

'Your luggage?' he asked, looking at the unstamped, crisp passport pages.

'I don't have any,' I said. 'I went to college in England. I still have my stuff there.'

'But you have a new passport?'

'Yes. I lost the old one.'

'We have to question young girls travelling alone. It would be better if I saw your parents. There have been cases of runaways. Parents come and question us about their daughters afterwards.'

Young girl? But I'm twenty-four today! I wanted to yell. 'I'm only going for a short visit to the UK. I think my parents must have left the airport by now,' I said even more calmly, looking over my shoulder disinterestedly at the exit.

He checked my passport again. He checked my ticket. I had a return ticket for ten days later. Finally, he gave me my boarding card.

Just before boarding the plane, I called my friend from the departure lounge.

'I'm about to leave. Call my parents in two hours,' I said. 'Tell them I've gone back to the US. I know this isn't going to be easy for you. I couldn't have done it without your help. I'll call you in a day or two.'

'Good luck, yaar. You're a strong woman. You'll be fine. I'll be praying for you.'

Strong woman or mad woman? I was walking out of madness. Or walking into madness? I couldn't tell what I was doing, or what was propelling me to action. I felt possessed, as if self-will had left me. And I was carrying out orders that my rational mind couldn't comprehend. Who's the strong woman here? Who was this man I was leaving the parental prison for? Would I be trading one prison for another? The parental one for the marital one? But at that moment, I wasn't seeking answers to complex questions. To me there was a simple solution in case things didn't work out: I could always end my life. I was willing to take risks for my principles, and for a man who said he loved me and would never marry anybody else. He said he would grow old waiting for me.

'What do you know about life's practicalities?' my father had once asked. 'Love is nothing when it comes to practical life.'

I disagreed wholeheartedly with him then. And do so even more now.

I met my Indian husband in the US when I transferred to college there from England. He believed in God but never worshipped in a temple. He was born a Hindu but had nothing to do with Hinduism. My father could not understand this: how could a Hindu not be a Hindu? But there was more to my father's opposition. As a Muslim youth, he had lived through the hate-filled Partition. He had to leave the beloved city of his birth, Calcutta, and seek his livelihood in a new Muslim nation. How could he now allow his daughter to marry a Hindu, and return to the enemy's folds?

My flight stopped in Dubai for an hour. I kept staring at the plane exit, scrutinizing the cleaners and the airline staff. I couldn't take my eyes off them. I was sure an airline official or a policeman would walk down the aisle and ask me to get off the plane. My father would have got in touch with the airport authorities by now and explained that I should be deported back to Karachi by the next flight. He didn't know which airline I was travelling by, but he could find out. He was infinitely powerful.

I hadn't been able to eat a thing from the in-flight meal. The man sitting next to me tried to be friendly but my answers remained curt. I stared past him at the night sky framed in the oval window of the plane. He wanted to know if I was married. Yes, I said, I was going to meet my husband in London. I was surprising myself with my self-composure, given how terrified I felt. What if a security guard entered, and whisked me away while I was telling my co-passenger about my husband? I imagined him getting all flustered as I was escorted out. I had forgotten I was twenty-four and wasn't obliged to tell anybody anything, and what I was doing wasn't illegal or immoral. It was easy to forget how old I was. It was easy to forget I had any rights. Most women I knew had never reached adulthood, not even after giving birth to several children. Not even after the birth of their children's children. My own mother was the saddest example of such infinitely stretched infancy.

~

My father assigned little value to love but in his youth he had fallen in love and asked my mother's brother, for her hand. They were neighbours in a crowded lane in Chittagong where immigrant families arrived from West Bengal to rent the narrow houses of former East Bengal. My mother was an orphan and her eldest brother had replaced her father. They were Muslims but not from the same ethnic community so their marriage was opposed by their families but my father was determined to marry her. For this act of tactless rebellion, they have my lifelong admiration. Their marriage was not 'okay' but it was a perfectly legitimate union from an Islamic point of view.

Mine was neither legitimate nor okay because I was marrying a non-Muslim. I was going against divine law, the sharia, the Islamic code of conduct.

I never quite understood the intricacies of my father's Islam. How did my father define practising Islam other than following rituals? Could he peer into the depths of the hearts of practising Muslims? If he simply said he dreaded the loss of his izzat, his honour, his standing among his relatives and acquaintances if his American-educated daughter couldn't find an eligible Muslim to marry and had to disgrace herself by running away with a Hindu, I would have felt infinite sympathy for him. I didn't want to run in the first place. But if he made such an admission he would have to admit his own vulnerabilities. And my father could never portray himself as a weak man.

The more he provided for us materially, the more he won rights to silence any opposition. He wrote to my academic adviser in the US to inform him that I would not be returning for the spring semester. He had in his possession my passport and return ticket. He had removed them from my closet. Rather he had had them removed.

And who did the removing? My mother, though she later denied her role in this theft. My mother, who was too low on self-esteem to ever exercise her own will in any matter, who could only cry and whine over his indiscretions with other women; my mother who believed no matter what her husband did, it was her religious duty to obey and follow his dictates; my mother for whom his commands were above God's; my mother the pragmatic woman who knew the consequences of going against his wishes. He could turn her out of the house. He could divorce her. He would have the full weight of the Islamic sharia backing him if he chose to divorce her for the crime of disobedience and abetting a haraam act like a daughter's marriage to a non-Muslim. Who would support my mother? Who would she turn to if turned out of her husband's house? No shelter, no state institution waited for her with open arms. She had no parental home to return to. Her father was dead. Her mother was a mentally unbalanced dependant living at the mercy of her brothers. My mother had no education to go out and earn a living. Her izzat lay in serving her husband in a society in which marriage was the only respectable career for women like her. She had already risked her reputation as a young woman by marrying him for love. That this love was a fleeting affair and now lay ruined by what my father called *practicalities*, didn't make her original decision to marry him any less heroic in my eyes. She had rebelled, and she had paid a price. Why didn't she dare support her daughter's rebellion?

I've asked her countless times. 'Were you afraid? What

were you so afraid of? Why didn't you stand up for me?'

She has nothing to say.

~

Raj was waiting for me at Heathrow airport. My taut body collapsed in his arms. But even then, I first turned round to see if some officials or police were coming after me.

'It's okay,' he kept murmuring, stroking my hair. 'Everything's going to be okay. You've grown so thin! Let's get you some food. Then we have to get some clothes for you.'

We went shopping, and I bought two shirts and two skirts from Oxford Street so I could change out of what I was wearing. We applied for a marriage licence. And took off for a vacation to explore Dorset in the time it took to process the licence. I sat and watched the ocean in Weymouth for hours. I glanced at the happy-looking vacationers chatting over their scones and tea, and I asked myself what I was doing? Was I doing the right thing? How would I know if I was doing the right thing?

A week later, we got married at the registrar's office in a Hertfordshire village, where our hosts, my boarding school chemistry teacher and his wife, stood in as our two witnesses. We celebrated our wedding with them at a small restaurant. The food was very bland, very English. But the sherry and champagne were sweet and forgetfulness-inducing. The next day we applied for a US visa for me and a few days later, we flew back to the United States.

Once again I was staring out the window of a plane at the

clouds. What was married life going to be like? From a PhD student, I had become a PhD student's wife. The man I had taken so many risks for was reading a mystery novel on the flight. His mission had been accomplished. But mine? I didn't even know what my mission was. I felt strangely distant from everything, including him.

It was as if the most exciting part of this romance novel had already transpired.

~

Soon after we returned to the US, my father arrived there. He did not talk much to me or Raj but he insisted on the formality of making us go through a Muslim marriage in a Chicago mosque. Raj was a student and he couldn't afford a ring for me, so my father bought a wedding ring and asked Raj to slip it on my finger. I have no idea to this day what the reason was for such extravagance. It was his way of showing me what I had got into by marrying a penniless student. I tried to sell that ring later when we were hard up, but jewellery had very little resale value in the US. Though he didn't think a Muslim marriage would absolve us of a life of sin, he still insisted on it! My father chose the Muslim name Rehman for my husband though he knew he wasn't going to adopt it officially. He was doing everything to mutate this aberration, this wart that my running away had grown on the blemishless skin of his respectability.

We went to a Thai restaurant after the nikah at the Islamic centre was over. I had just got married a second time to the same person. In the middle of the meal, my father looked at me and said: 'I don't give more than six months to this marriage.'

I wished I had never agreed to go through this ceremony for his sake. I wanted him gone from my life.

~

Life assumed a semblance of normalcy. My father returned to Karachi, armed with a copy of Raj's conversion to Islam certificate and our nikahnama. But after his return to Pakistan, he never called me. Nor did my mother. Raj was busy finishing his PhD and I had started working at a fast food restaurant. His meagre assistantship wasn't enough to pay our bills. When I wasn't at work, I cooked and cleaned our small apartment, and sometimes I went and sat in on philosophy and literature classes at the university. I felt listless, but carried a cheerful, thrifty, new-wife look about me and kept a tight lid over my tumultuous, confused emotions. I scarcely dared peep into my soul. I had dropped out of the graduate programme in Chicago. Though my adviser called and said I could come back next fall, I didn't have the emotional or intellectual strength to return to graduate school after what I had been through.

Plastic-wrapped DHL envelopes arrived from my father at the rate of almost one a month. They weren't letters. But I would still rip them open in the hope of finding one. Maybe there would be a short note asking me how I was getting on? Or a gift of money since he knew I was hard up. Could my little sister's drawings come out of one of them? The envelopes only contained clippings from newspapers and religious periodicals I had never known my father to read when I was a child. In my childhood his bookshelves were filled with Urdu fiction and poetry. The articles he sent me by DHL were about the duties and obligations of Muslims towards their parents, and the wrath of Allah that awaited disobedient and wayward offspring. There were never any articles about the high value Islam places on compassion and forgiveness or parents' duties and obligations towards their children.

I started tossing out the clippings without reading them.

~

'Who's a true Muslim in your eyes?' I asked my father many years later to see if he had grown inwardly in the long intervening years.

'A true Muslim is one who follows the five pillars of Islam and has blind faith in Allah and his Prophet. Does your husband have blind faith in Allah and his Prophet? Does he read the Quran? Does he pray five times a day? Does he fast? Does he give zakaat? Does he intend to do these things, ever?'

It was true that my husband and I didn't have blind faith though we did believe in the presence of Universal Intelligence. He was a scientist and a skeptic. He didn't say his prayers or fast. But neither did I. He didn't go to the mosque but neither did he visit temples.

'Your husband is not a true Muslim,' my father had said this again and again. 'And neither are you.'

It wasn't enough to believe in the oneness of God. It had

to be a Muslim God. If you didn't pray five times a day, you weren't a Muslim. If you didn't follow the sharia, you weren't a Muslim. Therefore, my husband and I weren't Muslims. Our marriage was a haraam marriage. And our children would be haraami children.

But the poetry I had read by Ghalib, and by Sufis like Bulleh Shah proclaimed that one who seeks truth and follows the path of universal love, one who practises compassion, one who is careful not to break a human heart, is a true Muslim, dearer to God than those with empty hearts who pray five times a day.

'I don't know who you've been reading and where you get your ideas from,' my father said.

'I'm reading the Sufis. I'm reading Ghalib.' I wanted to remind him that he was the one to introduce Ghalib to me when I was seven.

'The Sufis are not real Muslims,' my father pronounced.

~

The number twenty-four is strangely significant. My birthday falls on the twenty-fourth of the month. I initiated a life-transforming journey of madness on my twenty-fourth birthday. I took another twenty-four years to find the detachment to write about what I did at twenty-four. I had eloped—an old-fashioned word, an outdated concept. And though quaint it must seem—this old-world romance, marked by impracticality and recklessness, an anachronism in our pragmatic post-modern, security-obsessed lives, I'm still proud of what I did. Why did I wait so many years to write about it? Perhaps it's because I'm no longer as enamoured by the institution of marriage. I had to await my emotional liberation from belief in marriage to write about my marriage. Marriage is a time-bound formula for social development. In our time, it has failed to develop into an equitable institution that benefits both partners equally. For years, I braided marriage and love into one plait. And it was only after I unravelled the two strands, that I could write about both in a dispassionate way.

But Love in all its myriad expressions and relations remains the universe's eternal gift to humans. It's only humans who are driven to tears and transcendence, sacrifice and story-telling by the madness and gentleness of love. The unfettered pursuit of love in its manifold avatars seems to me to be the simplest and the only path to peace in the world. This book is dedicated to lovers all over the world and their beloveds, and may good fortune help them surpass all hurdles in the path of wasl or union with the beloved.

I began this chapter with Bulleh Shah's words and I end it with the words of the thirteenth-century master of mystical love poetry, Jalaluddin Rumi, who poured his love for his beloved, Shams, into his verse. Rumi's is one of the most soul-enriching cries of courage, cheering lovers on, both those seeking mystical union as well as those seeking human love. For both kinds of love are different facets of the same Reality.

How gracefully you move, oh essence of my soul,
    do not go without me.

Oh true friend in the garden of life, do not go without
  me.
Oh heavens, do not turn without me; oh moon, do
  not show your face without me.
Oh earth, do not rise without me; oh time, do not
  travel without me.
This world is delightful with you; the other world is
  delightful with you.
In this world do not be without me; in the other
  world do not stay without me.

—From Rumi, to Shams[3]

May the spirits of lovers like Rumi and Shams bless this
book. May the light of love light up our lives.

---

[3]*The Guru of Rumi: The Teachings of Shams Tabrizi*, by Mostafa Vaziri,
Pilgrim Books, India, p. 57.

2

Brides of the Shrine

Faqir near the entrance to Nizamuddin's shrine, Delhi

Nami danam chi manzil bood shab jaay ki man boodam;
Baharsu raqs-e bismil bood shab jaay ki man boodam.
Pari paikar nigaar-e sarw qadde laala rukhsare;
Sarapa aafat-e dil bood shab jaay ki man boodam.
Khuda khud meer-e majlis bood andar laamakan Khusrau;
Muhammad shamm-e mehfil bood shab jaay ki man boodam.

I wonder what was the place where I was last night,
All around me were half-slaughtered victims of love,
    tossing about in agony.
There was a nymph-like beloved with cypress-like
    form and tulip-like face,
Ruthlessly playing havoc with the hearts of the lovers.
God himself was the master of ceremonies in that
    heavenly court,
oh Khusrau, there (the face of) the Prophet too was
    shedding light like a candle.

—Translated by S.A.H. Abidi, from:
http://oldpoetry.com/opoem/98123-Amir-Khusro-
Nami-Danam

15th August 2010

I left Allahabad, the city where I have lived for more than a decade, on Independence Day. It was a sultry August night. Earlier that day on my morning walk, I had come across three rag pickers, boys with shoulder sacks as big as themselves. They squirmed and looked away when I asked if they knew what day it was. Only one, the tallest among them, answered. Then he too turned away, dismissing me. His deft hands continued scouring and sorting roadside garbage for recyclables. Maybe he feared I'd start preaching to him about patriotism and love for the nation.

What does 15th August mean to most of India's disavowed? And to India's women? Have they won the freedom to live and love freely? The day before, on 14th August, neighbouring Pakistan had celebrated its Independence Day. Do Pakistani or Indian women know what it is to live and love freely? What little freedom Muslim women of the subcontinent had acquired during the struggle to liberate their nations from colonial rule, has started to decline with the rise of the fundamentalist fixation with regulating women's freedoms. But privileged women, whether Muslim or not, have retained some of their freedoms: they can exercise some choice in who their future husbands will be as long as they choose men from their religions, castes, class, ethnicity. On the whole though the modern woman of the subcontinent is forced to live in a more careful, calculated way than ever before.

Compare the Muslim woman of today with a woman of early Islam. Compare her to the first Muslim woman, Khadija, the Prophet's wife. She was twice widowed, and much older than the Prophet. She managed her own business and it was she who proposed marriage to Mohammad, her young trusted manager. He was fifteen years younger than her. She was forty at the time of her marriage to the Prophet. I've yet to meet a twice-widowed or twice-divorced Muslim woman who marries a third time, and marries a man fifteen years her junior, and does so with her community's approval! Modern Muslim women have lost essential freedoms. Love has ceased to be an essential freedom. A good life has come to mean a financially safe life—a good marriage is marriage to a man who can provide the material goods of life.

I waver at the boundaries of a forbidden, sequestered world—the world of Muslim women's love. There must be Muslim women who risk religion, reputation, family, country, and career for love, but such women are largely missing from contemporary life, and the literature of the subcontinent on Muslim women. Much of classical Urdu poetry and fiction I've read is men's work. Women in them are only objects, never subjects of desire. Women writing women's desire in Urdu is sparse before the twentieth century. Even the canon of mystical love poetry by Sufis has largely been written by men for their male beloveds, whether earthly or divine. Even rekhti, nineteenth centrury Urdu verse celebrating erotic love between women, has been written by male poets. So where are Muslim women's voices?

When will we set out on a voyage into the assumed stillness of women's desire, speaking of ourselves through the risks we take, waging a jihad against forces bent upon erasing our distinctiveness? How long the wait before we openly speak and sing of the webs of love we weave in the disfigured landscape of meaninglessness and violence?

I jot down these random notes on the train from Allahabad to Delhi:

Blaming Islam for eroding women's freedoms would be simplistic.

Islam didn't restrict women's right to self-development.

The Prophet's wife's asserted her rights as a woman.

Why do contemporary Muslim women get punished for loving, for making choices?

Love is a dangerous emotion. Why?

To murder the errant woman in the name of honour is a power trip that allows Muslim males to preserve their dominion.

Imprisoning women out of the public sphere, keeping her behind the chadar and chardivari, the four walls of the home, keeps them helpless and confined to the veil and the home.

16th August

I've reserved this day in Delhi for visiting the shrine of Amir

Khusro and his spiritual mentor Hazrat Nizamuddin Auliya. I wanted to make a symbolic beginning with a visit to the tombs of these two Sufis. I wanted their blessings for my journey—Amir Khusro's and his beloved murshid or spiritual guide, Nizamuddin's.

It's a stifling day. Late monsoon torpor hovers over the squalor of the dargah. I go past the dilapidated Ghalib Academy. There's a display stand with books on Ghalib, but nobody's around to answer any questions. No attendant is needed as the junta filing past hardly stops to browse through the books. It looks less like a literary outlet selling books by and about Urdu's greatest poet and more like a neglected government bureau stuffed with publications worth nobody's time. Next to the academy, lies the mausoleum of the great poet my father introduced me to in childhood, but I don't have the heart to enter his mazaar and instead say a speedy fateha and rush to Nizamuddin's shrine. Ghalib deserves a day set aside entirely for him.

Outside the unattended Ghalib Academy, a sulky woman sits fanning herself with a straw fan. She's selling slippers from a cart. There are families next to her, seated on the bare floor, and there are women begging. Many of the women have babies clasped to their breasts. More beggars are seated outside eateries with large pots of cooked food, waiting to be fed by visitors to the shrine. Nizamuddin's dargah has evolved a complex support economy related to various rituals of the devotees. Touts outside the eateries try to sell me coupons. 'Feed the poor, Madam, feed the poor.'

The narrowness of the lane leading up to the dargah rankles and reeks of sweaty bodies. The essence is decidedly male. There's a whirling medley of local men and visitors—some of whom look like foreigners—and the mineral water sellers, STD/PCO booths, rose petals, ilaichi dana and chadar sellers, money changers, jalebi and samosa sellers are all vying for their business. I stop at M.M. Cloth Depot, which is selling prayer mats and religious books in Urdu and Hindi. I pick out two books, priced at twenty rupees each: *The Muslim Wife*, and *Guidelines to Sexual Intercourse—the Islamic Way*. As I leaf through the pages replete with long lists, outlining women's duties in the conjugal bed and marital household, I imagine translating some enthralling passages on the long bus ride I'll be taking from Delhi to Lahore.

The shop-lined street gives way to a narrower, people-packed, covered alley flanked by more flower and incense sellers, shoe-minders, and chadar sellers. The shoe minders start pestering me for my slippers: 'Madam, Madam, deposit your chappals here'—long before I reach the shrine's entrance. The chadar sellers call out, 'Come here, come here, madam.' The unceasing clamour unnerves me.

Just before the shrine's entrance, in a small, green verandah, an amiable-looking young man stands behind a long table lined with glass jars filled with sweet biscuits. He's watching the crowd disinterestedly and doesn't seem to care if I stop at his shop. I ask him if I could leave my chappals with him, and when he says yes, I collapse on a wooden bench and order tea and biscuits.

He prepares tea and I gaze distractedly at a faqir with tousled hair and strands of coloured beads, fast asleep next to the tea shop. His rubber chappals are stacked near his head. Nobody expects him to move. The laissez faire, all-are-welcome air lulls me into an inexplicable resignation. What will be will be, says the disorder around the shrine. A dusty, electronic security gate stands neglected and unused on one side of the entrance, as if pushed aside by crowds of impatient devotees.

'Do they ever use that security thing?' I point it out, and Shahid the chaiwala shakes his head.

'Only sometimes during the urs, the anniversary celebrations of the saint,' he replies, handing me a plastic cup of extra-sweet, extra-milky tea. 'When VIPs are coming, they get orders from the government to use it.'

I dunk my biscuit in my tea and muse: 'Good thing VIPs don't visit often.'

The unstoppable, scruffy multitudes, Muslims and non-Muslims, women and men, beggars and supplicants, crossing the threshold of the shrine day and night, are not worthy of special protection. Such indifference soothes me, makes me feel safer than I would entering a mall in Delhi, and more resigned to my anonymity and insignificance in the larger scheme of life.

I finish my tea and biscuit. Depositing my slippers with Shahid, I cross barefoot into the dargah, into a space filled with visitors of all ranks, losing myself in the crowd. Unprotected, here the privileged must share space with faqirs, tramps, the homeless and itinerants. I walk first towards the tomb of Amir Khusro,[1] who lies buried at the feet of his spiritual master, Nizamuddin. Toti-e-Hind, Parrot of Hind, says a sign outside Khusro's tomb, a title conferred on him as Hindustan's most well-loved literary parrot, for his literary, musical, and linguistic genius. Khusro, why are you not here with me in this darkness? Why have you, poet, Sufi, lover and devotee, architect of Sufi and bhakti syncretism, forsaken us in our dark times? Though it's Nizamuddin whose spiritual beneficence draws thousands of devotees to his dargah, it's Khusro whose charms as a poet has fetched me here. I say my fateha standing outside the cupola housing his tomb. As a woman I'm not allowed to go inside the chamber where his grave is.

Women are not allowed inside the domed tomb of Nizamuddin either. An ugly yellow sign in Hindi, Urdu and English prohibits women from entering. But what if I were cross-dressed as a man? Wouldn't they let me in? Accessibility is all about cleverly disguised appearances.

A group of bearded men in spotless white attire, the pir sahibs of the shrine see my camera and notepad and hurry towards me with thick donation ledgers. One of them thrusts an opened page at me, filled with columns, names and numbers—presumably a listing of the thousands of rupees received by them in donations.

---

[1] If there was one single person who could be credited with influencing Hindustani classical music the most, it undoubtedly is Amir Khusrau or Khusro (1253-1325). He was a Sufi saint, darvesh, philosopher, devout disciple, linguist, historian, warrior, inventor, a naughty humorist, lyricist, singer, musician and poet *par excellence* . . . the list is endless.

'Enter your name and address here,' he demands, handing me a pen, along with an offering of rose petals and ilaichi dana.

'Why aren't women allowed to go inside?' I ask.

'It's part of our religion,' he replies with a scowl.

'You're lucky women are allowed to come into the dargah at all,' another spotless one says menacingly. 'We could stop them at the entrance.'

'So why are you asking me, a woman, for a donation when I can't go inside and say my fateha?' I return the pen and ledger to him, and step down into the crowded pavilion.

Why do the shrine's caretakers restrict women's admission? Qawwalis are sung regularly at the shrine. So music is okay, as is trance-induced dancing by men, the burning of incense, kissing of the tomb (by men) or prostrating onself and asking the saint for favours, tying coloured strings to the marble jaali at the shrine—pagan rituals resembling what the Hindu *but-parast*, or idol-worshippers do. All that's okay, but not the defiling presence of women inside the inner sanctum! Nizamuddin, whose tomb is now off limits to me, had his most beloved disciple, Amir Khusro, dress in women's clothing, place flowers in his hair, compose songs and dance and sing for his sake. Not all Khusro's poetry was composed as purely spiritual verse, not all of his poetry was about mystical union with God. Writing and singing for his earthly murshid's love was as important to him as winning God's love.

As for his love for Khusro, Nizamuddin is known to have said, if shariat allowed, he would have had Khusro buried in the same grave as himself. Nizamuddin passed away first. And Khusro a few months after him. Though the two were not buried in the same grave, Khusro found a resting place close enough, at the feet of his murshid.

Khusro, the lover who transcended the worldly boundaries of gender and propriety to write such disarming poetry— you have to give me your blessings, I plead with him. Inspire me. Hold me. Protect me. Didn't you call out to your murshid, didn't you address God as your bridegroom, didn't you become transformed into a woman for your love, Khusro? Didn't you adopt a feminine voice? Didn't you say you lost everything willingly, your self-importance, your superior reputation, when your beloved's eyes met yours?

Chhap tilak sab cheen lee ray mosay naina milaikay
Prem bhatee ka madhva pilaikay
Matvali kar leeni ray mosay naina milaikay
Gori gori bayyan, hari hari churiyan
Bayyan pakar dhar leeni ray mosay naina milaikay
Bal bal jaaon mein toray rang rajwa
Apni see kar leeni ray mosay naina milaikay
Khusro Nijaam kay bal bal jayyiye
Mohay suhaagan kar lee nee ray mosay naina milaikay
Chhap tilak sab cheen lee ray mosay naina milaikay . . .

You've taken away my looks, my haughtiness, by just a glance.
By making me drink the wine of love-potion,
You've intoxicated me with a mere glance;
My fair, delicate wrists with green bangles in them,

• 43 •

Have been held tightly by you with just a glance.
I give my life to you, Oh my cloth-dyer,
You've dyed me in your hues, with just a glance.
Khusro gives his whole life to you Oh, Nijam,
You've made me your bride, with just a glance . . .[2]

~

Khusro and his Nijam—spiritual companions and soulmates.
But don't pollute their pious names by calling them lovers.
The question of pollution comes up only if we separate the
sacred from the profane. What we make of our discomfort
with questions about Khusro's relationship with
Nizamuddin depends on our cultural lens. Dualisms are
modernity's bane. Insisting on simplistic answers to complex
phenomena, making relationships one-dimensional and
flattening them out, rejecting the coexistence of contradictory
truths—isn't that what legalistic religion does? Things have
to be black and white. Fuzziness is intolerable. It becomes
sacrilegious to ask questions like, were Khusro and
Nizamuddin lovers? If they were both men seeking God,
one a seeker, the other a guide, how could they also be
seeking each other? Their union could only be a spiritual
one if they were holy men, unafflicted by earthly love. Our
collective shame and our fretful adoption of hypermasculine
heterosexism, the fervour with which we disown the
emasculated images of our revered spiritual figures, speaks

---

[2]Chaap tilak sab cheen lee ray mosay naina milaikay
YouTube: http://www.youtube.com/watch?v=paRmnYmt2z4&NR=1]

of us as colonized subjects. The seamless fusion of the sacred and the secular in Muslim poetry and cultural life was seen as a sign of moral decadence and was promptly excised from our consciousness by nationalist reformers, shamed by the contemptuous gaze of angrez—British—colonizers.

Eight centuries ago Rumi cried out for his beloved: 'Ya, Shams Tabrizi. Everything should intoxicate me but only you do.' For Rumi, yearning for the sacred and transcendental was an in the-body experience of longing, loving, and yearning for union with his beloved Shams. But we, who've been taught to degrade the body and its desires as profane, placing the sacred in a rarefied, out-of-the body realm, how can we, the colonized, the educated, modern Muslims fathom the multiple dimensions of a relationship such as Khusro and his beloved Nizam's? The delicate sensibility needed for such perception has been bludgeoned out of our souls. Indoctrinated with a hyper-rational morality, we've lost the taste buds for tasting the vagueness and wholeness of love.

The Muslim fundamentalists are a product of such tasteless, one-dimensional modernity. If they are unable to make room for the ghaibi, or unseen dimensions of love, or admit a fusion of contradictory impulses in their literalist minds, it's because they are well-schooled in the modernist school of rationality. How could they tolerate traces of earthly love between Sufis? They may concede that Khusro and Nizamuddin shared a sublime regard for each other as master and disciple, but even a remote suggestion of erotic desire between them is unthinkable. Erotic love between humans is a powerful sign of resistance to the status quo, it's a force that threatens to topple power structures. Love liberates. Love incites rebellion. Neither liberation nor rebellion is what the fundamentalists want for, or from the masses.

~

After I refuse to enter my name in the donation ledger, I lose myself among the women in the pavilion. The verandah circumscribing Nizamuddin's tomb is the women's place. In the verandah women sit, praying silently or reading the Quran. With the maghrib azaan, men enter the red mosque adjoining the dargah. I sit with the women in the verandah, resting my head against a marble pillar, breathing in the incense, listening intently to the soft hush that comes on at dusk, when the heart of its own accord turns inward for solace.

A young girl starts talking to me. She tells me she's come with her mother to say prayers of gratitude because her wish has materialized: Nizamuddin Auliya has helped her get into the journalism programme at Jamia Millia!

'What did you come for?' she asks me.

'I've come to seek blessings for the book I'm writing. And the long journey I'm going on.'

I leave the praying women and wander off towards the walled enclosure behind the pavilion, a sequestered space with a latticed marble partition separating it from the main pavilion. Several women and a man are sitting inside the marbled enclosure, holding on to the gaps in the filigree partition. In the gathering darkness their heads are pressed to the barrier. A young woman has her fingers curled tightly around the marble jali. She's swaying and crying softly. Suddenly, her soft whimpering turns into heart-rending wails. Her body swings faster, as if tossed about by unseen forces, and words tumble out of her, raw and frenzied. She jerks herself upright.

'Oh, Baba, oh Nizamuddin, do you hear the cries of your broken ones? I'm a broken one. I bow before your powers. I shall never try to win against you,' she moans, flinging herself to the ground.

As if in response to her tormented pleas, the qawwals in the pavilion begin to sing *zehaale-miskeen*, one of Amir Khusro's love songs. Khusro composed it in Brij bhasha and Persian, the first line of each couplet in Persian, the second in Brij bhasha, a unique fusion of two languages.

> *Zehaal-e-miskeen makun taghaful,*
> *Duraye naina banaye batiyan.*

> Do not overlook my misery, by blandishing your
> eyes and weaving tales.[3]

I listen, marvelling at Khusro's genius for so smoothly blending Persian and medieval Hindi, two wines from very different vineyards.

The woman at the wall of wailing becomes Khusro. Khusro is the bride who pines for his beloved—he's the tortured

---

3. See http://sufipoetry.wordpress.com/2009/11/06/zehaal-e-miskeen-amir-khusro

lover who yearns for one look, one glance from his beloved. His feminine sensibility comes alive in his words depicting the lover's utter helplessness, the fatal brokenness of a lover's heart filled with longing that drives him to madness. In separation from the beloved the only ecstasy he knows is the ecstasy of imagined union. It is in longing and in desire for this union that his love reaches expressions of divinity.

Ke taab-e-hijran nadaram ay jaan,
Na leho kahe lagaye chatiyan

My patience has over-brimmed, O sweetheart!
why do you not take me to your bosom?

The young woman rises, still swaying, still crying, her words coming in gasps between her sobs. When she can speak, her voice is gravelly. She's flinging her long hair from right to left. Some wisps of hair stick to her tear-stained, sweaty face. 'Don't you hear me, Baba? Won't you release me? I'm your slave. I shall never win against you. Won't you pronounce your judgment today, O Nizamuddin? You win, I lose. I wouldn't win even if I tried to win against you, Baba.' She speaks as if the jinn inside her is speaking and she's only a medium.

Shaban-e-hijran daraz chun zulf,
Wa roz-e-waslat cho umer kotah.

Long like curls in the night of separation, short like
life on the day of our union.

She's the tormented lover, begging her Nizam to subdue the evil jinn that resides inside her. The jinn who possesses her and torments her, is soon reduced to pleading with the Nizam through her.

'Hazrat Nizamuddin, never shall I disobey you. I bow before you, I say my salaam!' She prostrates and straightens herself puppet-like, hair falling and rising like a tidal wave, as if rendered helpless, unable to control her own movements or speech. 'You have turned me captive, Baba Nizamuddin. Will you not give your verdict today? I have gone mad in this captivity, Baba, release me, let me go. I'm a broken soul.'

At one point I wanted to ask her what had brought her to the shrine. But after a few minutes of listening to her I instinctively knew what was wrong. What was wrong was life and to probe more deeply into her life seemed disrespectful and intrusive. Like the other wailers gathered in the courtyard, I listened to her grief and, like them, I shared silently in her grief.

Sakhi piya ko jo main na dekhun,
To kaise katoon andheri ratiyan.

Dear friend, how shall I pass the dark dungeon night without your face before me.

The qawwals have repeated this last verse with plaintive, subtle variations. I've been listening to the qawwals and the woman, my head buried in my knees. I too am pleading silently for her with Nizamuddin.

Can the dispossessed pass life's dark dungeon nights without the grace and beneficence bestowed by their beloved saint and saviour? My eyes mist over. Light from the chandeliers in the pavilion lights up the top of the woman's hair. Her agitated frame, the crying, pleading people in the thick, damp darkness fill me with foreboding. The qawwals go on singing, and their repetition has a hypnotic, silencing effect on me. I am momentarily transported beyond the present, beyond the squalor and disorder of my surroundings to a world where neither pain nor ecstasy, justice nor injustice exercise any hold over my spirit.

Later, when I'm writing this chapter, I'll recall this strange vision I had after my visit to the dargah. I am lying on the floor of my room. Dazzling particles of green light are dancing behind my closed eyelids. I'm sitting on the ground of the spacious pavilion where the qawwals are singing. And Khusro, dressed like a woman in a long sequined gown, with flowers in his hair, is whirling and singing passionately with the qawwals and Nizamuddin is watching him while a half-smile lights up his face. Dancing and whirling, Khusro twirls over to where I am seated and bends down to speak to me: 'Listen, I'm living and loving like this so you can write about my love one day. Because the world will need to hear about us in your times.'

Had Khusro really spoken to me? Or was it purely my imagination? I wasn't sure if my mind was playing tricks with me, or was this a real communication from the spirit of Khusro? It felt like Khusro had spoken to me. It felt like I was embedded in that space in that time. It was only a feeling and I wanted to dismiss it. But what if, what if, dispersed across aeons in the vastness and connectedness of the universe, life and death and time were merely illusions which we mistook as unalterable reality?

Did it matter if my vision wasn't real? What's real? What's normal? In that imaginary, visionary, transcendental space created by my mind, Khusro's presence and his poetry and music and his speaking to me had felt real. There's a part of me that thinks what goes on in this world, what we call reality, and the inordinate significance we attach to that reality, is nothing but a fixation on a particular kind of reality.

The woman's outburst dwindles down to a soft purring, and then stops. The others have ignored her muttering and nobody looks up even now. Deliberate disregard for fellow wailers has evolved as the unspoken etiquette of shrines. The shrine is one of the few places in the world where public display of grief is not frowned upon. The young man sits motionless with his face stuck to the marble partition. The other women keep up their muttering and swaying and sobbing, resting their heads against the partition. All are alone and all are in company.

A little boy who's been waiting behind the woman, as if he's used to waiting for her, now approaches her. She turns towards him and with complete poise, the demons of her soul mollified for the moment, says: '*Chal, aath baj rahe hain*—Let's go, it's almost eight.' I'm shattered by her poise. She picks up her plastic bag from the floor, holds the boy's hand and they leave, leaving before I have time to fathom the change in her. I've barely recovered from the acuteness of her publicly-expressed pleas. Her transition from mental and spiritual anguish and so banal a return to normalcy unsettles me. I feel humbled by the beauty and grace of a place like this to bring peace to the poor and the broken-hearted who have access to few alternative healing spaces.

The unadvertised, do-it-yourself healing is what the shrine provides, with Nizamuddin's blessings reaching out to all those who cry out his name in earnest. I walk out and cross the courtyard into another sequestered space which, unsought and dark, also on the margins of the shrine, seems like a women's space. It takes a few seconds in the dimness to see the women there. But my ears pick up their fast-paced, expletive-encrusted verbal exchange immediately.

The qawwals are still singing and the sound of the dholak and their rhythmic clapping from the shamiana-covered pavilion is a strange backdrop to the women's abuse-littered exchange. I stand unnoticed in the space between the women and the graves.

'*Haan, haan, chudwa lijyo, apne baap se. Tu to waise hi besharam hai, sattar bapon ki hai,*' the older one says. Yes, yes, go on, get me fucked by your father. Anyway, you are shameless, born of seventy fathers. She's squatting on the floor between the graves, nursing her infant. A chickpea-sized boil on her chin bobs as she speaks.

'*Tu chup reh, tu to chillay pe bhi jaa ke chudwati hai!*' You shut up. You get yourself fucked even at the chilla, barks the younger one. Now that I can see her face, I'm shocked. She couldn't be older than fourteen. She's my daughter's age, and already exposed to linguistic brutalities best reserved for adulthood. She's standing defiantly over the woman suckling the infant. Her thinness and matted hair are matched by the sharpness of her speech.

I squat on the floor between the graves near the entrance, exhausted by the heat and entranced by the fighting women. I've never heard women bandy about the Hindi word for fuck so unreservedly. This is no ordinary exchange. It's happening inside the holiness of a shrine! The complexity of the space, the dargah, begins to unravel itself like a Chinese scroll. None of it hidden, all of it spilling out if you care to peep into the crannies. The women continue cursing, getting each other fucked by several men, multiple times.

'You're a randi (prostitute). Your mother was also a randi,' the young girl says triumphantly.

'She just called me a randi! And my mother too,' the older woman shrieks. And finally, she enlists my help. 'She said it in your presence! You heard her, didn't you? She called me a randi.'

I nod helplessly.

Finally, a man appears from somewhere in the back. He's the father of the young girl. 'What right have you to say such things to my daughter?' he yells at the woman. 'You have fun with strange men every night. Have I ever accused of you of wrongdoing?'

The father exchanges place with his daughter in the fight.

I step out, and his daughter steps out with me.

The qawwals in the pavilion are singing a qaul, a short hymn by Amir Khusro, devoted to Hazrat Ali. *'Man kunto maula, haza Ali maula, Ali maula.'*

'Have you come to collect the children?' a beggar woman sitting on a plastic mat asks me.

'No.'

'Are you Punjabi, madam?' another one asks.

'No, I'm just a visitor.'

'Come away from them. They just want your money,' the young girl says to me.

'What's your name?' I ask, following her to the green and white wall.

'Shabnam.'

'That's a nice name. It means dew, you know?'

'Yes, I know.'

'Where do you live?'

'Here.'

'Here?'

She turns towards a line of low quarters behind the dome of the shrine. 'I sleep over there. In the qawwal's house.'

'And that man, he was your father?'

'Yes. He's a khadim for the pir sahabs. He works for them. Can't you see them? They're sitting over there.' So her father worked as a servant for the pirs.

'Yes, I see them,' I say, remembering my disagreeable conversation with them. 'They were also asking me for money.'

'They take out all the money from the collection boxes at night and take it home.' Her eyes sparkle, reflecting the chandeliers.

'What do you do here all day?'

'Nothing.'

'No school?'

She shakes her head.

'Where do you eat?'

'Here,' she says. 'On Thursdays, the langar is good. You get rajma-chawal or puri-sabji. Sometimes we even get sweets when people bring them. Will you come for langar?'

'Yes, some Thursday I'll come and we'll eat together. If you're still here.'

'I'll always be here. Where can I go?'

'Why was that woman so mean to you?'

'She's always mean to me. She fights with everybody, not just me. I told her not to kick the boy. Did you see the boy? He was sleeping on the floor in one corner. You saw him? And she went and kicked him in the head with her foot. You didn't see her do that? Anybody can sleep in this dargah,' Shabnam expresses the right for all to the democratic spaces of the shrine. 'This isn't her house. She had no business telling him to get up and leave. That's all I said. I said you have no right to kick the boy. It's not your house. And she started fighting with me.'

Afterwards, I met another homeless woman who's an expert at making homes at shrines. She begs at them, moving from shrine to shrine, following the urs (death anniversary) celebrations of the saints when devotees come in large numbers and alms are easier to get. It's safer than being on the roads. And food and accommodation is always free.

'She's not from here,' Shabnam went on about the older woman. 'She has a husband in Bareilly but she's run away from him. And now she lives at the dargah and sleeps with another man.'

'Do you two fight often?'

'Every day,' Shabnam says smugly, her eyes glinting in the glow of the chandeliers. 'We fight every day.'

Like the wailing women, Shabnam seems emptied out and liberated after the verbal duel. She's at ease now, answering my questions without any rancour or resistance. She has very little curiosity about me. Perhaps she already had an idea of the kind of life I led. I asked her about her mother.

'My mother died in a fire when I was small,' she said.

And she doesn't remember much more. They lost everything in that fire. Her father, brother and she moved to the dargah and started living here. Her father started working for the pir sahibs.

'He's sick often. He can't work every day,' she said about her father. 'His stomach was split open from here to here,' she made a vertical line on her shirt.

I give her a hundred rupees and promise to come back to eat with her one Thursday.

The sanctimonious air of the shrine its caretakers are so careful to project and preserve, barring women from entering the inner chambers, is undone here in the fringes where Shabnam and I stood and talked. In the not-so-visible peripheries of the shrine, it's the wailing women, the cursing women, the unchaste and outcaste women, the questioning women, the mad women, the fighting women, who add to the shrine's pathos, garlanding its beauty with their strange pluck, mixing madness with resilience, resignation with resistance. It's women like Shabnam and her fighting partner, they are the real brides of the shrine, lacking visibility and possessing no power in the hierarchical administrative structures of the shrine. Like the world outside, here too, they strive to carve out an existence on the margins.

It's the women I met and watched who reflecteded the sublime, hidden, and nuanced beauty of the shrine for me. It was their presence that blessed the journey I was about to embark on. It's in its overwhelming femininity that the humanist ethos of the shrine lives on despite the overt misogyny and tasteless greed of its caretakers. That they haven't been able to turn the shrine into a rich-only, males-only space, though they might desire to do so, speaks of the classless, genderless spirit of this and other Sufi shrines. It's stubbornness on the part of women that makes Nizamuddin's shrine into a womanly and women's space. And I felt it was the right sort of beginning for me to start my travels from this sacred space, a sheltering space, a musical space, a healing space, an irreverent space.

3

Dilli se Lahore

Church wall, village near Kasur, Punjab, Pakistan

In the pre-dawn dark, I arrive at Delhi's Ambedkar bus terminal. It's 4.30 a.m., two hours before the bus to Lahore is to depart. For security purposes, I was told to come at least two hours early by the ticketing clerk. A big blue sign proclaims: 'Delhi-Lahore Bus Service: A bridge between two nations.' Once inside the building, the security checks are time-consuming and verge on the comical. I'm asked to open both my bags, and turn on my laptop. When it comes on, I'm asked to shut it down. What could be the purpose of making me turn it on only to make me shut it down?

'Where are you coming from?' the immigration man interrogates me.

'Allahabad.'

'Where do you live?'

'Allahabad.'

'Madam, where in Allahabad?'

'You mean, my address?' I'm intimidated by his questions, not sure why he wants to know my address.

'Yes!' He sounds impatient. 'Do you live close to Tagore Town?'

'No, not close to Tagore Town. But,' I try to placate him, 'in a small town, you know, nothing is far from anything.'

'So you know Tagore Town?' he says, sounding somewhat

relieved. 'You know Nehru's mausi's (maternal aunt's) house? She used to be my uncle's neighbour in Tagore Town.'

'*Accha*? No, I don't know Nehru's mausi's house.'

'I was posted in Allahabad for the Kumbh Mela, thirty years ago,' he says proudly. 'You were? That was a long time ago!' I reflect his wistful longing for his uncle's house back to him. 'And you haven't been to Allahabad since?'

'No, just once. But I remember my uncle's big house in Tagore Town.'

Noticing his emphasis on 'big', I say: 'Tagore Town has many big bungalows.'

He's happy when I say that. 'There are only a few passengers, madam,' he proclaims, as if justifying this lengthy digression about his uncle's bungalow. 'Very few people travel to Pakistan during Ramzan.'

'What's this, madam?' he asks, removing my bag of wheat bran from the duffle bag.

'Wheat bran.'

'*Atta ka bhoosa*?'

'*Arre, yaar*, it's dalia,' a colleague standing next to him corrects him.

'Dalia?' He examines the bag, his scepticism unquenched. '*Accha*? Dalia? But this dalia looks different. My dadi ate dalia every day for breakfast. And what's this?' He holds up my spiky acupressure foot-roller.

'It's a foot massager. For back pain.'

'A foot massager for back pain? Madam, why do you massage your foot if the pain is in your back?'

'*Abbe yaar*, you don't know,' his colleague tries to show me how much better-informed he is. 'Those who live with pain know about pain. If the doctor tells you to massage your feet, you massage your feet even if the pain is in your back. *Samjhe nahi*?'

'My dadima never had any kind of pain,' says the man who was posted at Kumbh thirty years ago. He rolls the foot-roller in his hand and examines the spikes on it as he speaks of his grandmother. 'She wished she would fall sick so she could come to know what pain is. She prayed to Ishwar to send her pain. But for a long time, she got no pain. Then He listened to her prayers. She got ill, and then she was in so much pain, she never got off her bed. And one day she died from pain.'

I shake my head as a gesture of commiseration as I rearrange the bag of bran, the foot-roller, the clothes and books, and wait for the bag to be weighed.

The Kumbh mela man smiles patronizingly: 'It's 9 kgs over the 20 kg allowed limit. Madam, 120 rupees per kg for excess baggage. That comes to one thousand and eighty. You can pay a thousand.'

'Really? That much?' My disbelief reflects in my voice.

After studying my shocked face, he has a change of heart. '*Chaliye, koi baat nahin*, madam. You're from Allahabad. I'll let you go this time.'

I thank him profusely for his generosity and thank God silently for our Allahabad connection, but I also have a feeling the scales weren't accurate.

After he lets me go I enter the waiting area where a lady

checker wants to frisk me. First she checks my 'ladies samaan', my purse.

'Weren't you here last year? You were writing a book, na?' she says conversationally, rummaging through my purse.

'I'm still writing it,' I reply.

'You're still writing it?' she exclaims, wide-eyed.

'Yes. I'm still writing it. But you remembered me. Your memory is good.'

'Yes, I remember you. You said you were a writer going there for some interviews for your book.'

I nod.

She asks me to climb up on a low wooden stand and starts frisking me. My body tautens in an obedient T. She admonishes me in a sisterly way:

'*Aur aap phir akeli jaa rahi hain wahan?* You're going there alone, again?'

'*Ji hanh.*' I try to appear unfazed as she swipes the detector over my arms and legs.

A smile was probably not the right response but in that awkward position, I couldn't think of doing anything else.

'Your book, is it in Hindi or English?'

'English.'

'Then I won't be able to read it,' she says sternly as I climb down.

'If I can get it translated, I'll bring you a copy in Hindi.'

'You have to remove your camera battery. You can't take pictures on the bus,' she says, suddenly remembering that I had a camera in my purse. She sounds distant and bitter and not happy with me. I can't tell if it's about my travelling alone, travelling to Pakistan, carrying a laptop and camera, or writing the book in English.

I am not the only woman on the bus but I am the only woman journeying alone. I survey the other women in the departure lounge: all are accompanied by males. It would be a euphemism to call the waiting area a lounge—pesky flies, no fans, nailed-to-floor orange chairs and a single cooler whirring disconsolately in a corner of the long hall. The seats closest to the cooler are taken up by the security guards. There is a small TV high up on the wall, tuned to an old Bollywood hits channel. Rajesh Khanna is singing to Mumtaz about her conceited, coquettish ways. They are frolicking, rain-drenched, in a garden and she's dancing in an alluring lemon-wet sari. The security guards hum along with Kishore Kumar:

Gorey rang pena a itna gumaan kar
Gora rang do din mein dhal jaega

Don't let your fair skin give you such airs
Your beauty is transient, will fade with time

~

Around 5.30 luke-warm tea and Marie biscuits arrive.

'Not for me,' the older woman next to me waves the tray aside. 'I'm fasting.'

I take a cup and dip a dry Marie into it. I glance at her to check if she disapproves.

Her hair is henna-orange, and rosary beads move swiftly between her fingers. After giving me her version of verbal frisking (Where do you live? Are you married? Do you have children? Why are you going *there*?) and feeling satisfied with my answers, she tells me she is going to Lahore for her brother's funeral. As I listen to her I realize that she, like the security guard, isn't interested in me beyond the categories of respectability she has just slotted me into. She simply wants a willing listener to recount her own tale to.

'I'm going to Lahore after twenty-three years but I can't stay more than a week. My brother passed away so I have to go. My daughters-in-law just don't know how to manage without me. And my grandchildren will cry for me. And then there's Eid preparations so I'm coming back in a week.'

Of her five sons, the youngest is accompanying her. He looks bored, a beefy lad with a beard, fiddling with his phone.

A group of four women in black attract my attention. They sit silently, so close to each other, they look like they have flowed and morphed into a single mass on the orange seats. I don't know why my eyes keep returning to them. Perhaps because I am concerned if they can breathe. Their faces are covered with black veils. Their burqas are black. Their socks are black. The gloves they wear are black. I am sweating and fidgeting in the humid room and their head-to-toe cover makes me even more fidgety.

'Who are those women? Why are they all in black?' I whisper to my neighbour who seems well-informed about everything.

'They're Tableeghi Jamaat ladies.[1] They've come from Burma. They're going to Pakistan.'

'I didn't know there was any Tableeghi Jamaat activity in Burma!' I say, amazed. Wasn't Burma communist? 'And those men? Who are they?'

'Their husbands probably.'

The husbands are men with stern faces, sitting a few seats from us, in a separate group. The only thing black about them is their beards. They are wearing white caps, white kurtas and checkered lungis.

I comment on the folded prayer mats all the Tableeghi husbands are carrying. In response, my neighbour pulls out a pocket-size sunglass case from her purse and flips it open to unfurl a full-size ja-namaaz, a prayer mat. The lettering on the case is COOL.

'When I travel, I make sure I have everything I need.'

'Cool!' Awed, I ask if I can inspect it. She is pleased to see how impressed I am by the prayer mat's compactness. Made

---

[1] Tableeghi Jamaat (society for spreading faith) is a religious movement founded in 1926 by Muhammad Ilyas al-Kandhlawi in India. The movement primarily aims at Tablighi spiritual reformation of Muslims across all social and economic spectra to bring them closer to Islam. Tableeghi Jamaat encourages its members to spend at least forty continuous days in a year on tableeghi missions. Accompanied by a close male relative, women members are also encouraged to go out and work among other women and family members while following the rules of modesty, seclusion and segregation. They are made to observe strictest rules of hijab by covering their faces and hands. From http://en.wikipedia.org/wiki/Tablighi_Jamaat

in China I expect, and Made in China it is. Muslims praying on mats manufactured in godless China?

By the time I finish the tea and Marie biscuits, it is time to board the bus. I am glad for the air-conditioning inside the bus, and even gladder to have an unoccupied seat next to mine. I don't want to make conversation on the trip. I had planned to read and nap but the excitement of the border-crossing, even though it is not to happen for several hours yet, keeps me preoccupied. I had made this journey last year, and there must be a reason I am doing it again. I need to meet people for the book. But that is just one of the reasons.

There's a certain compelling charm and pathos in crossing the man-made border between enemy countries. It's a challenge, a daring act. Years ago, my father had threatened my survival if I married a man from the other side. I had defied him and survived though he kept waiting for me to return defeated to the parental fold. From fatherland to husbandland, and back to fatherland—as a banished heretic, I've been flitting across this border, belonging to both lands and to neither, fitting in neither here nor there. Each time I go across the border into Pakistan, I feel I'm crossing imagined lines because the landscape in Amritsar and Lahore isn't that different. There are no markers other than the border checkpost to tell you you've entered a different country. It doesn't feel like I'm returning to my fatherland. Nowhere is where I feel I'm from. Travelling by plane simply doesn't have that literality—the extraordinariness of the journey that comes from slowly progressing towards the border. By plane the journey from Delhi to Lahore is over in fifty minutes, before you've had time to absorb that you're going across countries. The flight from Delhi to Lahore simply doesn't feel grand enough to encapsulate the grandness, or the horror of this crossing made by those millions who were displaced, killed, looted, so Indians could call the land on the Indian side of this border India, and Pakistanis could call the land on the other side of the border Pakistan! If you fly over the border, thousands of feet above it, you lose out on the immediacy of so colossal a piece of historical idiocy. Flying has none of the starkness, the imagined terror that renders the bus journey non-trivial, and makes it an event to mull over.

The best-known Partition story by Saadat Hasan Manto[2] hinges on the exchange of lunatics between India and Pakistan. The story's hero, Toba Tek Singh, a Sikh inmate of Lahore's insane asylum, is forced to migrate to India. The officials of the newly-formed nations decide to exchange their lunatics and move them to India if they are Hindus or Sikhs, and to Pakistan if they are Muslims. On the designated day, Toba Tek Singh is overcome with confusion, not sure which side of the border he belongs to, because he's not sure where his hometown is, anymore. He refuses to walk across the border to India; he collapses between India and

---

[2]Saadat Hasan Manto (1912-55): Controversial 20th century Urdu short story writer. For a special issue on Manto's centenary and my essay titled 'Manto, My Spiritual Father', see the April-May 2012 issue of e-zine, *Muse India*, at http://www.museindia.com

Pakistan, in no-man's-land. When the bus crossed over from India into Pakistan, I felt like Toba Tek Singh— belonging to no-man's-land, hemmed in by hollow subscriptions of nationhood.

Is there a patch of the planet I can call my own? Can the planet be cut up into pieces and owned by individuals and nations? Ownership of the planet sounds quite ridiculous when you think the planet is a celestial body swirling round its sun, and has been swirling for millions of years before humans came into existence and will perhaps do so for millions of years after humans cease to exist.

~

As we go past the Red Fort ramparts I see the homeless of the planet asleep on the roadside. They don't have pretences of owning any patch of the planet. A shy sun peeps out, lighting their curled-up bodies. They look like bags of grain under clay-coloured sheets.

Soft rain starts to fall as we merge with the national highway, heading north to Haryana. Raindrops, as if mad with ecstasy, land on the glass of the window and race downwards, propelled by breeze and gravity. Perhaps they will merge with the ocean eventually, become one with the ocean, like qalandars, faqirs who turn away from the lures of this world and wander deliberately into obscurity, in search of God. I watch the racing droplets and descend into some inner, hypnotic, veiled world of my own.

Two police jeeps and two gun-carrying guards escort us, making us feel we're precious or dangerous cargo. The

Indian guards on the bus are chatting with their Pakistani counterparts in Punjabi. It's their camaraderie that eases me into more relaxed breathing, and I go back to watching the droplets of rain that scramble like dervishes on the window pane.

I'm reminded of my plane journey to England more than two decades ago. There's a difference though: I'm freer now, at least mentally, though the world around me isn't. I felt completely defenceless then though the world had seemed a trifle safer. Words like terrorism and suicide bombings were non-existent then. I feel unsure of how to handle my newly-acquired personal freedoms in an increasingly unsafe, uncaring world. The freedom I experienced for a few moments in the colourful chaos at Nizamuddin's shrine was stamped out soon enough—there too, I was declared unfit as a woman to go near the tomb, ending that momentary feeling of freedom. I had been pushed back into my place. Women aren't meant to be truly free.

The soft rain becomes a steady downpour, and a silver-grey mist hovers over the green fields flanking the highway. Airtel welcomes you to Haryana, beeps my mobile. Muddy villages blur past, momentary disruptions in unbroken swathes of green. There's no escaping Bollywood: the Indian and Pakistani security guards in the front rows are once again watching the racy dance and song sequences on the small TV screen. Most of the passengers though are nodding off. I wonder if the four Tableeghi Jamaat ladies are also watching the videos, and if this wouldn't pollute their fasting, and what do they make of so much exposed female flesh?

The non-fasting passengers are served breakfast in Haryana and lunch in Punjab. The meals included as part of the very reasonably-priced ticket are somewhat surprising, a gesture of goodwill on the part of the two governments perhaps. Into the parking lot of Magnolia Restaurant, run by the Punjab Tourism Department, the bus pulls up for lunch. There's a painted sign to greet passengers. Two men, representing a Punjabi Sikh and a Muslim, the former in a turban, the latter in a Turkish cap, are embracing each other, standing in the no-man's-land between India and Pakistan. The Sikh guy is Toba Tek Singh, I like to imagine. And he's embracing his Muslim brother, after they both meet and refuse to migrate to one country or the other. Instead, they compose a poem on love and brotherhood, standing on land that is neither India nor Pakistan.

Painted above the heads of the two of them is this verse that reads like a prayer that Toba Tek Singh might have recited:

Dil ka darwaza khol ke jaana
Par wapas jaa ke bhul na jaana

Open the heart's doors wherever you go
But do not forget me once you depart

Outside the ladies' bathroom, the old lady with the COOL Chinese prayer mat, sputters breathlessly: 'You wouldn't believe the low neckline of one of those Tableeghi Jamaat ladies. Yes, yes! I could see everything when she threw back her naqaab and bent over the sink to wash. *Tauba, tauba.*'

'Really?'

'I'm not lying. Allah forbid that I should tell lies in the month of Ramzan,' she says, hurrying back towards the bus.

I rush towards the ladies' room so I can also claim to be an eyewitness of a Tableeghi lady's bosom but the Tableeghi ladies file out it in a black line just as I enter the women's toilets.

~

Back on the bus, I take out my notebook and the little Urdu paperback I picked up near Nizamuddin's shrine in Delhi. It can be roughly translated as *Islamic Etiquettes of Sex: Sexual Relations between Husband and Wife*—penned by a Dr Aftab Ahmed Shah of Itawah, a homeopath and a specialist in women's skin diseases. This little paperback lives up to its promise of livening my hours on the bus. Its preface proudly proclaims it to be the second Indian edition and there's also a highly successful Pakistani edition. The pseudo-scientific undertones of the book and the author's medical degree justify its medically peddled misogyny. Dr Shah fills it with health, diet, and nutritional advice for a sexually successful life. A sexually successful life is one that leads to successful procreation. Sexual pleasure is to be engaged in primarily for begetting children, preferably sons. True to his goal of making the Muslim ummah more populous, Dr Aftab Shah includes several calorie-rich recipes for increasing sperm count. I found this testicle-strengthening halwa quite irresistible:

'Using one large egg, add carrot juice the equivalent of one hollowed-out egg shell, and add one egg shell equivalent of ghee and honey. Mix well, and cook on low heat until the mixture turns to a soft, halwa-like consistency. Eat daily for at least twenty-one days. Avoid sour, flatulence-producing foods, and refrain from eating meat and fish during this period. With the halwa's use as prescribed, even elderly men can recover the vigour of their youth.'

Women, writes Dr Shah, are objects of beauty that are not meant to be displayed in public. Therefore, they should be kept in seclusion at all times so that their honour and physical beauty can be preserved. This advice for women's purdah is for some reason included in the section titled Night Emissions. The rest of the chapter discusses the causes and cures for wet dreams. If they are limited to two or three times a month, there's no cause for worry. However, if they occur more frequently, the sufferer is advised to have dinner early and avoid going to bed on a full stomach. Dr Shah suggests the following as palliatives for morning ejaculations: sleep on the right side, get up early, never use a soft, foam mattress, think only clean, pure thoughts, shun the practice of going to the cinema, and avoid hot drinks at bedtime.

Masturbation is a heinous, forbidden transgression, Dr Shah warns. It's better to marry a slave girl if you have unbearable sexual urges rather than dirty your hands with this haraam activity. He doesn't discuss women's masturbation, perhaps because it's a non-issue, or not much of a problem, or simply not worth discussing. Another reason might be that even if women masturbate, it can't affect their ability to reproduce, whereas male masturbation means loss of valuable seed.

Sex with the wife during menstruation is to be avoided,

writes Dr Shah. Anal sex, or 'penetration from behind', is also haraam according to him. Sexual activity that is engaged in for any other purpose than procreation, such as pleasure, is unnecessary, and therefore, forbidden.

He provides detailed instructions to the bridegroom for initiating sex on the wedding night. The proper procedure includes prayers which must be recited first, if truly Islamic sexual etiquette is followed. In a rare display of concern for women, he advises the groom to wait a few days if the bride is menstruating because sometimes, during menstruation, intercourse can be painful for women. But sex on the wedding night need not be delayed for any reason other than menstruation. Nowhere does he mention the etiquette of ascertatining the woman's degree of desire, or obtaining the woman's consent before initiating intercourse.

Doctor Shah's advice to Muslim bridegrooms on their wedding night:

'When you are left alone with your wife, and before you consummate the marriage, recite Bismillah and Sura Ikhlas thrice. Then recite this prayer: O Allah, I begin with your name, and may you guard us from Satan's evil influence. And also protect our progeny, male or female, which you grant us, from Satan's manipulations.'

Just before ejaculating, he advises the groom to recite this prayer: O Allah, do not grant Satan access to the child you grant us from this union.

Failure to recite these prayers, Dr Shah warns, will invite Satan's wrath and your children are bound to grow up quarrelsome and become mischief-makers.

He discusses the merits of the many prohibitions, precautions and restrictions, and wherever possible, cites medical jargon and quotes vague hadith[3] to add stature to his assertions:

'As for the most natural position in which to have sex, it's best to have the man on top. All animals have sex in this position and it is most effective for successful impregnation.'

Both the man and woman must relieve their bladders post-coitus, or they risk getting infected with incurable diseases (names of these incurable diseases are not mentioned).

If you have a wet dream and desire to have sex with your wife right after it, you must bathe first. Otherwise the son she conceives from such intercourse will be born insane.

Do not drink water right after copulation. Doing so can give you asthma.

Do not copulate in a vertical position. Doing so gives birth to retarded children and according to Greek medicine, can also cause trembling sickness.

Do not gaze at the genitals of the woman while having sex. Doing so can cause the progeny she conceives to be blind.

Do not converse with her while having sex. Doing so can make your child speech-impaired.

Use some kind of fragrance before sex, especially if you are smelling of perspiration or cigarette smoke, because this is undesirable.

---

[3]Hadith: collections of sayings attributed to Prophet Mohammad.

Do not face in the direction of the holy kaaba when you have intercourse.

Do not disrobe completely. Complete nudity will make the conceived child immodest.

While ejaculating, recite this prayer: O Allah, if this copulation leads to birth of a son, may Satan not harm him.

After ejaculating, do not separate immediately from your wife. Wait till she climaxes. Women take longer than men to climax.

You are allowed to kiss, suck on, tickle, and rub your wife's breasts. This is often very pleasurable for her. However, beware that if you take her nipples into your mouth, do not swallow her milk. Doing so is highly objectionable.

The man who follows these instructions, and after copulation partakes of some high-calorie food such as carrot halwa, egg halwa, milk sweetened with honey, cream barfi, or if none of the above is available, then at least eats two or three tolas, approximately 11.6 grams, of plain jaggery, such a man will never experience fatigue after sex, and will always retain his potency.

After reading and marking out passages for translation from Dr Shah's manual of Islamic sex, I sat back, closed my eyes, and prayed to the Almighty that newlyweds may never lay their hands on this manual: Dear God, please don't condemn Muslim men and women to a life of erotic sterility, and do not allow this book further editions. And dear God, if a third edition is inevitable, exercise your omnipotence and omniscience to prevent Muslim males of the

subcontinent from following the instructions in this manual.
Ameen.

The hours pass pleasantly in reading and translating the
Islamic etiquettes of sex according to Dr Shah. Around two
in the afternoon, we enter Amritsar, and an hour later, we
are at Attari, the border village on the Indian side.

The immigration hall is dark as there is no power. It takes
two hours to get our passports stamped and our luggage
checked and reloaded onto the bus. Part of the delay is
caused by the Tableeghi ladies who refuse to unveil their
faces to a male immigration officer. A lady immigration
officer had to be found to match their passport photos with
their unveiled faces.

We pass from India into Pakistan, walking through the
no-man's-land, and reboard the bus in Wagah on the
Pakistani side.

There's no power in Pakistan either. But the authorities
turn on the generators. The immigration and customs
building on the Pakistani side is definitely cleaner, newer,
and quicker and we get through passport control and luggage
screening in a few minutes.

We're back on the bus again, and during this last hour
before reaching Lahore, I try to enumerate the differences
between the Indian and Pakistani sides of the border. The
Indian sky was the same shade of overcast grey as the sky in
Pakistan, and the moisture-laden August air in Attari just as
stifling as Wagah's. The rice fields held the same greenness,
and the villages looked just as rustic on both sides. But there
were exceptions—the shop names were in Hindi over there

and they are in Urdu here. I saw more women there and less women here.

~

We reach Lahore at dusk.

'*Chalo baccho*, Pakistan *aa gaya*! Put on your slippers,' a passenger with several children exclaims.

Lahore is crowded with autorickshaws, but they aren't decorated with glittering flaps like the rickshaws of India. Like Delhi, the number of vehicles of all sizes in Lahore is soul-shrivelling. But Lahore still has relics like donkey carts from an era that is already passé in Delhi. As our bus crawls to its final stop in the pre-iftaar rush of cars, rickshaws and buses, its progress is blocked by one of these carts. The cart driver is daring enough to hold up the traffic in a fashionable street. He's tugging at the reins of his donkey and talking frantically into his mobile. He could be part of a poster titled 'modernity and tradition brush shoulders'. Two colossal cauldrons of rice, which he was probably trying to deliver before iftaar, are on the cart like two out of place, old-world ladies, stranded on a fast, impatient street.

In Lahore I am the guest of a friend at the Formation House that belongs to Franciscan friars. In this all-male friary, I am the only woman among fifty men. They're thrilled to have a lady visitor, a writer, as a guest from India. Never mind that I'm not really Indian or Pakistani. They don't ask and I don't tell. Precise identities are not too much of an issue in this space.

A Christian village close to Lahore has been ransacked a

couple of months ago by a mob over rumours of a Christian girl desecrating pages of the Quran. It happened in Kasur, the home of the legendary Sufi poet of the Punjab, Bulleh Shah, who believed the worst sin was not the demolition of temples and mosques, but the shattering of a human heart.[4]

Brother Lamaan, my friend and host, asks if Christians in India feel discriminated against the way they do in Pakistan. His parents migrated to Pakistan from India. His birth name is not Lamaan. A Sufi baba with whom he feels a deep spiritual connection gave him this name and he prefers his friends use it rather than his Christian name.

'If you talk of feelings, maybe you should ask if there's any place where people on the margins don't feel discriminated against,' I reply. 'There's discrimination everywhere, especially when it comes to acting on feelings and desires. Christians in India can't fall in love with non-Christians and live a life free of fear. Not unless they're rich and influential.'

'Our students are scared after these recent incidents in Kasur,' Lamaan says. Lamaan teaches English and Personality Development to incoming aspirants. 'I make my class read *The Road Less Travelled* by Scott Peck in Urdu first,' he says, 'and we take a whole year over it. We go through the book very slowly. I have to go slow when I am introducing spiritual concepts like love and I have to let them discover that true love can only flower in the absence of the ego.'

'Do the boys get it? About love and the ego,' I ask.

---

[4]See the Bulleh Shah quote at the beginning of chapter one.

'Some of them do. It takes them time, that's why I take a year. Most of the aspirants come from the poorest villages, and they've been told Christians are uncivilized bhangis, untouchables. They grow up having internalized a lot of self-hatred.'

Later that day Lamaan hands me the manuscript of John O'Brien's book on the construction of Punjabi Christian identity.[5] The more I read, the more ashamed I feel. The Christian boys who've grown up hearing they're uncivilized, greet me, carry my bags up to my room, bring me cold water, and ask me if I would like tea. Dignified and quiet, they go about their classes and turn their eyes downwards respectfully when they meet me in the dining hall. From my window, I watch them sweeping the pathways, watering the vast garden, feeding the dogs and cleaning out the bird cages. Where's the trace of uncivilization in them? They go about their chores with a gentle grace. They could be monks from another universe. It must take a lot of dying to live so gently.

'I want to go to Kasur,' I tell Lamaan. 'Can you arrange for me to visit the Christian community there?'

Early next morning, I board a van popularly referred to as Hiace from outside the Daata Durbar shrine and am on my way to Kasur. Daata Durbar, located near the Bhati gate of Lahore, is one of the oldest Muslim shrines in the subcontinent. It houses the remains of a Sufi saint, Abul

---

[5]John O'Brien, *The Unconquered People: The Liberation Journey of an Oppressed Caste*, Oxford University Press, Pakistan. http://www.oup.com.pk.

Hassan Ali Hajvery (more commonly known as Daata Ganj Baksh, meaning the master who bestows treasures). He is said to have lived on the site in the eleventh century. In July 2010, two suicide bombers blew themselves up at Daata Durbar shrine on a Thursday, the day when thousands of (mostly poor) devotees throng the shrine. Many died and many more were injured. Absence of safer alternatives had returned the homeless to their nightly shelter on the traffic islands outside the bombed shrine.

The homeless of Lahore are asleep on the traffic islands. Like their Delhi brethren, they are concealed from head to foot under dirty sheets that keep away mosquitoes and visibility.

In Kasur, a dusty little town surrounded by green villages, about an hour's ride by Hiace from Lahore, I am met by the nuns from the Convent of Our Lady of Sorrow and Our Lady of Joy. Their church is a red brick building, sitting serenely in a compound filled with ancient neems. The nuns run a school for five hundred children and live behind the church in a simple house. We sit down to tea in the parlour. They tell me how terrified they were on that July night when the women from the village came crying to tell them their homes had been attacked and looted by the mob.

'Why did this have to happen in Bulleh Shah's land? How soul-broken he must be,' I say.

'You know, I grew up in Lahore. Lahore's patron saints are Daata sahib and Madho Lal and they preached love for all,' one of the nuns says. 'I grew up in Lahore but we didn't know they were Muslims and we were Christians. But now, it's very different. What is our future in this country? Where has love gone? Where is tolerance for one's neighbours?' Her eyes turn moist.

'Sister, you're still running your school even though you see no future here. That's where love is. That's the answer to your question,' I say, almost on the verge of tears myself.

After lunch, the nuns take me to the village to visit the Christian families. There's a strange hush over the village. Corn cobs are drying in open courtyards. A broken-down door swings on its hinges as we step down into an aangan. I feel like I've come to a cemetery. An old man struggles to get up and greet us. He sighs and shows us broken trunks, smashed walls. He says he is still waiting. For what?

Waiting is a hopeful word.

One woman talks without meeting our eye, as if she's remembering a loved one, or something that has vanished forever: 'We were cooking—it was getting dark when they came. We ran and jumped over the walls. We hid during the night in the fields. Everything became different afterwards. We've stopped attending one another's weddings and funerals. We don't even send our children to their school anymore. What if they find an excuse for starting another fight and beat up our children?'

The mob was made up of men from the village, men they knew well, men who had been their neighbours for years. Isn't this reminiscent of what Hindu neighbours did to Muslims in Gujarat in 2002? Except there the victims were Muslims, here the perpetrators are Muslims. It's a Friday afternoon, and pious Muslim men of the village are making their way to the mosque for prayers. The maulvi's voice crackles over the loudspeaker and rends the silence.

'Is this the mosque where the announcement was made?' I ask, repelled by the brazenness of the loudspeakers.

The Christian villagers accompanying us nod silently as we rush past the mosque's entrance. Christians are kafirs, unbelievers, they should be destroyed because they have sullied the name of Islam—the maulvi had announced, inciting the Friday afternoon crowd, and erecting the Us and Them boundaries.

Later that afternoon, I make it a point to visit the dargah of Kasur's custodian poet-saint, Bulleh Shah, to register my protest with him. Abida Parveen sings *Yaar Subha Shaam* in my head and I need her voice to buoy up the dead spaces of my heart. The approximate translation from Punjabi of the opening lines of this Sufi kalaam by Buleh Shah is:

> If God could be found by roaming the forests
> God would have been found by beasts and fowl
> Mian Bulleh, only they find the true God
> Who are true themselves and pure of heart.
> You learnt so much from reading
> a thousand books
> But have you read your Self?
> You go and sit in mosque and temple
> But have you visited your own Soul?
> You are so busy fighting Satan
> You never wage war with your Self
> You may have reached the sky
> But you failed to glimpse your heart.

There are beggars in green kurtas with dreadlocks who beckon for alms from the shade of trees. A drainage channel overflowing with sewage and puffed-up polythene bags runs alongside the dargah's entrance. The material poverty of Kasur adds sadness and riches to Bulleh's mystic verses. He lived here, he danced here, he loved here. So what if two centuries have gone by since he lived and loved? His verses are no less powerful today and even more relevant.

To Baba Bulleh Shah, the mystic mad with the ecstasy of love, I stand and pray with folded hands. I stand on the women's side of the shrine, where several women are seated. 'It's just as well that you are not alive to see what passes for religion in our times. But, I suppose you knew this was going to happen so you left us your poetry. You departed from this world of lies and illusions. Oh Bulleh, will you not cast your loving eye towards us once more? Will you let love perish in this land of yours? Then what good is that soul-wrenching poetry of yours?'

~

I get back to Lahore that evening. At the Formation House, I wait out the routine power cut in Lamaan's narrow room. The country is experiencing its worst power cuts, several hours a day. There's only a mattress and a few cushions on the floor and Lamaan's woodworking tools, otherwise the room is bereft of furniture. Lamaan has painted the square window panes in bright kaleidoscopic colours against a background of black. When sunlight spills in, the room fills with many-coloured splendour.

The night is sharp and silent, sweaty and sad. But Lamaan's room has a soft, sacred grace about it. The only light is candlelight. There's a clearing of consciousness, a heightened silence in the absence of lights and fans, making small sounds like cricket chirps louder.

My friend, Ghazala, has come to take me home to meet her mother. Lamaan brings her a plate of roti and sabzi. There's always food at the friary for guests who drop in.

'Religion has failed, but so has science, to solve humanity's problems,' Lamaan says, placing the plate before Ghazala on the floor. He's a tall, broad man. Outwardly imposing, you could say. Hearing him articulate something so profound in such a perfunctory, humble voice, unnerves me.

'And you're still churning out fresh crops of Franciscan monks every year?' I laugh. 'What for?'

'In the impractical hope of ushering in a new universal spiritual consciousness at some point. Isn't that impressive sounding? And because, in the spiritual quest we're all heading towards The One. But the paths to The One can be infinite.'

'I'm a living example of failure of religion,' Ghazala says, her dark eyes catching a gleam of candle light. Her pensive, attractive face betrays pain she can't speak of.

'Haven't you been fasting like a good Muslim to atone for your sins?' I ask her.

She nods as she eats. 'I have! But fasting is hard on smokers. I'm dying for a cigarette. Is it okay to smoke in your room, Lamaan?'

'Only if I can borrow one,' Lamaan chuckles. Ghazala passes him the pack.

'How's Amma? What does Amma think of your fasting?' I ask Ghazala.

'She loves it,' she says pushing aside her plate. 'She's the one who wakes me up for sehri! She gets up to make fresh parathas for me. You should see her on Eid—how she dresses up and makes seviyan with such enthusiasm, as if it's her festival.' Sehri is the pre-dawn meal eaten during Ramzan, and seviyan, sweetened vermicelli, cooked in milk, is served on Eid.

Ghazala's mother is Catholic and Ghazala at one time was also a Catholic, but when she married a Muslim man, she decided to convert to Islam. On her mother's side, her grandparents used to be Muslims until her grandfather changed his religion and converted his whole family to Christianity. Ghazala's mother resisted, but later, when she fell in love and married a Christian, she too became one. These challenging and dizzying religious crossovers don't end here. Ghazala's Christian father's family in the village were Hindus before they converted to Christianity!

'Are you saying you're a failure because you're all mixed up as far as religion goes? Because you aren't this or that?' I ask Ghazala.

'No, it's not just that. I am who I am. I wonder if any of this matters,' she says, gazing distractedly at the glowing tip of her cigarette.

'Don't you know, you are the object of my admiration because of your mixed-up-ness?'

'That's not something most people admire me for!' Ghazala grinds out the stub on the floor. 'Have you packed? We'll leave as soon as the lights come back.'

I patted my purse. 'I've packed my toothbrush.'

When the lights come back on, Ghazala and I walk out of the Formation House and stop an autorickshaw. She's been jobless for a good part of the year, and has only recently found work.

I have to lean into her to hear her above the roar of the rickshaw. 'Amma and I were living in one room all these months. We've just moved to a two-roomed place. But we still haven't unpacked. Don't mind the mess.'

Ghazala married a married man, changed her religion to Islam for his sake, but has never lived with him. They meet on weekends and holidays. I ask her about him. Her life is mixed up on many fronts from economic to emotional.

'He's all right,' she says, 'But I can't do the wifely thing for him all the time. For that he has his first wife. I'm happy with this arrangement. He's not a typical husband, but he's a good human being and a loving friend, and I like his company. We had a good time when we celebrated his birthday at my house the other day. Amma wants me to live like his proper wife, have a home and all that. But if you ask me, I prefer this, living like a married single woman. I like my independence. I don't want to be tied up in fake and unnatural relationships.'

The rickshaw enters a narrow, unpaved gali. Untidy, unpainted grey facades of tightly-packed houses gives the gali a choked look. Sweet shops, general stores, video shops and mobile phone shops are well-lit and open, imparting a garish cheerfulness to the greyness. The rickshaw bumps along till Ghazala asks the driver to stop next to a high iron gate.

'This is our new home.'

We enter a small, dark courtyard. Amma throws her arms around me.

'Beti, I've been waiting for you. Now quickly tell me what would you like to eat? Have you had dinner?'

We sit on the durrie in a dark room. It's load-shedding hour here. In a matter of minutes, working in the light of a battery-powered lamp, Amma has served us tea and suji-ka-halwa, and as we're eating halwa and drinking tea, sitting on the floor of the little room that serves as living room and Ghazala's bedroom, Amma keeps fanning herself. The second room of the house is Amma's bedroom and kitchen.

'Use this pillow. Don't lean against the wall,' Ghazala warns me. 'The wall is shedding paint.'

'It's because it rained so much,' Amma says, embarrassed.

'Amma, Ghazala tells me you get up to make parathas for her at sehri. I'm envious!' I try to take her mind off the peeling walls.

'If you stay here, I'll make them for you too,' Amma perks up. Her smile lightens her eyes and deepens her faint wrinkles. Her warmth feels like a cocoon I want to burrow into. 'So what if I don't fast? I was a Muslim until I got married. I've lived around Muslims all my life. I know their customs,' she asserts enthusiastically.

'Wah, Amma, *aap ki isi baat par mai qurban*!' I say. 'Don't let the Taliban hear you say that! In fact, what if some Talibans in the mohalla are spying on you?'

Amma chuckles and shakes her head vigorously. 'The Taliban? The Taliban can never rule this country. Jesus came to me in a dream and told me that. I dreamt that a Tsunami was coming to our shores. It's a huge wave that is about to destroy everything in its wake. Everybody is running for their life and suddenly, Jesus appears. I'm standing there alone. And he addresses me and says: 'There's no need to be afraid. The Tsunami rises higher and higher till it reaches the sky. But nothings happens to the people. The wave doesn't come into the city. What that means is that the Taliban can try all they want but they can never take over this country.'

'That's a powerful dream,' I say.

'It's a message from the Saviour,' Amma says emphatically. 'Jesus doesn't make false promises. Both my religions are my heritage. I practise them both. I can't leave one or the other.'

'That's why we celebrate Eid and Christmas, *hai na* Amma?' Ghazala gives her mother an adoring look.

'*Aur kya!*' Amma agrees. 'And on Thursdays, I buy sweets for niaz. And I believe in the power of Aab-e-zamzam.[6] When my sugar was really high, do you know, I went to a hakim who told me to drink Aab-e-zamzam daily after reciting an ayat, lines from the Quran, over it. And it worked. I'm a firm believer in spiritual cures. But I also go to church on Sundays. You need to have faith otherwise nothing works.'

---

[6]Aab-e-zamzam: water from the Zamzam well, situated near the Holy Kaaba, in Mecca. Muslims believe Zamzam water to have special healing properties.

Lights and fan come back on. Amma potters about getting ready for bed, and Ghazala and I look at the pictures of the birthday party she hosted for her husband last week. From time to time, the computer screen goes blank.

'It has a mind of its own,' Ghazala says.

Then it goes blank and stays blank. 'Why did you get married if you prefer to be single?' I ask her in the interlude.

'I didn't want to get married, but he did. He thought it wasn't right for us to be in a long-term relationship without marriage,' she replies.

'And love? Have you found love?'

'Love is too vast a topic and I can't explain what it means,' Ghazala says reaching out for a cigarette. 'Sometimes love only gives you pain. I can't say I've found the love I was looking for. I haven't. I realized something after going through so much pain: I've loved without conditions but I didn't get unconditional love in return. I always feel an emptiness in my heart. I tried to find real love, but all I've found is love with conditions, and if I deny or challenge it, I risk losing that love too.

'I have the love of my friends, my mother, my brothers and to some extent you could say, my husband's, although he doesn't show it much. So you can say love has come in various shades and expressions through different relationships. I express my love for my family by spending money on them. I express my affection for my husband in words and gestures, which makes him feel happy and secure, but it does nothing for me—marriage has just hindered my idea of love. It's meant getting stuck in a set pattern which I must follow, and if I break out of it, I'll get labelled a rebel.'

'You are already a rebel!' I say. 'I don't see you as stuck. You're just not proud enough to be who you are.'

We spread out mattresses on the floor and Ghazala, Amma and I lie down and watch one of the food channels, which Amma likes. Chef Zakir is preparing a fish pulao on Masala TV. The glistening pink boneless fish steaks, the colourful spices in little glass bowls, and the way chef Zakir chats with callers to the show, while he chops, stirs, fries and swoons over the aromas he's generating, keeps us riveted.

There's a commercial break before chef Zakir's pulao enters its second phase of preparation. More out-of-reach-of-most, glamorous food is advertised—kiwi slices and luscious strawberries swirl down into crystal bowls of whipped cream.

I ask Ghazala: 'Have you ever eaten a kiwi?'

'No, what is it?'

'It's that green fruit with black seeds in that fresh cream ad.'

'Oh! That's a kiwi? Have you eaten it?' Amma asks.

'When I lived in America I did, but I've never seen one in these parts.'

'You could probably buy them in one of the big supermarkets in Lahore,' Ghazala says. 'They import all kinds of fancy things from Dubai.'

The kiwis and strawberries and fish pulao are for a handful of princes among paupers who patronize the specialty supermarkets. In August 2010, a fifth of Pakistan's land mass lay submerged under the worst floods in the nation's post-colonial history. Twenty million people became refugees in their own country. Sugar and flour were selling at jaw-dropping prices. Those twenty million aren't buying kiwis or fish.

I fall asleep waiting for chef Zakir's fish pulao to get done. My last thought is: how many Pakistanis can eat kiwis and fish?

A couple of days later, I'm on an air-conditioned bus speeding north on the smooth, four-laned motorway to Abbotabad.

I recall a conversation with the rickshawala in Lahore. On the way to the Daewoo bus station, he got carried away expounding his horror at the forty-five people killed in the Shershah scrap market in Karachi the previous day. Lamaan had packed me some sabzi to eat on the way. I had asked the driver to stop at a tandoor for naan.

He forgot to stop at the naan shop. 'Baji, Amrika is coming, I tell you Amrika has plans to take over Pakistan,' he yelled above the traffic, almost hopefully. 'And it won't be bad if they came. Then we might make some progress. You watch, Amrika will take over our country soon. Our leaders get our votes with promises of roti, kapra, makaan, but which of them has ever given us anything? Sugar is selling at ninety rupees a kilo. Rents keep going up. Who's going to send my children to school? I'm only educating one child. Who's going to help me send my other three children to school? If Amrika comes, may be things would get better for us.'

Amma had seen Jesus in her dream. Jesus told her nobody, not even the Taliban would ever be able to take over Pakistan. But did Jesus mean to exclude the Americans too? What would the poor of Pakistan look like if Amrika ruled it? Would they be able to buy fish and kiwi? What would it mean for women after the Americans came? Would they feel 'liberated' like the women of Afghanistan and Iraq were supposed to feel after the Americans went in there to liberate those lands?

~

That night was a special one for me. And it had been a special day too. So much learning in so short a time, and I wasn't sure of the multiple nuances of all I had absorbed. Struggling humans, their dignity tattered and endangered in the midst of intense hatred, and faltering love jostling for space in ever-growing alienation of humans from humans. And, yet the glories of ongoing co-existence—in the vast, whirling dance of existence, in the subdued villages of Kasur where some no longer feel like they belong to Kasur, in the downward gaze of the gentle friary boys, and in the room with peeling paint where Ghazala and Amma live and practise Christianity and Islam side by side. Peace and love, ordinary and unglamorous, thrive in the most drab, undramatic settings. Its flag bearers are Ghazala and Amma, Brother Lamaan and the rickshawala, and the Sisters of the Convent of Our Lady of Sorrow and Our Lady of Joy in the town where Bulleh Shah rests.

A few months after my meeting with Ghazala, Amma

passed away. She went peacefully, while she was saying her prayers, as if Jesus himself had come for her, Ghazala emailed me. Her email was characteristic of the admirable mixed-up-ness of her creed, defying definite labels: 'I meet Amma very often. She is very happy, beyond the pains and problems of this world. She loved red roses, so on her chaliswan,[7] I presented her a bouquet of red roses from all of us.'

---

[7]Chaliswan is the fortieth day after death observed by South Asian Muslims as a ceremony marked by special prayers and distribution of food to the poor.

4

Eid in Oghi

Embracing the Asokan edicts in Mansehra

Last Friday in Ramazan

A mountain-blue, hot September day. I reached Abbotabad from Lahore two days ago. Today I am embarking on a journey from Abbotabad to Oghi. I say *embarking* because it feels like I'm going on a pilgrimage. The village I am going to is close to the Taliban belt, in the North West Frontier Province (NWFP) of Pakistan. NWFP was renamed Khyber Pakhtunkhwa in 2010. I refer to the region by its former colonial name because that's what it was called when I visited it. And because the old name has an alienating foreignness to it, which resonates with the continued presence of imperialistic foreign forces in the area. Oghi isn't more than 50 km away from Abbotabad but it's going to take me almost three hours to get there. First to Mansehra, then to Oghi, and from Oghi to the village where my friend Laila lives. Laila has invited me to her house for Eid. I met Laila a couple of years ago in an art therapy workshop for earthquake-affected women. Her village, like most other villages in Mansehra district, was devastated by the 2005 earthquake, for which the cumulative death toll stands at 70,000. The number of homeless and internally displaced stretches to hundreds of thousands of families scattered across eastern NWFP and parts of Azad or Occupied

Kashmir, depending on which side of the Indo-Pak border you're speaking from.

~

Laila and I had been in constant touch on our mobiles during the last couple of days.

'Is it safe for a woman to travel to Oghi?' I asked her.

She went quiet. 'Why do you ask, baji?'

'Because my foolhardiness is no match for the Taliban's madness.'

The Taliban had entered and established their rule in the neighbouring district of Buner six months back. My paranoia was justified: Oghi borders the dreaded tribal region of Kala Dhaka, where many of the Taliban have gone into hiding after the Pakistan government conducted a military operation to root them out from Swat and the Federally Administered Tribal Areas (FATA), regions of NWFP adjacent to Pakistan's border with Afghanistan.

'There are no Taliban in our village!' Laila said confidently.

Thinking her too young and naïve, I asked to speak to her father. According to my socially-conditioned South Asian reflexes, a man's knowledge about the Taliban is likely to be more accurate than a twenty-year old village girl's.

'What Taliban?' her father sounded offended as if I had attacked his Pashtun honour. 'Just come. You don't have to worry about any Taliban.'

Reassured, I purchased a black head scarf and a grey chadar from a shop named Insaaf (Justice) Cloth Depot. The shopkeeper tried to figure out the purpose for my purchases. It was early in the morning, around ten. I was the first customer at Insaaf, at an hour when women were busy with housework. A woman not wearing a chadar but wanting to buy one, and my mohajir Urdu, gave me away.

'From Karachi?' he asked.

I nodded.

'Work for an NGO?'

I nodded again, letting him make what he would of my geographical origin and professional affiliations.

I walked back to my host's apartment. She gave me a quick lesson in chadar-wearing. She was an old Karachi acquaintance who moved to Abbotabad for work. The head scarf and grey chadar were to make me look stolid, respectable and inconspicuous, but my image in the mirror wasn't convincing. The black head scarf and the chadar concealed my hair and body admirably but when I stretched the chadar over my nose and mouth, it kept sliding down.

'How can I keep this thing in place?' I asked frustrated.

'You need lots of safety pins,' my host advised.

'Safety pins?' I doubted safety pins could keep the chadar in place. 'Safety pins won't keep it fixed over my nose!' I recalled the women in the streets. 'I've been watching the women here. They never need to adjust their chadars. And they don't use safety pins.'

'How long have you been wearing a chadar?' she quipped.

'Yes, I get your point. But there's got to be an easier way of chadar management. I'm not using safety pins,' I said grumpily. From my observations of chadar-clad women in

the past two days, I thought I had figured out the perfect
way to keep chadars in place:

- they stay in place if you walk with your nose slightly up
  in the air
- if you combine upward nose tilt with a slow gliding
  walk
- if you make no sudden turns of head
- if you don't walk or talk too fast or try to run
- if you're very patient

~

Next morning, it's time for my departure to Oghi, and my
host calls an elderly taxi driver she trusts. She feels I'd be
safe with him, travelling alone. The narrow two-lane, tree-
lined highway leading out of Abbotabad towards the smaller
town of Mansehra is crowded with bride-like trucks
decorated with dazzling truck art—horses, peacocks, lions,
flowers and calligraphed lines of poetry. Suzuki vans and
cars and impressive SUVs owned by international aid
organizations zip by. Falling away below the highway are
the neatly-terraced fields of young wheat, corn cobs drying
on rooftops, and clumps of dark pines casting their shadows
on grassy slopes; an occasional donkey loaded with sacks
trudges up the hilly shoulder of the road, and crowning it
all, is the poetry of the splendid sapphire sky. Light-haired
boys gaze passively from the shoulders of the road, hoping
tourists will pull up. They're selling roasted corn, Made-in-
China toys, tents, and colourful umbrellas, but in this season

of violence, vacationers aren't venturing out into the breath-stopping beauty of these valleys. There are war cries everywhere but not on these mute mountains, not in the sun-reddened faces of the boys selling toys—in their languid reclining postures is reflected only the perfection of nature. As I lean against the window, I know I'm glimpsing another reality not visible in the insensitivity of global media's war coverage. We pass little towns and dull streets with shuttered shop fronts squinting quietly in the vivid light coming off the sharp-rimmed mountains. It's the last Friday of the holiest month, and most of rural NWFP has shut down. We pass the town of Qalanadarabad and the taxi driver tells me you get the best chapli kebabs here. We don't stop because no roadside kebab stalls are open for business. It's Ramzan, whispers the tranquil air of the shabby bazaars. And yet, it's a tranquility fraught with duplicity: a proud people have become dislocated, disowned refugees in their own land, and the world looks at them in self-righteous indignation: they have no right to dislodge the world from its comfortable, unthinking routine, or shake us awake from our stupor, our daily intake of apathy. Those villagers sheltering the Taliban and other terrorists-in-the-making must be rooted out, and dropping bombs from drones on them is the safest way to restore the world back to peace!

I read the anti-American slogans chalked on the walls during the drive: *Go America Go, Stop Colluding with America, Drone Attacks are a blow to Pakistan's sovereignty, Death to American Culture*—splashed in bold, black Urdu letters in town after town—signed Jamat-e-Islami, the country's largest religious political party. I wished to see counter-slogans, slogans of hope and change, from civil liberty groups. But human rights organizations do not take risks of public self-expression. What would they say, anyway? You're either with the Americans, or against them in the post 9/11 world. Any middle ground, any sane alternatives to this either-or option have been wiped out.

At the time of writing this chapter, in 2010, I happen to glance at the Pakistani edition of the *International Herald Tribune*. Imtiaz Gul, a senior Pakistani journalist and think-tank director, an expert on NWFP, is about to release his new book on NWFP titled the *The Most Dangerous Place: Pakistan's Lawless Frontier*. In his newspaper article he comments on the growing militancy in NWFP, referring to the tribal regions of the province as the 'nursery of global jihad' and blames the Pakistani government for allowing all kinds of national and international jihadist, terrorist groups to take up residence in NWFP. Surprisingly, he doesn't mention anything about the American government's role in spawning the Taliban phenomenon in the first place.

At the Mansehra lari adda, in the dusty disorder of buses and vans, I find a ladies' seat in the front row of one of the Hiace vans leaving for Oghi. Mansehra is named after Man Singh, its seventeenth-century Sikh governor. All the back seats are filled with men returning to their villages for Eid. My eyes, hungry for the sight of women to make me feel like I belong to this space, scan the bus depot, but except for my lady co-traveller and two burqa-clad women who are hurrying behind their male guardian with hushed, diffident steps in the throng of vehicles outside, I see none. I stare at the rows of once-white towels hanging outside a hot hammam. What if I'm returning from a grimy trip and need a shower? The hammams are for men only. My left hand is clutching the end of my chadar, stretching it taut across nose and mouth and my right is holding my voice recorder, under the chadar. My bulging tote bag which has my clothes, notebooks and a water bottle, is perched on my lap.

~

She and I are squeezed into the ladies' seat, which is optimally designed for one. She is covered from head to toe in a heavily sequined, shiny black burqa. And not once does she seem flustered, or have to raise her hand to adjust her gauzy naqaab over her face. Her delicate hennaed hands rest in her lap and dozens of gold and red bangles sparkle on her wrists. Her richly painted toe nails leap out at me from her dainty sandals. I hadn't expected to see such riotous femininity in this grey, mostly male chaos.

The conductor lures a couple more passengers to fill the van to capacity. The driver dumps a big bag of spinach and onions next to our feet. Finally we get going. I know I can't last much longer on the winding mountain roads, without medication. I swallow a pill with a sip from my water bottle, defying established custom. You don't eat or drink in public during Ramzan.

'Keep your shoes away from the vegetables,' the driver addresses me. I don't miss the disdain in his remark. I stare dispiritedly at my sneakers. Is it because I am travelling without a male, or because I drank from the bottle, or is it my unfeminine footwear, or the inescapable fetidness of big cities that I carry in my unchaperoned presence? Why had he addressed me, and not my companion seated between us?

~

'How far are you going, baji?'

She speaks Urdu! There is a strange intimacy in her voice.

'To Oghi. And you?'

'To Oghi,' she smiles through her translucent naqaab.

She seems relieved that we are both travelling to Oghi, and I am travelling alone like her. I want to ask her more about herself but I'm not willing to disclose too much about myself, so I stay silent.

An hour later, when she gets out in Oghi, she has more surprises in store for me. The driver and conductor get out in a hurry and run after her. They start arguing and I am worried because she looks too frail to win arguments.

'What happened?' I ask when they return, two large men, shaking their heads and waving their fists. She, my fairy-like van-mate, in the meantime, has vanished down one of the side lanes.

'She didn't pay her fare! She told me she was coming to Oghi to get her son,' the driver blurts out, reverting to Pashto-tinted Urdu. 'I trusted her. She said she'll pay when we get to Oghi. And now she says she has no money! I lost fifty rupees.' He grunts and shifts gears and the Hiace lurches towards Oghi's main bazaar where Laila had instructed me to get off and ask for her uncle, Janbaz Khan.

'Here's her fare,' I say, removing a fifty-rupee note from my purse. 'Maybe she had some majboori,' I pronounce, almost chuckling at her brazenness.

Inwardly, I applaud her audacity. Going by her timid, tantalizing appearance, the driver and conductor might have hoped to receive payment of another kind from her. But she had duped them both and hitched a ride in a place where women barely ventured out of their homes. I regret now remaining distant when she had tried to engage me in conversation.

Oghi is a small market town in Mansehra district. The highway into town turns into its main street and is lined with small businesses—clothing and shoe stores, bakeries, poultry, vegetable, fruit and milk stalls. Milk and vegetable shops also sell mobile phone cards and painted signs advertise cards of various companies. Many of the shops are owned by Afghan refugees who moved here after the 1979 Russian invasion of Afghanistan. The absence of women in the street is hard to get used to. I don't see women even in shops that are selling women's clothing.

Janbaz Khan, Laila's uncle, runs a taxi service from Oghi to the surrounding villages. His fleet consists of a few small, battered pickups, called *carry* in local lingo. He is standing in the crowded market with his mobile sandwiched between ear and shoulder, getting instructions from Laila, I suppose, because as soon as he sees me, he runs across the street and

waves down our Hiace. It turns out the Hiace driver knows
Janbaz Khan well since everybody in the local transport
business knows everybody else. It is time for the Friday
prayers, and fearsome sermons over loudspeakers waft out
in the bazaar. Maulvis in mosques all over the country at
that hour are exhorting errant Muslims to mend their ways,
give up the life of sin and revert to the path of prayer and
fasting. Surprisingly, all the khutbas are in Urdu, not Pashtu
or Hindko, the two dominant languages of this region.
Would the maulvis ever speak about the environment and
climate change in their sermons, or the rights of women in
Islam? Could one suggest more urgent khutba topics than
lapses in a five-times-a-day prayer regimen to them?

Janbaz Khan's nephew drives me to the village, a twenty-
minute ride on a winding, dusty, dirt road that bifurcates
the pine-covered hillside. Chickens cluck and goats hastily
get out of our way as we speed past, raising dust storms
behind us. An impassive old man sits on a boulder holding
up a placard asking for donations for rebuilding a village
madrasa. A colourful plastic canopy is stretched across the
top of the carry, making it a sun-proof, waterproof, and
male-proof enclosure. When the two benches inside are
filled with passengers, men clamber outside, hanging onto
the side rails for support.

'How many kilometres to the village?' I ask the lad.

Out of shyness or bewilderment, he stares stiffly at the
blue air outside the windshield.

I repeat my question.

'Four,' he replies tautly.

'Shouldn't take us too long then.' My attempts to be friendly are met with silence for the rest of the ride.

The distance from the edge of the village to Laila's house is a ten-minute walk down a narrow path. Mud houses that look like their walls have been sewn to each other flank the serpentine path. Janbaz Khan's nephew trots ahead with my bag while I try to disregard my dizzy head and match his pace. Women lean over their walls and children peep from door jambs. By the time I reach Laila's house, I am dropping with exhaustion, and half the village knows about my arrival.

'Why do you have such a thick chadar on?' Laila's mother exclaims in Pashto as soon as I enter the courtyard. All the women of the large family gather in the courtyard to hug and kiss me. You are kissed on both cheeks and the back of your hand and then you do the same to your kisser. 'This?' I address Laila's mother, unwrapping the chadar. 'You don't like it? I bought it for this trip especially.' I speak to her in Urdu, which she understands, thanks to Urdu and Hindi films and plays on TV.

'Take it off, take it off! It's too hot.' She yells instructions to one of her daughters. 'You don't need to wear it inside the house.' I gather her meaning from her Urdu words: chadar, ghar, garmi. One of her daughters brings me a light cotton dupatta and hangs up my chadar and head scarf on the wall. And there they remain till the day I leave.

'Laila's saying her prayers. Aren't you going to pray?' Her mother asks in Pashto-Urdu.

'I have my periods,' I lie. Ritual prayer is more than what I can contemplate after the torturous ride through the mountains. I am feeling woozy and more tired than after the twelve-hour bus trip across the border from Delhi to Lahore.

I slump on the charpai and remove my sneakers. Laila's little sister brings me a pair of chappals and deposits my unsightly sneakers in the store room.

When Laila finishes praying, she rushes out, her white dupatta still wrapped round her head. 'I never believed you'll come. I thought you'll change your mind. Only when you smsd me after sitting in the Hiace, I believed you.' She kisses me on my cheeks, clasping my hands in hers, and turns my face to the wall. 'Look! We've been painting the house! That's all we've done since sehri and we've just finished.'

The women had been painting the patio and courtyard walls for Eid. The pale green, lime-washed walls look creamy and inviting in the late afternoon light. How did they manage to stand and work in the sun while fasting? In the coming days, I witness how exalted their endurance is, how they can scrub and cook, soothe and reassure, wait and serve, squat at the stove, with faces set, backs sore.

'Didn't any of your brothers help?'

'No, they slept after sehri.' When she laughs, Laila's brown eyes light up. 'They got up late and went into town with Abbu.'

Two years ago, her Abbu returned from Saudi Arabia. He lost his job there as a driver with a transport company and used his savings to set up a children's clothing shop in Oghi.

'Business is slow,' Laila's mother says. 'Times are bad. Who has money to spend on clothes?'

But sales had picked up a little in the last few days before Eid, she says. She is a graceful woman with flushed cheeks, proud stature, and a smile that advertises contented motherhood. She has raised seven children. Her husband left, like many men from the villages do, to look for work in Karachi. And from Karachi he found his way to Saudi Arabia. He used to come home once in two years and leave her pregnant after each visit. In fourteen years, she gave birth to seven children. Now, he was done with Saudi Arabia and was trying to make a go of the shop in Oghi.

I wash from the bucket in the courtyard, and tired and drowsy from the anti-sickness pill I'd taken, fall asleep on the floor. There is no electricity that afternoon and the tin roof transmits the sun's heat magnified several times, but at sunset, the ceiling lets loose its hoarded heat and the air mellows out. The way a cruel day transforms into a velveteen evening in the valley never ceases to surprise me throughout my visit.

I am awakened close to iftaar time by the warm homey smells drifting in from the kitchen. Across the courtyard, Laila is busy in the kitchen, preparing iftaar, the meal eaten at sunset that signifies the end of a fast. Curls of thick smoke swirl skywards into the gathering dusk from chimneys dotting the village. I feel as though I have stumbled onto a page in a charmed picture book, so small and perfect seem the scale of things. Laila is the gentle, strong princess of this fairy tale and I the wayfarer. She has cooked chicken biryani and is now mixing the batter for pakoras. I squat on the floor beside her and peel and chop potatoes and onions. I watch her as she pokes the fire and adjusts the logs. The flames surge with a crackle and bring back memories of fires from my childhood. She adds potatoes and onions to the pakora batter and drops spoonfuls of the batter into sizzling oil. Ethnicity, age, language and education are the differences between us. She will never know the land of rice paddies, rivers and cyclones I was born in, and would perhaps feel alienated by the idea of separate bedrooms I had grown up with, in my nuclear family. And yet, a miracle lies in our quiet communion. We are sitting, like two travellers who've been brought together on a kitchen floor by a series of chance happenings, and found unity in a vision which we share but cannot articulate clearly.

In the next few days, I learn to light the mud stove. It is easy once you get the hang of it. Every unneeded bit of paper, as well as plastic unfortunately, is tossed in as kindling. Very little of anything is wasted. Dishwater is used to water the plants, rain water is stored in a drum, and kitchen refuse feeds the goats. The kitchen is a lovely space of infectious warmth, a warmth that emanates from something deeper than the mud walls or the stove. A curious quality of caring, an inexpressible sense of the sacred, hovers here in the early mornings, when Laila's mother milks the buffalo and bends down to light the stove and make tea and paratha for me because I am not fasting. All her movements, which I watch entranced, are elegant and calm. The filling of water in buckets, the babble of birds and bleating of goats, and the crowing roosters, are all part of an unhurried grace. These endearing sounds mingle and pour into the kitchen with light from the high-up square window. Beyond the window, the sun kisses the tops of the walnut trees and they sway softly. The family's three goats are tethered to their trunks.

At iftaar, the whole family gathers in the kitchen. As soon as azaan is heard from the mosque, we can eat. Iftaar on my first day is dates, fruit chaat, pakoras, and biryani. Laila's father and her brothers eat from one plate, and we women eat from another. Family members usually eat from the same plate. When Laila asks if I would like to eat from their plate, I smile inwardly.

Every day, Laila's cousin, Zeenat, comes in just before iftaar with a bowl of curry or walnut chutney. Laila's two uncles, her father's younger brothers, and their families live on the same ancestral property. The original house has been divided into three parts. Each uncle has constructed a set of rooms, kitchen and separate toilet for his family. Laila's family is prosperous enough to have toilets. Most of the villagers are not. Women rise early and go out into the fields. The three houses are interconnected through their courtyards. The uncles each have many children and their wives are harried women, but they seem proud of their large families.

The evenings are dark and lovely. The crickets chirp loudly. And the stars—I have never seen so many in any city—millions of them pinned to a dark dome, flicker benignly. Something fragrant from the courtyard infuses its faint scent into the night. Laila is a proud gardener and her ardour is apparent in the profusion of red and white and pink blossoms. I sit in the verandah in the early mornings, drinking in this delightfulness, grieving as this cool softness changes from delicateness to the harshness of a new day.

The delicacy of those dawns leaves you unprepared for the hot days. The reality of a civil war raging in a place so peaceful leaves you even more nonnplussed. The same issue of the *International Herald Tribune* where Imtiaz Gul denounces Pakistan as the nursery of global jihad, reports of fresh bombs dropped by the US in the tribal areas, to root out 'suspected militants'. How can pilotless, unmanned, bomb-dropping machines target militants with unfailing accuracy? There have been thirty-three Predator drone attacks since January 2010 in this region, and drone attacks have killed 900 people since 2008, the same newspaper reports.

~

Is it so difficult to connect the dots between growing resentment towards American interference in the region and the locals who support the Taliban for being the only group daring to oppose American military presence here? Bombs are supposedly dropped on high value targets. A high value target (HVT) is defined as a 'target the enemy commander requires for the successful completion of the mission. The loss of high-value targets would be expected to seriously degrade important enemy functions throughout the friendly commander's area of interest.' The *Herald Tribune* also reports: 'It is not known if any high value target was present in the area at the time of attack.' Not known if any HVTs were present? Why drop bombs if chances of hitting an HVT isn't high enough to begin with? Bombs on villages that have no hospitals or even a rudimentary first-aid unit for the wounded? I imagine the drone operator, a young man sitting in front of a computer terminal at some military facility in Arkansas or Nevada, who tries to ascertain if his remote-controlled drone will bomb an HVT in some village in NWFP which appears as a grid filled with dots. Dots stand for houses on his screen. What kind of a village is his imagination capable of conjuring up? Can he not imagine homes, families, gardens in those villages? If the US military has the technology to tell a village militant hideout from a non-militant home, all the way from Arkansas or wherever their drone operators sit, they deserve my deepest respect. But since they aren't sure if they're hitting HVTs, the ire and bewilderment of an impoverished but dignified people, when bombs drop on them from the skies, seems just.

~

Laila, Zeenat and I are sitting on the charpais in the verandah. The conversation turns to marriage and love. Both Laila and Zeenat have recently become engaged.

'Have you ever seen or spoken to your fiancé?' I ask Zeenat.

'No.'

'But he's your cousin! And he's from the next village. Hasn't he tried to call you or see you since your engagement?'

'No, he works in Karachi.'

'Doesn't he have a mobile? Don't you want to know what he looks like, what he sounds like?' I am astounded by her impassivity.

'No,' she shrugs. Then smiles. 'I've seen his photo. That's enough. They showed it to me just before they said yes to his family.'

'Bas? What if you don't like him after marriage?'

The last time I met her in the art therapy workshop with Laila, Zeenat had wanted to study archaeology because this land of hers is the home of the ancient Gandhara Buddhist civilization. She was made to quit college recently because she was to get married.

'What if you don't like him?' I persist.

'Compromise,' Zeenat pronounces the English word. She's only nineteen and knows what compromises are all about. What the inevitable is all about.

'I told his sister when they came for the engagement to give me her brother's number,' Laila blurts. 'So Zeenat could talk to him. But she didn't. She's a mean one.'

Zeenat glances shyly at the bold Laila, but there's something calm and maternal in her stooped shoulders and her slender frame, and her tentative smile is all about the advantages of submission to pre-determined fates. She appears aged compared to Laila's fiestiness.

'My friend says if things are good on the wedding night, then the future will be good. But if things don't go right on the first night . . . but I say it's all kismat,' Laila laughs.

Laila is engaged to a distant cousin. He fell in love with her when she was fifteen. In a culture where girls are betrothed at birth, and often to first cousins, she's considered a rebel, too modern for having waged a three-year jihad with her father, uncles and grandfather to get engaged to a distant relative who fell in love with her. He works in a factory by day and sms's her love poems by night. Recently, he's been laid off, and is back in the village. But they are forbidden to meet. Later that night, as Laila and I are talking, huddled under the quilt in a little room next to her grandmother's, his sms's start beeping in. Laila types replies, lying down. She hardly sleeps. She keeps checking her mobile and fires rapid replies. Then he gives her a missed call, and she climbs out of bed and goes into the next room to call him back.

'I don't want to get married. At least not for a couple of years,' Laila says after she returns and climbs back into bed. 'I want to work and earn some money.'

She has just finished a three-month training in community health. And will soon start making visits as the first Lady Health Visitor of her village. Her job will take her to village women to tell them about health and nutrition, and slip in contraception advice. Her community health text book has a chapter on family planning, which explains how contraception is not against Islam. The State pushing the ideology of smaller families, despite the maulvis who consider all attempts to curb procreation unnatural and un-Islamic, seems like quiet good news.

'It doesn't pay much but it's a secure job, once they make me permanent,' Laila says.

'You don't want to marry him but you're in love with him?' I ask Laila.

'With my fiancé? I am and I'm not,' she says quite honestly. 'My mother says I've cut off my feet by getting engaged to him. He doesn't even have a house for me and now he's lost his job. And his family is so huge. You'll see how they live. Their house is messy and full of children. I don't know how I'll live with them.'

I've heard her whisper *I love yous* on the phone.

'How do you say it in Pashto?' I ask.

'Nobody says it in Pashto anymore.'

'Nobody says I love you in Pashto anymore?'

I'm feeling sad at the cultural losses incurred by the mobile phone era. Children speak Pashto at home but learn only Urdu at school. So none of them can read or write their mother tongue. None of them is likely to read their iconic poets like Rehman Baba or Khushal Khan Khatak in the original.

I'm tempted to quote a Rehman Baba poem because this most-loved and revered mystical poet of Pakhtun culture is so little known outside the Pakhtun world:

Whether it involves kindness, love or enmity,
I have trusted the friendship of my friend.
Though in separate bodies my friend and I are really one.
Thousands of houses make the city of Baghdad.
There can be no separation between my lover and me;
All events have their own appointed time.
It is not dependent on the beloved's beauty at all;
The lover's heart is content with his own love.
I ask God for passionate sighs;
Whether the lover's heart is of wax or steel.
For those who are not dispersed like the beloved's braids,

The communion of their hearts is a heinous crime.
Those who have no strength to complain or sigh,
Each silence of the powerless is a sigh and a complaint.
Ishq has a hundred more names - like
the names of Majnun and Farhad.
It sits and stands wherever it likes,
Love is the true son-in-law of intellect and cleverness.
In love kings become Malangs,
Who remembers the likes of you and me?
If excellence is in proportion to humility,
Then the position of the student is above the teacher.[1]

'Can't you break off the engagement?' If Laila ran a three-year campaign to get engaged, she's surely empowered enough to run another campaign for an exit strategy.

'No, *yaara!*' Laila gasps. 'I can't do that! I can't break off this engagement! I was the one who fought for this engagement. If I break it off now, I'll dishonour my family. People will say I've become too modern. Nobody's going to marry my sisters if I do something like that. I made my choice. Now I must live with it.'

'You don't know if your family chose a husband they would've made a better choice.'

'I told you, it's all kismat. My kismat. But I feel a little safer because my fiancé says I can work after marriage and I

---

[1]*The Poetry of Rahman Baba: Poet of the Pakhtuns.* Robert Sampson and Momin Khan (translators), University Book Agency, Peshawar, 2005.

told him I won't have children for five years. I've told Zeenat she should do the same. I'll give her the contraceptive so she won't get pregnant right after marriage,' she says pragmatically.

'Are you really going to do that without her husband's knowledge? You thug! Lady Health Worker!'

'You know what I think the difference between love and marriage is?' Laila stares into the dark, after shooting off another sms to her fiance. 'Life is like a glass of soapy water. And love is the foam on top. When the foam fizzles out, what's left behind is marriage.'

We chuckle under the razai. But behind her facetiousness, Laila, like her cousin, seems a melancholy, aged spirit to me. At twenty, of slight build, with a captivating, vivacious face, pensive and passionate brown eyes, and doubts and desires that I had barely begun to articulate at her age, she seems much older than I was at her age. She has attended the village school only up to class eight. The wisdom she whispers in the gloom of the night can't come from what they taught her in school.

'Well, since you have to marry somebody, if you marry your fiancé, at least you would have tasted some love bubbles!' I console her.

'But I don't know why I feel sad inside about my future. And why I get mad at him,' Laila struggles to understand her own conflicting emotions. 'Then afterwards, I apologize. I sms him. I say I'm sorry. I love him more when he's all quiet. But my mother thinks I made a mistake to choose him. It's his family. You know I love my garden. If anybody messes with my plants, I yell at them. I can't do that in their house. I'll have to come to my mother's house and take care of my garden,' she says with resigned certitude. 'But if things really don't work out, I can go my way, and he can go his.'

'So you'd better retain your garden in your mother's house!'

It takes me several days to understand the survival value of her pragmatic fatalism and her dance back and forth across thresholds of autonomy. Her feigned docility is wisdom she has absorbed from the tradition-encrusted chadar of her culture. It takes creativity to challenge the kind of unchanging social facade she is trapped in. But with each bold belief, even if she cannot always act on it, she is rending the fabric of millennia-old customs.

Eid Shopping in Oghi

The day after my arrival, Laila plans a secret shopping trip to Oghi. She says we'll go into town under the pretext of visiting the hospital where she's been training as Lady Health Worker. The bazaars are crowded just before Eid and her father wouldn't approve of us going into town. But her mother tells me calmly to wait till her husband leaves. Laila takes off for the hospital with her father early and tells me to come later with her sisters and Zeenat, who also has to wait till her father leaves for work. Laila's aunt from next door also joins the party. Laila's two brothers, aged fourteen and sixteen, accompany us. Women from respectable families don't travel without male companions, even if the accompanying male happens to be the youngest child of the family.

Autonomous women are an anomaly, and not just in villages. I recall the separate immigration counter reserved for unaccompanied women at Karachi airport. The sign above it says *tanha khwateen*—which translates into lonely women, women unaccompanied by males, women in need of special protection.

We wait at the side of the road, our faces covered with chadars, our backs turned to the male gazers in the passing carrys. It's hot and though I'm thirsty from the walk up the hill, it wouldn't have been right to carry water when others are fasting.

Finally a carry that has room for three, but can squeeze in five, stops. We pile in and the two boys hop on to the roof. I'm holding Laila's little sister on my lap, and my knee is four inches away from the genitals of the man opposite. I wince at the thought of accidental contact if there's a bump in the road. I shut my eyes and pray. When the man and his women get down, I open my eyes and take my first deep breath.

The Pathans are a poetic people, and poetry is everywhere—on the backs of vans and trucks, and engraved on gravestones. The Urdu couplet inside the carry reads:

Hazaron baar phul khile, hazaron baar bahar aai
Duniya ki wahi raunaq, dil ki wahi tanhai

A thousand blossoms bloomed, a thousand springs came,

Amid the bustle of the world, the heart's loneliness
remained.

The metaphor sinks softly into me—a thousand springs
have come and gone, symbolizing hopelessness, poverty,
and soul-enriching beauty. When will a spring beyond the
thousandth spring come to announce the end of poverty
and war? Will it take a thousand more years for the uncaring
and bustling world to open its eye of compassion? A thousand
years of war before peace comes to this land?

We get off in Oghi bazaar and walk down a side lane to
reach the hospital. It's the last day of classes before Eid
holidays, and Laila's teachers haven't showed up, since it
was assumed none of the students would. I meet Laila's
classmates. They're an animated group of young women
from neighbouring villages and they aren't shy of talking
about contraception and sexual practices. They know about
the X and Y chromosome and know women aren't
responsible for the sex of the child.

'But it's common for a man to bring a second wife if the
first can't give him a son,' one woman says. 'Men want sons
because lineage continues through sons.' She's pregnant
with her fourth child in the hope of a son. She's better
educated than the rest of her teammates but her anxieties
about her worth as a woman are clearly expressed by her
inability to produce male heirs.

She laughs when I say: 'Tell your husband there can be
no lineage without daughters.'

Laila introduces me excitedly to her teammates as the *baji* who's writing a book about us 'women and our problems'. We leave the classroom and walk back to the market, through narrow lanes and dark bylanes that make up the entrails of the main market. Tiny shop fronts are bulging with women's clothing, bangles, cosmetics, and lingerie. Women who were missing from the main street are to be found here. But men outnumber them here too.

'What business do men have here?' Laila mutters loudly under her naqaab.

'Of course men have business here,' replies a young fellow in passing.

'Did you hear him? His business is to harass us,' Laila says. 'It's like the son who told his mother not to go to the bazaar. And when his mother went out, all covered up in a burqa, he was the one caught teasing her!'

There's a palpable sexual energy in the dark, covered pathways of the bazaar as men brush past us and chadar-clad women try to avoid their touch. The girls want to buy sandals. We hurry into the first shoe shop we see. The Pathan behind the counter is tall and good-looking and extremely adept at selling shoes. He manages to find something for everybody, including Laila's sister who attends college in Mansehra and is no longer a country girl who can be easily pleased.

'These are all last year's fashions,' she whispers.

'Last year's?' The salesman overhears her. 'Who says? These are the latest designs. If you don't like it, bring it back after Eid,' he says thrusting a shiny silver sandal into her hand.

'Bring them back after wearing them?' jokes Laila. I'm scared by the casualness of the exchange taking place through the naqaab in this grid-like rigid space.

The good-looking Pathan laughs. He's enjoying the banter too, though he appears impatient.

I buy Laila a pair of walking shoes as a gift for becoming the first Lady Health Visitor of her village. 'You should give us a good discount,' I say to the shopkeeper. 'We've bought so many pairs from you. And I'm a guest from Karachi.'

'Karachi?' He shrugs, unimpressed. 'I get customers from America.'

We scurry down the dim, men-packed lane to another shop to buy bangles. Bras are hanging in glass display cases. I recall a politically incorrect joke, about a Pathan who goes to buy a bra for his wife:

Shopkeeper: What's her size?

Man, handing him his topi: I don't know her size, but she made two caps for me from her old one.

'Do women ask the man in the shop to show them bras?' I'm incredulous. Yet another stereotype about life in the hinterland has to go. 'You can't do that even in Karachi.'

'Anything goes in this place,' is Laila's casual reply.

The girls buy bangles and mehndi cones, eye liner and nail polish. Laila calls her brother. He's waiting for us at the entrance to the bazaar, in a graveyard where many faceless, veiled women are hugging shopping bags, and waiting for their men to come and get them.

Day Before Eid

We are watching the news on TV that evening to find out if the Eid moon has been sighted. The local Moonsighting Committee in the capital, Peshawar, announces it's Eid the next day, going by the moon's sighting in Saudi Arabia.

'So it's Eid tomorrow?' I seek confirmation from Laila's father.

'No, it's not,' he says contemptuously.

'But they just announced it on TV!'

'For us it's Eid the day after tomorrow, with the rest of the country,' he says. 'Those maulvis in Peshawar are not real Muslims. They want to prove they're more devout than everybody else, so they follow Saudi Arabia.'

I'm impressed by his reply and awed by this villager's audacity, from a tiny village of a hundred families, to declare solidarity with the rest of the nation and defy the status quo of Peshawar maulvis. Laila's father lights a cigarette and proceeds to do a leisurely socio-cultural and political analysis of the current unrest in NWFP. I listen respectfully for the next half hour or so. This is the only real conversation he has with me. He's a short, intense-looking man, with soft, kind eyes, and gentle manners. It's his impassioned way of speaking, I think, which Laila has inherited.

I include a heavily shortened synopsis of his conspiracy theory, which explains the unrest in the country:

Mullah Fazlullah and Baitullah Mehsud are American agents. The CIA paid Baitullah to kill Benazir Bhutto. The CIA wanted to make Zardari the president because he would let them do as they pleased in this region. The United States wants to break up Pakistan. The United States wants to make NWFP a part of Afghanistan, Baluchistan a part of Iran, and Sind a part of India. Only Punjab will remain as Pakistan. The US will set up military bases in NWFP to keep an eye on China and India. China needs watching as it is going to declare itself a superpower by 2013. Obama is no different from other American presidents. He won't change American policies, his government will create trouble in any part of the world if it benefits America. The Afghans, especially, the Farsibans (Persian-speakers) can't be trusted at all. They're on the side of the Americans.

I don't know what to make of his conspiracy theory so I join the girls who have started preparing for Eid even though they'll celebrate it a day later. Laila brings out the henna cone, and starts tracing an intricate pattern of flowers, leaves, and delightful curlicues on my palms. I watch the emerging artwork and think how far I've had to travel to find such unguarded warmth—all the more overwhelming by its virtual absence in the urban spaces where I grew up, where we are ever so careful not to puncture one another's privacy. Privacy is an alien concept here. So is solitude. Laila's cousin who arrived from a neighbouring village calls her Gautama Buddha because she goes quiet and likes to be by herself but a similar request from me is seen as a lapse in their duties as hosts. Girls sit up half the night stitching shiny, dangling things on their dupattas. Laila's chachi slides glass bangles onto our wrists. She's an expert at doing this without breaking them. A neighbour drops in to ask Laila if she could wax her arms and pluck her eyebrows.

'Come tomorrow. I'm busy right now,' Laila tells her. 'I haven't done my own eyebrows yet, how do you expect me to do yours?'

'You village girls are so fashionable!' I say.

'Only city women can be fashionable?' Laila's shakes her head.

The next day is thankfully the last day of fasting. The lie about my periods as an excuse for not fasting or praying has to be stretched no further. It's Eid in Peshwar, a couple of hours away, but not in Oghi. In the evening, we get the house ready for guests. We spread new sheets on the charpais. Laila sweeps the yard, and smears a layer of fresh mud on the blackened walls around the stove. I pound rice in the mortar for kheer. Her younger sister sits down to iron the entire family's new clothes before the electricity goes. Everybody has new outfits. A new shalwar-kurta has been stitched for me too, miraculously, in one day. Toes are blackened with toe henna. Laila's youngest brother dunks his four pet chicks into a bowl of food colour. The chicks shiver and huddle near the stove, turning into fuzzy balls of pink as they dry out. One of them doesn't withstand this drastic makeover and dies in the night.

Eid Day

The household is up while it's still dark and cold. Laila's

mother has been in several times, tugging at her toes to wake her up. I stay in bed curled up under the quilt's warmth, trying to gauge what's wrong from their hushed whispers. The rooster crows. The Eid khutba can be heard from the village mosque. It's in Pashto so I don't follow a word. Finally, I get out of bed. The stars are still out at six-thirty. I get my toothbrush and walk across the courtyard. I have to wait for my turn to use the bathroom. The water's freezing, but after the first few tumblers, I stop shivering. I put on my shiny new silk outfit, and am surprised that it fits quite well. Today, there's no getting out of praying so I go into the room and join the women. Peace, peace, peace. Please God, please restore peace, I entreat as I prostrate myself on the prayer mat.

The whole family assembles in the kitchen for tea. I wish Laila's father and uncles Eid Mubarak. Laila laughs and tells me what she and her mother were discussing earlier—the loss of four kilos of meat. The cat devoured it during the night.

'The cat had her Eid while we slept. No biryani today,' Laila says, unruffled. The meat must have cost several hundred rupees. The good humour, the generous acceptance of loss, and lack of blame surprise me.

Laila asks her aunt to give her a chicken. Instead of biryani, lunch is chicken curry. The men take off for Eid prayers. And the women start getting ready. Hair is oiled and braided. Earrings and rings slipped on. Lipstick and kajal applied. The new sandals are taken out of their boxes. Laila slides three golden rings onto my fingers. And makes me put on two dozen more bangles and lipstick. I keep staring at my unfamiliar fingers with the three large, shiny rings. By the time the eyelash curler is produced, I resign myself to my fate. Laila curls eyelashes by squeezing them between the blades of the eyelash curler.

The men come back, eat, and take off to visit relatives in neighbouring villages, and we visit the nearby women. We are force-fed biryani and halwa everywhere, and I have to answer the same set of four questions: Are you married? Do you have kids? How many? No sons? Then the shocked look, followed by genuine sympathy for my sonlessness.

Laila gives family planning advice to someone who's just had her fifth child.

'What should I do?' the woman smiles. 'Block the entrance between my legs?'

'Get the shots,' Laila scolds her. She translates what the woman just said in Pashto. 'You need just one shot every three months. Can you help them if they don't want to help themselves? These village women!'

'Can't their husbands use condoms?' I ask Laila as we clamber up the narrow path to another relative's house. If women can talk about sex in such a jaded way, as if it's no more exciting than housework, can't they also talk about condoms?

'The women are the ones who have to stay home and take care of all these children. They should insist their men use condoms.' Laila sounds exasperated with women's passivity. 'But they don't. My uncles' wives are the same. They just keep having babies.'

The last stop is Laila's fiancé's house. Laila waits at her aunt's house and we climb up the hill to her in-laws' house. She's not allowed to meet her fiancé before the wedding but he does come over to see her when her father is out. Her mother knows about his visits and doesn't object. Laila was right about the disorder in her fiancé's house. There are clothes and dirty dishes lying on the floor. There are no traces of festivity, none of the cultivated loveliness of Laila's courtyard garden. One of her future sisters-in-law, a woman with dough-streaked hands and wisps of hair escaping from under her crumpled dupatta, greets us.

'How are you? You look tired,' I ask her.

'*Kaisi hun? Wahi haal, wahi chamri, wahi khaal,*' she smiles. To translate what she said is to kill the poetry but I'll try: why ask about me? I'm in the same state, same old skin, same old hide. She used to live in Karachi. And I can see her Urdu is accentless and her language carries that city's tart humour. 'You know, we women are *qurbani ki bakriyan* (sacrificial goats)—there are twenty-three people in this house,' she names the household's children and adults. 'We have to make breakfast for them, get hot water ready so the men can bathe, polish their shoes. Where's the time to put on Eid clothes?' she says. I look at her, amused and sad. She's a thin woman, with sallow, anaemic skin, a mother of five. Her husband left her in the village and went to Dubai three years ago. She awaits his return like millions of women do in villages all over the country, raising his children in his absence, longing for love and companionship.

Day After Eid

The day after Eid is the busiest for the women of the household. They are busy cooking and serving guests who keep arriving throughout the day.

Laila is irritable. She kneads dough and as we're approaching the tandoor in the back yard to bake the naans, she blurts out: 'I want to pile all these men into the tandoor and set them on fire!' She wants us to go to an engagement party but we can't go because the guests have to be served.

When her father comes in, Laila snaps. 'We're tired of working. We can't go anywhere. We have to keep feeding your guests. Is this how we're to celebrate Eid?'

Her father is taken aback at her anger, especially in my presence. 'I'll see to it that you can go,' he says gently. 'Go and get ready.'

Laila smiles triumphantly after he leaves. 'I'm his favourite daughter. He can't bear to see me unhappy. Come, let's go and get ready!'

Once more we go through the elaborate routine of putting on our Eid outfits and the jewellery. The rings and bangles, lipstick and eyeliner are spread on the bed in Laila's mother's room. The engagement party is an all-women affair in the next village. Laila wears her flat sandals and packs her stilettos in her purse to put on once she arrives at the party. Darkness falls on our way back, and the carry drops us quite a long way from the village. Laila laughs as I snap a picture of her removing her stilettos and putting on her flats for the long walk back home.

'Are we safe in the dark on this lonely road?' I ask.

'Don't worry,' Laila reassures me. 'We're very safe. Nobody would dare do anything. We are known here.' They've told me how safe the village and its surrounds are. Women walk all over the village, gathering firewood and fetching water, going out to the fields. Nobody would dare harass their own village women. It's only in the anonymity of bazaars that the ancient code of conduct, the Pakhtunwali, is broken.

Laila's absence from the house has been missed. Her grandfather is distraught and asks her to do dumm for his toothache. I've hardly spoken to him since my arrival. He spends his days watching TV, feeding the dogs and goats, and yelling at his grandsons for climbing the walnut trees and for getting into fights. The day I am to leave, he produces a dozen walnuts from his shalwar pocket, and says: 'Take them with you. They're from our trees.'

'He scolds the kids all day long,' Laila whispers, as she sits down next to him. 'No wonder his jaw hurts.' She recites a prayer and blows on his hurting jaw. The dumm is done. And the old man leaves, leaning on his walking stick, looking dazed but comforted.

The men of the family seem lonely and in need of being ministered to, even though they remain distant and inscrutable. Are they aloof because they need to conceal their inner frailness? They seek women's services, but they say very little to them at mealtimes or any time. Roles are well-defined and a good life means performing those roles. I have the feeling everybody is in a silent movie. It's the men's job to command women's submissiveness and devotion and in return, the men provide for them. Laila's father sits smoking silently on the charpai in the evenings with a restless, far-away look. His wife sits near him, but they hardly talk. He too wants Laila to do dumm because his stomach hurts from eating half-cooked sweet rice at the maulvi's house. I've seen him sit beside his mother in silence. He comes in when Laila is feeding her milk and cornbread. He sits for a few minutes, kisses her on both cheeks, and leaves.

I want to ask the silent men what becomes of the latent lovers and poets in them? Do those fumbling, embarrassing, half-clothed, smothered encounters with their wives that pass for sexual intimacy, those precursors to necessary, frequent pregnancies that continue the geneology, stone them into such silence? Homo-erotic relationships among Pathan men have probably evolved to fill the lacunae of emotional intimacy between men and women. Keeping boys instead of mistresses for sexual pleasure is an accepted practice among heterosexual men of means, and is not taken to be an indication of homosexuality or bisexuality. I have no way of finding out whether women also resort to relationships with other women for emotional and sexual fulfilment. I feel such relationships may not be unusual in heavily gender-segregated spaces. Village women may not advertise themselves as sexual beings, but what they resort to for sexual bliss is another matter. Laila tells me of a classmate who's been smsing her, begging her for 'lip-kisses'!

Out in the Fields

By the fifth day, I'm restless for contact with the outside world. In the real world, I shirk newspapers, especially front page news. But here my isolation from the outer world as well as my inability to access my inner world is making me restless. This is evident to Laila and she keeps an even closer watch to make sure I am not alone, which makes me somewhat more irritable. There are no newspapers, no internet, no email. I didn't even bring my laptop. I can't go out for solitary walks since it's improper for a woman guest to go wandering on her own. I can't sit by myself without somebody from the family enquiring, Are you all right? Are you bored? Do you need something? My mobile is my lifeline but its connectivity is erratic. What's going on in the world? There's a TV—but it's hardly ever tuned to the news except when the men are watching it. When the girls are watching, they switch over to the saas-bahu soaps, revelling in the mother-in-law-daughter-in-law conflicts.

'Baji, you're getting bored, aren't you?' Laila wants to know.

'No, not bored. Just need to know what's going on in the world.'

'Why? Why can't you forget what's going on in the world? We don't make you happy? Why do you want to bring the world's worries here?' Laila asks, genuinely puzzled. 'You told me you felt sad about all the bad things happening in the world. What's there to know, when all the news is bad news?'

'Maybe I'm addicted to bad news,' I say, and I wonder at

my addiction. Why do I really need to hear or read more bad news?

'Tomorrow I'm going to show you a really beautiful place. You'll never forget this village then. Then you'll say to your friends in the city what a *zabardast* time you had in the village. They'll be envious.'

The next morning after everybody has had tea and parathas for breakfast, the courtyard swept, Laila's plants watered, and the various buckets and drums filled with water, we go out in a large group, just us women, with all of Laila's sisters and cousins, including the youngest, who is only four. The weather changes from early morning frostiness to mid-morning piercing sun. We walk on narrow, twisting paths through the trampled undergrowth, the girls chattering gleefully, showing me places in the woods where they used to stop on the way back from school and the fig trees they climbed.

In the village, there is no need for chadars. It is enough to cover our heads with dupattas, which keep sliding down in the up and down walk on brambly paths. But nobody seems to care. 'No chadars as long as you stay within the village limits,' Laila tells me.

'When did you stop climbing trees?' I ask Zeenat.

'Two years ago,' she says.

'Can't you climb one now? How can I believe you ever climbed one?'

'No! The villagers will think I've gone mad,' she shakes her head vigorously, as if embarrassed to even contemplate it.

'Come on, nobody's watching,' I urge her.

'No! No!' She's getting married in two month's time, and can't risk village gossip. No girl who's about to get married climbs trees.

Recollecting that walk is a journey to a feeling that defies definition—the laughter of the girls, the prattling steps of the little ones in their too-small slippers, the timid gurgling streams, the birds, the mottled shadows that dot the forest floor and mingle with scant light from the unbroken canopy of pine trees—and Laila's and Zeenat's restless, breathless chatter. They are relating childhood anecdotes—the churail, an ugly witch, the ghost of a woman who died during pregnancy, their grandmother had seen her sitting on a rock when she used to come to the woods to gather grass, when the woods were denser and the streams fuller, and the churail with her wild hair and fiery eyes had made her grandmother drop her scythe and run back to the house in fear. And how her grandmother sat and meditated and prayed for forty days, how she learned the special dumm to crack evil spells cast by churails. And how she returned, emboldened with her new knowledge and overpowered the churail, who never dared to come back to these woods ever.

'Dadi has taught me how to do the same dumm,' Laila says. 'That's why everybody in the family asks me to do dumm if they're ill.'

She holds her slippers in one hand and jumps across a ditch. I hesitate at the mouth of the ditch. Laila stretches her arm out to me.

'Hold my hand,' she says, extending her arm towards me and pulling me across. I land on the other side, awed and unsteady. She is laughing.

'Why are you laughing at me? I didn't grow up in the village,' I say, embarrassed.

Laila can't stop giggling at my clumsiness, my fears, and the others join her. This is their chance to show off their nimble-footedness before a city lady. Even her little four year-old cousin jumps the ditch, unassisted.

Is Laila a child or an elder? She hops across ditches like a schoolgirl and she's a healer of pain. Laila—the brave woman, healer and rebel, ready to leap across ditches without a moment's thought, but unable to break out of a relationship she feels tied down to. I watch this amazing woman's forays into independence and her retreats into dependence. Terrified by her own intrepid ways, how long will she hold herself back, how long will she continue to remodel herself to fit into her family's cocoon?

~

A couple of days after Eid, amid great protests from Laila's family, I hug and kiss all the women of the family, and walk uphill to the highway. Laila's two brothers accompany me. I click a picture of the message painted on their school wall:

Talib-e-ilm mein sharm munasib nahi kyunke sharm jihalat se badtar hai.

Observe no modesty in your quest for knowledge for such modesty is worse than ignorance.

~

The Hiace lets me off at Asoka Park café in Mansehra. I offer the driver a fifty-rupee tip for dropping me at a point beyond the designated stop but he refuses to accept. I've asked my friend from Abbotabad to meet me for lunch at the café and then we plan to visit the Asokan edicts next to the café.

The menu at Asoka Park café boasts a little bit of everything. It's Pakistani and Continental. The waiter is so polite, he makes me wonder why I seldom come across such well-mannered men in big cities. He doesn't meet our eye, and starts each sentence with 'excuse me'. It takes him a very long time to produce the two hamburgers and fries we ordered. The burgers surpass McDonald's burgers in slimness. The buns are sweet and cold. The cook has left, and the substitute cook is not good, the waiter confesses, when we complain about the sweet, cold buns. Serves us right for ordering burgers in a place where they spell it as Bargars on the menu.

Our amiable waiter accompanies us to Asoka Park after lunch, carrying my bag. The park gate is locked. It's a little after 4 p.m.—closing time for the park.

'*Ab kya hoga*?' I'm alarmed. I forget momentarily that in South Asia all regulations are merely suggestions, not restrictions.

'Madem, come with me,' the waiter says confidently. He ambles up the hillside, along the park fence and points to a ledge.

And while he looks the other way, my friend and I haul ourselves up as gracefully as possible, and lower ourselves over the fence into the park.

We are happy to have the officially closed park to ourselves. The Asokan edicts are not quite what I expected. They're overwhelmingly large, grey rocks, mammoth granite boulders, resting in a lovely landscape of trees and stone, overlooking the busy Karakoram Highway, the Silk Road that Asoka's monks travelled to take Buddhism all the way to China.

I'm ending my pilgrimage at this peaceful oasis in the midst of a land at war, where the great Buddhist king inscribed his message of peace, tolerance, and love in the third century BCE. Asoka came to this wisdom only after the horrors of a war in which hundreds of thousands were killed, but the fact that such wisdom is possible to come to, that a war-mongering king can become a devout follower of non-violence and devote his life to spreading peace and prosperity among his people, makes me hopeful.

This is where I'm saying my fateha, I tell my friend, hugging the cool face of the granite boulder. I close my eyes and kiss its weathered surface, placing my lips upon the Kharoshti script that has faded into mere nicks and scratches on the rockface after two millennia of exposure to wind, dust, rain, and snow. My prayers are similar to Asoka's for the future of humankind:

I have had this Dhamma edict written so that my sons and great-grandsons may not consider making new conquests, or that if military conquests are made, that they be done with forbearance and light punishment, or better still, that they consider making conquest by Dhamma only, for that bears fruit in this world and the next. May all their intense devotion be given to this which has a result in this world and the next.

~

I've left the village but Laila keeps texting me. I'm on a Daewoo bus to Peshawar a few days later, when my mobile beeps. Her poetry mirrors her feelings for me, which she doesn't mask, and her candour is more poignant than merely sophisticated word wizardry:

Safar dosti ka chalta rahe
Suraj chahe har sham dhalta rahe
Kabhi na dhalegi apni dosti ki subha
Chahe har rishta ham se jalta rahe

Let friendship's journey never cease.
The sun may set every day,
but never mar our friendship's dawn.
Let all others in the world envy us.

5

Siraat-e-Mustaqeem—The Straight Path

Cartoon: S. Ahmed

The social engineering project

'I don't see what women see in other women,' I'd told Dr Nolan in my interview that noon. 'What does a woman see in a woman that she can't see in a man?' Dr Nolan paused. Then she said, 'Tenderness.'

—Sylvia Plath, *The Bell Jar*

'Making love with one's likeness is a strange, delightful thing.
Even if you get entrapped, being so consumed is comforting.'

—Shaikh Qalandar Baksh Jurat [1748-1810][1]

---

[1]For Shaikh Qalandar Baksh Jurat's Poetry *see* Vanita, R. & Kidwai, S.(Eds.) (2001), *Same-Sex Love in India*. Delhi: MacMillan India Ltd.

Nusrat: poet, visual artist, stage designer, college lecturer—
one of the few 'out' lesbians in Pakistan who was willing to
talk to me about being out. I had emailed Nusrat about this
book before I reached Karachi, and explained how I got her
contact through a mutual acquaintance. Nusrat was cautious:
she mailed back to say she'd meet me, but she wanted the
first meeting to be at her workplace and she wanted me to
reassure her about the confidentiality of information shared.

We met on a Friday afternoon in late October. Classes
were done early because of Friday prayers, and it seemed
like a quiet time to chat about fruitless topics like love.

On Friday afternoons even banks close down for three
hours, and Nusrat's college campus seemed to have shut
down too. There was a decidedly dull, safe air for forbidden
conversations. Most male students had left for mosques and
most women had gone home. We sat down in the college
canteen. It was a warm afternoon; though October was
drifting towards its end but in Karachi, it still seemed like
summer. The man who could serve us tea had gone to say
his prayers. We spoke in deliberately low tones, in English.
There were a few student couples lingering on benches but
they were too absorbed in themselves to bother with us.
Nusrat's attire was a litany of fashion failures. She had on a
striped beige kurta, white shalwar, a plain white cotton

dupatta and a men's watch, hair pulled back in a ponytail. No make-up, no frills, no ribbons or laces that Pakistani ladies were laden with that season. Her style of dress and speech were charmingly defiant.

We sat across from each other and I got to my questions immediately.

'Any organized lesbian groups or movement in Pakistan?'

'You don't waste much time!' Nusrat chuckled. 'No, there's nothing of the sort here. No official movement or groups. The silence is startling. But then, lesbians are not separate creatures from women. Everything that afflicts Pakistani women afflicts Pakistani lesbians—lack of freedoms and the denial of desires—most women don't have the freedom to make any choices, whether to marry, or study, or work. So how can we talk of a lesbian liberation without a heterosexual women's liberation first?'

'And what about literature's acceptance of women's love for women? Is there any positive depiction of such love in Urdu writing? Other than classics like Ismat Chughtai's[2] *Lihaaf,* and rekhti poetry.'

'Ismat Chughtai's depiction of love between women wasn't positive at all! She considered lesbianism an aberration from the norm—a social evil that erupts only when men fail to satisfy women's sexual needs. And rekhti? Those are

---

[2]Ismat Chughtai (1915-1991:) feminist Urdu writer. Her short story, *Lihaaf* (The Quilt), published in 1942, explored same-sex desire between women living a sequestered life in a middle-class Muslim Indian household.

nineteenth century erotic poems written by men as soft porn for straight men.'

'I would argue rekhti is a lot more nuanced and sophisticated, and far more ambiguous than porn! What do you think of this couplet?' I said, opening my notebook and quoting a couplet by the Urdu poet Insha:

Choti yeh teri hai saanp ki hi lahar dogana
Khaati hun tere vaaste mai zeher dogana

This plait of yours is the wave of a serpent, Dogana,[3]
I am compelled to take poison because of you, Dogana[4]

'Pretty! But it's still men's portrayal of love between women. Speaking of lesbians in contemporary Urdu literature, there was a writer of detective novels in Karachi. A Mr Humayun Iqbal. His protagonist was a woman detective called Sabiho Bano. Way back in the 70s, Sabiho rode Karachi buses looking for young girls to seduce! Iqbal's books were really popular until the Zia-ul-Haq regime clamped down on the publication and he went out of business!'

'A lesbian detective on the crime scene in Karachi in the 1970s! Urdu homo-erotic poetry depicts male to male love. But love between women hardly surfaces as a literary theme.'

'Aside from rekhti, there isn't much I know of. No literature of ours, as far as I know, valorizes long-lasting romantic relations between women. Nobody remembers

---

[3]Dogana: a woman's double, intimate companion, a woman's woman lover.

[4]Vanita, R. (2005). *Gandhi's Tiger and Sita's Smile: Essays on Gender, Sexuality and Culture*. Delhi: Yoda Press.

detective Sabiho Bano anymore. A very gentlemanly writer friend recently asked me after umming and aaahing. Umm, tell me, Nusrat, are you women really capable of, umm, satisfying each other?'

Nusrat mimicked him, leaning towards me, paraphrasing his questions in highly ornate Urdu, the way an older literary generation used to speak.

It was my turn to giggle.

'What he wanted to know was what we women do in bed! He was pretending or maybe he was genuinely confused. Like he just couldn't imagine how two women could make love! Maybe he was demolished by the thought that women don't need men in bed to make them happy.'

'The rekhti poets were men but they were less egotistical than your friend!' I said. 'Look at Insha's use of the word *lahar* in that couplet. Does *lahar* mean the beloved's plaited hair or was he hinting at her wave-like orgasms? He's deliberately ambiguous and that makes it all the more charming. Why is there so much ignorance now about alternative sexual practices?'

'Well, it's intolerance towards different ways of loving. That's worse than ignorance. But I console myself with this: it's only recently that people came to know that men can land on the moon!' Nusrat smiled. 'So a woman can land on top of a woman and,' she winked, 'create a better experience than she could ever have with a man, that's something you come to know only if you've been there! You can see that society's notions about sex are entirely penetration-based. And if that's the definition of good sex, well!' she shrugged.

'The erotic goal for women is gentleness and caress. But we can even achieve penetration. There are all kinds of toys and tools in the marketplace!'

'Is being lesbian and Muslim okay?'

'For me it is. I've discovered this parallel hyper-consciousness about sexuality that accompanies all the religious restrictions. It's a silent parallel but a very strong one—the notion that god and love do coexist in all forms is dangerous. But that's the mystical truth. The central dogma of mysticism in Islam is *ishq* (loosely translated as love), the state of absolute madness at the height of love. In ishq there are mystical openings for the lover. And the object of your love becomes the eye of the needle through which the entire world can pass, and transform around you. You are endowed with a new gaze. And codes emerge through which you decipher experience and matter. You can read mystical poetry or formal texts, and you can hear Sufi music. They all tell us that religion is about love. And yet we're trapped in our mundane interpretations. It's about time we let go of this *rata pata*, Ten Commandments kind of religious code of conduct.'

'But people increasingly feel very threatened by liberal interpretations of religion.'

'Yeah, there's a lot of anxiety in an insecure world that social structures like the family will fall apart with too much freedom. The heterosexual family unit is the last bastion of patriarchy whether it's Protestant, Catholic or Muslim patriarchy. People wonder how children will be born and raised if gay marriage gains legal status? But they refuse to see how the problems of the planet are being compounded because children continue to be born mindlessly.'

The canteen man came back but he was out of milk so he couldn't serve us tea. Nusrat suggested we move to the staff room for greater privacy. I gathered my notebooks, pen and recorder and followed Nusrat across a grassy quadrangle to the main college building. The room we entered was dim after the sun-dazzled lawn. We were in a long, lonely room with a long table that took up most of the room. Hard-backed old-fashioned chairs stood like displeased elders. Nusrat turned on one of the fans. I pulled up a chair and sat down close to a large window which looked out onto the quadrangle. The quadrangle was shaded by neem trees and on one side of it, the darkish grass lay serenely in their shadows. An oblong of light fell on the floor below the staff room window whose shutters opened out into the quadrangle. The rest of the room lay cloistered in greyness. 'I don't usually come here when the other lecturers are here. Their banal conversations no longer amuse me.' Nusrat pressed her hands to her throat and feigned fainting.

I smiled and switched on my recorder. She sat up straight—legs crossed, confident, ardent and brash in her fervour to take on the world. The light from the window lit up half her face and the other half remained in darkness, giving her countenance an intense, divided look.

'So where were we?' she said, resuming self-assuredly. 'But wait! Let me show you something in today's *Jang*,'[5] she

---

[5]*Jang* is Pakistan's oldest Urdu language newspaper, with a circulation of over 800,000 copies daily. http://en.wikipedia.org/wiki/Daily_Jang

said, reaching out for the newspaper from the long table. 'We don't believe in love regardless of how much our romantic poets write about it. This sort of thing makes our leading daily's front page: *Andhi Mohabbat: Nabeena jore ne court marriage kar li.*

'Love is blind! A blind man and a blind woman get married in court. I mean, what is so newsworthy about two people falling in love and getting married? Why does it have to become front page news just because they happen to be sightless? Should the visually challenged have no right to fall in love or marry? You see, that's where we are in terms of acceptance of love.'

I glanced at the report. The black and white thumbnail photos of the couple seemed unnecessarily and cruelly inserted to shame them and their families. The boy and girl seemed very young and innocent, perhaps in their late teens. Their unseeing eyes seemed to be questioning the insensitivity of the sighted.

'At least the court honoured their right to marry! Even though the reporter doesn't seem in favour of such marriages,' I said.

Nusrat grew impatient and crossed and uncrossed her legs. 'Do write about this couple though theirs is not a story of same-sex love. But if we can't tolerate cross-sex love, what room does that leave for same-sex love? You started with what's going on with lesbians in Pakistan, but that word is not known to most Pakistani women. It's a very delicate thing you have to carefully build up and you have to say: I've accepted myself as I am. That's all you need, really.

That is the revolution, like this young couple—they ran off and got married! To hell with society—it's not society or the state granting you some right, or religion giving you sanction. Love and identity come together for a woman when she says: I'm a woman-loving woman. You're not born one. You evolve through attractions and loves and relationships. But you have to start with your own mind.'

'But that sort of opportunity to evolve exists mostly for middle- and upper-class women, right? They have more privileges, more freedoms. What about working-class women?'

'Obviously, if you're from the less privileged sector of society, you'd have less cultural and social capital. Gay and lesbian, we don't have an equivalent vocabulary for these identities. We used to be a very traditional society, but one which could tolerate same-sex relationships as long as they were kept hidden under the cover of heterosexual relationships. Intense and close friendships between women across all classes were the norm. You can blame colonialism, nationalism, modernism, feminism—all the isms we've been liberated from and victimized by for the demise of gender-segregated spaces within families! Some elderly women still lament the fact that they've lost their zenanas or women's quarters, where they could be away from men and have their own worlds. The range of expressions you could have if you had a purely women's space is gone. Old ladies reminisce about how much fun they used to have—they played women's games and celebrated women-centred rituals in the zenanas. People had fewer expectations from their marriages, in terms of it being what is now called a symmetrical marriage. Marriage was not meant to be a romantic, emotional and intellectual partnership. Earlier, men and women didn't have any of those expectations. The traditional extended families had a lot of room for acceptance of love between women, all of it undeclared and unlabelled, of course.'

'Don't most women get married because they want kids? What about maternal instincts?'

'I can't speak for all women. But I didn't have it in me. I've found other ways of relating to young people. That's why I teach. I can love other people's kids. And I love them for their essence, not as investments for my retirement plan.'

'One could make a case for same-sex relations being good ecologically. It could be promoted as an austerity measure along with contraception!' I said. 'Going gay might be a more fun alternative than swallowing contraceptives.'

Nusrat chuckled, 'Okay, you can make a case for population control but I'm not gay because I want to save the planet! I'm gay because I find women beautiful.'

My hour was up and we had only just begun exploring the convoluted business of love between women. Nusrat had to trek home from South to North Karachi. I asked if we could meet again.

'We can have brunch next Sunday,' she said. 'I'll sms you the address. You can meet my other half, someone I call soulmate.'

The brunch offer was a risky invitation but I was thrilled.

I must have won some trust. I had to go to Hyderabad the following week but I made sure I was back in Karachi before next Sunday.

~

I got into a cab for the long ride to North Karachi, the city's seamier side, far from the tree-lined, garbage-free lanes of Karachi's spacious sea-front bungalows, well-watered lawns and armed guards sitting outside gated compounds. Karachi's traffic was slightly less terrifying on a Sunday morning. I looked out as dusty, oxygen-depleted air blew into my eyes. I tried to make sense of the changed city as the taxi criss-crossed from one flyover to the next. Flyovers define the new Karachi, making it an alien city I don't recognize or relate to. The city I spent my teenage years in was a landscape of openness, and on its fringes, stretched a treeless, desolate desert. Images from those years seem to be real only in my memory. Girls could ride a bicycle in Karachi then. There were cheap lending libraries I could cycle to, to satisfy my reading lust. There were no flyovers then. Many of the streets had different, colonial names. Chaotic growth has altered the city, and the labyrinthine flyovers meant to streamline growing traffic reminded me of a many-limbed monster that had wound itself around the buried heart of the city. The city is no longer a walkable city. The flyovers have no footpaths. No dreamy strolls for peddlers, the slow, the disabled, the aimless. The focused, intolerant, efficiency-driven development agenda steamrolls itself, and chaos worms its way into the city's soul, hollowing out its core.

The spacious bungalows began to disappear as soon as we descended onto the other side of the flyovers. Multi-storied buildings with box-like apartments, stacks of greying highness and narrowness crowded the cityscape as we exited into the northern suburbs. Apartments that looked grim, uncared for and carelessly constructed, loomed on both sides of the street, as if ease had fizzled out of them. Clothes flapped restlessly on lines strung across cluttered balconies. Everything seemed short of breath, staring helplessly at the fast, impatient cars. The road twisted and stretched out like the splayed entrails of some just-sacrificed beast.

I asked the gatekeeper where C-29 was when the taxi dropped me off in front of a huge apartment complex. The painted sign above the iron gates matched the name in Nusrat's sms. The guard gave me directions to Block C. The lift filled me with foreboding. It looked like it got stuck habitually. I said Bismillah under my breath and entered the dark, tiny box and pressed the number six on the panel. It stuttered its way up and belched me out on the sixth floor.

The other doors on the sixth floor were doors you saw everywhere—barricades concealing gloomy lives. But the brief passageway to Nusrat's door was lined with potted plants and terracotta lamps. C-29 was calligraphed in black on the wall to one side of the door. My eyes came to rest on the antique brass knocker.

The one to let me in was not Nusrat.

'Hello! Nighat? I'm Quratulain. Follow me into the kitchen. Tea's almost ready.'

Quratulain? The partner, the girlfriend, the soulmate, the

other half? Her old-fashioned name was at odds with her breezy welcome, her T-shirt and jeans, and her short, almost too short hair.

I followed her across what seemed like an artist's studio—a mattress along one wall, the floor littered with magazines, tubes of paint, canvases and tin cans holding brushes, and palettes—and then we entered the kitchen. Nusrat was pouring out chai into large black square mugs. She was wearing a man's embroidered kurta and white pajamas. Onions, tomatoes and peppers were strewn on the kitchen counter. Nusrat looked strikingly androgynous. There was an ease to her oddness, she didn't seem edgy and caged the way she did on her college campus.

In the space between the stove and the kitchen door was a small, square dining table—a flat board atop two columns of old tires. And on this table was a sparkling glass jug of long-stemmed tube roses. Everywhere was light, but not the sort of harsh light I had just come in from.

'Welcome to our Sunday morning show!' said Nusrat. 'I've made my best elaichi-flavoured doodh-patti chai in your honour. To compensate for no tea at the canteen! And we have flowers too!' she pointed out the tube roses.

My mug of tea was large, fragrant and steaming. I felt like a victorious general receiving a medal for a stunning war performance. I had woken up late and set out with some apprehensions, not knowing if I could locate the address easily, and whether it was safe to get into a taxi alone, or what to expect from the meeting. There was no time for my morning dose of caffeine at my host's house as the household was barely awake when I left at 10 a.m. This hot cup of strong tea was the palliative I needed like a steadying hand.

'Great chai! And a nice kitchen—lots of light and space,' I said gratefully.

It was a genuine pleasure to be served such fine tea, to be welcomed with such familiarity into a home, a unique home, an exclusively women's space, where all seemed light and airy and nurturing. How had they managed to create such a treasure in the bowels of a megacity?

'This isn't ordinary light and this isn't ordinary space,' Nusrat said gently, turning towards Quratulain. 'It's QT's light. I call it her noor.' Her voice dropped to a quilt-like, caressing softness.

QT?

'Quratulain.'

'That's you? Quratulain?' I asked the tall, pretty, short-haired woman who was removing eggs from the refrigerator. Her face had flushed from the compliment.

'QT's fine with me. Quratulain is very impassive. Nusrat says it lacks intimacy.'

'It's a mouthful besides,' I said. 'QT blends better with your persona.'

I let my eyes rove over the kitchen. My domestically-trained eyes sought out the sink. Angled light fell onto the sink from closed glass panes stretching up to the ceiling, illuminating an assortment of unwashed dishes. A sink full of dishes says a lot about priorities. I inhaled the cardamom-rich aroma of my doodh-patti, not wanting to finish it too soon, in case they didn't have refills, and contemplated what the dishes in the sink revealed about Nusrat and QT, while Nusrat stood at the counter, peeling and chopping.

'All yours now, babe,' Nusrat said, sliding the chopping board towards QT and joined me. Waiting for the omelettes to cook, Nusrat brought out a bag of rusks. She offered me the bag and took one herself, munching noisily. The crunching and munching and the undone dishes in the sink became freedom songs that morning. There was something fragile about the three of us in that kitchen, as if we could be lost if not cared about, sitting in a flat in a city with serpentine flyovers. The uncouth chewing, the dirty dishes, and the light she had called QT's noor stood out as delicate, about-to-vanish values. I dipped my rusk into the mug, and sneaked glances at Nusrat. She deliberated between noisy mouthfuls on the questions of love and love-making between women. Bereft of self-consciousness, she had abandoned herself blissfully to eating and talking simultaneously. Watching her was a new dimension of sensual experience. The light and space and her voice carried unmistakable stamps of something rare. How had she escaped the self-censoring, the self-vigilance wired into most female neurons? Was she the hero of a new age novel or a forgotten one? One with chapter headings like Nusrat and food; Nusrat and art; Nusrat and messiness; Nusrat and love.

'The other day you were saying women are not empowered enough to ask for sexual pleasure. So sex for most women is just a duty?' I asked.

But it wasn't Nusrat who answered. QT set down the egg beater and walked over to join us at the table.

'Did Nusrat tell you I'm divorced? I was married for seven years. And the sex, to put it bluntly, was disappointing. And especially so after my son was born. I was the one responsible for taking care of him and the house. With time, there was a growing dissatisfaction, which threatened to turn into life-long disappointment. I think a lot of women have desire, but it's men who are the leaders in bed. The woman has to lie back and receive the love-making. Most women don't even think of themselves as sexual subjects. And men only see them as sexual objects. It was only after I met Nusrat that I realized how desire and emotional and sexual fulfilment could go hand in hand.'

'It was so strange,' QT continued, standing behind Nusrat. Her hands pressed down on Nusrat's shoulders. I thought she was about to cry. Nusrat tilted her head back and gazed up at her. 'For Nusrat the whole sexual act was geared to pleasing me and knowing my desires from the way I responded.' QT spoke with a faraway look, but with such tenderness, her voice reminded me of dew-topped leaves. 'She would read my face, my body, my movements, she'd know how I was feeling, where I was in my journey. With every bit of touch, she'd know how I was feeling—she knew how her caresses felt to me because she could imagine herself in my body. It came out of this physical knowing, knowing the wiring of the other woman because you're a woman yourself.'

QT could be any straight, modern, urban woman. Yet she wasn't. There was an untamedness about her femininity, a frail certitude in her voice that expressed the profoundness of what she had discovered. There was something remote, reverential, and almost sacred about her, as if she had received an intimation of something transformative, something she had stumbled upon in her emotional universe. The softness of her voice, the sheen on her face, the non-servile femininity—the kind that didn't appear interested in pleasing men, or caring about their opinion of her as an object—all hinted of the discovery she had made.

'Most women's bodies are never explored enough by men,' Nusrat said after a few minutes of silence. 'Objectified like hell. That's all you see in pornography, but hardly ever explored. Men can't give up their own restlessness about their own orgasms. There's fast food, and there's slow food, and we all know the difference!'

QT smiled faintly, gazing at something in the distance, as her fingers tucked back stray strands of Nusrat's hair behind her ears, and when she spoke there was a poignant sadness to her voice. 'Nusrat's right. My husband only indulged me to get to the real thing. Foreplay felt like I was forcing him do it, just because I needed it. I wanted to be touched everywhere but that was not his idea of sex. Our marriage wasn't a partnership. I don't know what it was, but it felt most ridiculous when we were having sex.'

'Yesterday was special. We celebrated our first anniversary!' Nusrat pulled QT to the front, encircling her with her arms. 'A year ago this beautiful creature and I committed to each other in a very private ceremony. And we moved into this flat and yesterday we completed our first year of togetherness. That's the real reason for the flowers.'

'Congratulations to two girlfriends, spouses, or partners?' Nusrat spoke after a long pause. 'Well, we have many terms of endearment but since we don't live by any preconceived roles or standards, we don't use the usual labels. I've used "girlfriend" before, and it seemed just right when I was younger, but now, girlfriend seems too immature. But neither can we be husband and wife—that's too corny and we don't follow those roles anyway. And lovers sound like we're naked in a jungle, singing mating songs. Like we don't have to go to work in the morning or come back home with groceries and cook and wash. There's no one word, really, but we think of each other as saathis—companions, or fellow travellers on the path.'

I glanced at QT as Nusrat spoke. She was the younger of the two, maybe in her early thirties, but she had already been through a marriage, motherhood and divorce. I was curious about her life and her work.

'I started looking for a job and finally this bank job materialized,' she said. 'I moved to Karachi to get away from my family. And a year later, I met Nusrat. Initially, I had to move back to my parents' house after my divorce. My husband agreed to the divorce if I left my son with him and never tried to get in touch with him. That's all he wanted— his male heir all to himself! They didn't think I was a good mother because I was not an obedient wife or daughter-in-law. The only regret I have is leaving my son behind. I had a Bachelor's degree, so I knew I had to reeducate myself. I enrolled for an MBA programme but my parents wanted me to remarry since they thought I was too young to live alone. But I was adamant though it was tough to ward off their pressure. They kept introducing me to divorced men and widowers. They were such bores, but they were the only men interested in marrying a divorced woman.'

'Don't you ever get to see your son?' I asked.

'No. His father won't let me. I'm supposed to be a bad mother,' QT's voice broke.

'Don't you have a legal right to see him?'

'After the age of seven, the father becomes the legal guardian. I tried many times but they won't let me. My husband and in-laws have poisoned my son's mind against me. I have no choice but to wait for him to grow up. Maybe that's when he'll want to know the truth about his mother.' She added in a quiet voice: 'Maybe. Maybe not.'

'Wait till he falls in love. I know that's when he'll come looking for you because you would understand him the way his father won't,' Nusrat said with an exactness, a prescience that can only be a gift of a soul that has forged ties of shared pain with another.

QT nodded absently but I could tell Nusrat's voice had a settling effect on her.

'Let me tell you how we met. Our first meeting was very special,' Nusrat blurted, looking apprehensively at QT but QT had suppressed all traces of pain by then. 'I was standing by the door of a bookstore, and I was on the phone, when she interrupted me. I've had quite a career with women. I know what it's like to be with different women but it's rare that I should get so love-struck after the very first meeting. QT's eyes lit up and found a life in mine. I was attracted by her nervousness, her eyes that had made that admission of desire and her anxiousness and readiness, her smile and the certainty of having given up all pretences. We were both wondering where this madness was going to lead to, but once that bechaini, that restlessness, had arisen, we both knew somehow it was going to express itself. Rationally, there were commonalities that fed the relationship—our shared politics and aesthetics, our sense of humour—but all that came later.'

'Why don't you recite the anniversary poem you wrote?' QT said deflecting attention from herself. She was her somewhat withdrawn, calm self again, moving back to the counter and picking up the egg beater. 'I'll get the omelettes ready.' She turned to me. 'You're in the presence of one of the best woman-loving poets in the country.'

Nusrat's voice was deep and strong, the voice of courage and craziness. She was right about the light in the kitchen: it wasn't ordinary. The light mingled with her voice and wove threads of pain and beauty into our morning. Something sacred and luminous was coming to life, beaming down from the kitchen windows. I closed my eyes. Her voice incited a parallel awareness, one that directed my mind away from the meaning of the words, and set it adrift. She recited and I sensed what their bond of pain was made of, the difficult-to-name union of theirs, how delicate it was, how it rested in an elemental space. It was a bandhan, a relationship too jaded for labels like girlfriends, lovers, spouses.

Here are the first few lines of the poem she recited and her translation.

Tum Noor Meri,
har pehloo main,
jahan vaday thay
puri dunya say,
vahan phoonk diya
tum nay rooh ka rishta,
yeh rishta kya, yeh tum say hai,
ya phoonk dya tum nay rishton main
mitti ka aur khoon ka rishta?
badan ka rishta, rooh ka rishta.

You, my Noor, O Light of Soul
In every aspect touched upon
Where there were promises to the world
There you blessed them with a breath
A link with the soul

Is this a link with you?
Or with a breath have you blessed
All links with a whiff of earth and blood?
This link with body, this blood bond with soul

The gift of lips on skin like silk
God knows what lies in this chain of beauty

You my Noor, O light of soul
Stay like a painting I can hold in my eyes
Stay in my breaths and
I in yours every moment

It is mine—
Call it the sweet love of knowing you like I do,
Call it the blind passion of a Majnun of the wild
So Unique is this—
Without saying much I'll say—
This union with you—
Has forged
A greatness like no other

QT announced the omelettes were ready.

'We'll say a silent prayer,' Nusrat said, when all three of us were seated.

We sat silently for a couple of minutes before the food. It was a novel, mindful way to begin a meal. The omelette was delicious, seasoned with cumin and coriander leaves, onions and peppers. I complimented QT, spreading butter and jam on my toast.

'What do the neighbours think of you two living together?' I asked.

'We don't ask and it doesn't matter what they think, as long as they don't bother us,' Nusrat replied. 'One of the ladies on the fifth floor was curious when we moved in. Basically, women worry about their husbands. But when she realized we had no interest in her husband, she calmed down. She even sent us iftaar during Ramzan. Some of the neighbours admire us, I think, the ones who have daughters. They want their daughters to get educated and have jobs like us. Our landlord's happy with us. We're always on time with our rent, we keep the place clean, and no suspicious-looking men come here. And anyway, professional women living and working in the city, is an accepted reality nowadays.'

'In fact, there was a TV serial written by a woman, and it aired on one of the cable channels. It was based on three single women sharing a flat—and it was quite popular,' QT said. 'The characters were all very mainstream of course, and one of the women even gets married in the end. But the point is, that single women, working women living independently as an urban phenomenon, were shown on prime time TV and it was okay! The writer's name is Firdaus Haider.'

Firdaus Haider? I already knew her. QT mentioning her name made me get in touch with Firdaus after many years. I think I was destined to include Firdaus in this book so the coincidental mention of her name by QT turned out to be just another of those many happy accidents.

After the deeply satisfying omelette plus walnut halwa for dessert, we stacked the dishes atop the unwashed ones already in the sink. From the kitchen we moved into the studio with fresh mugs of tea. Nusrat wouldn't hear of my helping with the dishes. 'We didn't win such a sinful Sunday to squander it on a pile of dishes! We'll do them later. Let me give you a tour of our ashiana, our little haven. This is supposed to be the living room but I've converted it into my bedroom and studio,' Nusrat said. 'The real bedroom is over there and it's QT's. There's the bathroom and that's the study. And that's the balcony.'

'Virginia Woolf would approve! Two women with rooms of their own.'

I moved closer to the walls to get a look at the artwork. There were charcoal and pastel sketches by Nusrat, portraits, and plenty of Urdu calligraphy, newspaper clippings about Sind's threatened cultural heritage and a huge map of Sind taped to the wall. And prints of famous paintings—two of them by Sadiquain: his fasting Buddha-artist and a self-portrait. The tortured, lonely artist, holding his decapitated head in one hand and a paintbrush in the other.

'Sadiquain's work has an understated, pained homo-eroticism,' Nusrat said.

'How did he get away with it?'

'Artists have always led their alternative lifestyles regardless of what the mainstream thinks,' Nusrat replied. 'This is also by him,' she pointed to a framed, calligraphed quatrain.

I read out loud:

Hum husn paraston ki shariat saqi
Is mein hai yahi tarz-e-ibadat saqi
Hum nay khad o khaal-o-mah-o- saal mein
Ki hai ayat-e -jamal ki tilawat saqi

'How does one translate this paean to Beauty? What does one call the *saqi* in English? And where does one draw the line between the spiritual and the secular?' I said.

'Forget it. It's untranslateable!'

'Nusrat, help me translate it. Poetry is not a luxury. Audre Lorde's words. Even if we risk losses in translation.'

Nusrat flopped down on the mattress, sipped her tea and dragged out a notepad and pen from underneath the mattress and started to scribble. She stared at the paper, frowned, paused, crossed out some words, wrote over them. Finally

she handed me the pad. 'That's as close as I can get!'
She had left saqi untranslated.

> For us, the devotees of Perfection, saqi[6]
> Our rule, our means of prayer and worship, saqi
> Over the sensuous turns of moon and months,
> Are chants caressing the sacredness of thy Beauty

Nusrat and I leaned back against the wall on the mattress.
We were both resting in some sacred silent space to which
the quatrain had transported us. QT mentioned something
about checking her mail and disappeared into the study.

For many minutes I kept staring in a fuzzy,
uncomprehending way at a shimmering red and gold chadar
draped over a long mirror. Light from the window opposite
was making its gold strands glint and its folds rose and fell
gently with the air from the fan. I was thinking about
Sadiquain's religion, his worship of Beauty, and I said: 'You
know I recently read a story from the life of the Prophet
where he's known to have said that the highest form of
religiosity is *ihsan*, or worshipping god's loveliness. It's above
ritualistic prayer, above faith. *Ihsan* is the mystic's worship
and the artist's quest for god's beauty.'[7]

'I think religion and language, music and poetry, always
come together to form that mixed bag you call culture—the

---

[6]Saqi: wine-cup bearer, the beloved, God.

[7]Safi, O: Is Islamic mysticism really Islam, http://www.huffingtonpost.com/
omid-safi/is-islamic-mysticism-real_b_841438.html

tender soil of imagination that nurtures you, and through which the metaphor of love gets played out. It's really heartening to see a few older women couples in this country. I don't necessarily look up to them like family members but you do feel like a community. You share the same odds, the same pressures, the same binds, the same religion and culture, and when you see them, how they have struggled to find alternative lifestyles, and how they've been able to overcome the odds, it gives me hope. It means that one can create room in this culture for oddities like us.'

'Sometimes, current debates on sexual rights seem like such a small thing compared to the magnitude of larger tragedies looming ahead,' Nusrat continued dreamily. 'And at other times, it seems like everything. Because love is everything, and your heart is everything, and how you feel as you walk down the street is everything. I could be sitting on top of a glacier that's going to melt—the end of all the snow which feeds all the rivers which feeds all of life. And yet, I could feel love in my heart and accept life even if it's ending. And thank God or nature for this love. Or I could be wealthy and lonely, and be someone who's never known love. And I could die from feeling barren emotionally. I think that would be much worse.'

I listened without interrupting. 'I'm recording this, okay?' I said.

'I know I'm blabbering. And my views on everything could be shredded by some other cultural critic,' she said. 'But I have to say this: you're patient. You're different from the other journalist types who zip in from abroad to interview us, like we're some endangered species—the Pakistani lesbians! Most times when I'm asked to give an interview, it's someone who's got very little time and who's flown in with a very directed set of questions, and unchallenged assumptions—based on the biases of whatever media house they're working for. They just assume there couldn't be functioning lesbians in oppressed Pakistan. They don't even see me as a real person. They talk to me as if I were a label—affirming their views, their stats. Theories are okay, I tell them, but you shouldn't just go by theories. The reality is I'm able to live with my love, and that's my definition of happiness.'

I don't know what else we talked about that afternoon. We listened to Abida Parveen's Sufi kalaam and I was convinced that she's not a person, she's a phenomenon. I heard her sing Kabir's *mann lago yaar faqiri mein*—my heart seeks the life of a faqir. More tea was made, more music was listened to. The November afternoon was beginning to cast longish shadows on the studio walls when QT got a call.

'I'll have to go to the DIC,' she said. 'There's a kid who needs to talk to me.'

'We'll walk with you,' Nusrat said, explaining. 'QT volunteers at a drop-in-centre for street children.'

We went down, crossed the street and entered the municipal park. QT had changed into a very sedate shalwar-kurta. And Nusrat had wound a thick dupatta around herself, almost hiding the men's kurta she was wearing. We could have been three ordinary women out for a walk except we weren't. There was a self-sufficiency about us that set us apart. There were some kids on the swings and slides. Watchful mothers sat on the weedy grass supervising them, and they eyed us as we walked past them. Heavy-set, well-fed men and a few women with covered heads, strolled on the path along the periphery of the park. We walked across to get to the park gate. QT said goodbye. The drop-in centre was in a lane on the other side of the park. Before she left, QT turned to me: 'You asked me if I missed seeing my son. I see my son in all the boys at the DIC.' She walked away hurriedly, before I could process what she had just admitted, before I could respond with something polite and affirming. In that moment I glimpsed the courage and compassion of QT as a mother, and came to know her more intimately than in all the hours we had spent together.

Nusrat and I continued walking.

The plants and trees and the path and the sky stood perfectly quiet and at peace with one another in the fading light, a light that wasn't glaring or punishing. It was a faultless November afternoon. The shrubs along the fence were bright like children. Their leaves were a glossy green, and the older neem trees near the gate stood dark and wise, holding their gnarled and brown selves aloof.

'Each tree, each plant, has its own integrity like people, don't you think?' Nusrat said.

I stopped next to a jasmine bush and found a solitary white flower; the only unplucked one, a little dot of a thing. I plucked it, smitten with its quiet beauty. A little thing like that—so fearlessly announcing its existence.

'I used to have a high school sweetheart once,' I found myself saying to Nusrat.

'And?' She said calmly as if she was used to such confessions.

I held up the jasmine to my nose. Encouraged by its softness against my skin, I said: 'I was ashamed of my feelings for her. We went on to different colleges, and . . .'

'And?'

'And we both got married and lived happily ever after.'

'You mean you both got married to men?'

We left the park and walked towards the autorickshaw stand. I watched the jasmine's whiteness transmute into a mottled brown as it fluttered in the dusty, smoky breeze during the long ride home. I was imagining the light in Nusrat's kitchen at that pearly evening hour. Evening light, tinged with departing gold.

The fragrance from the lone jasmine resting in a small bowl of water by my bed was a reminder about resilience. It still had its jasmineness even though it was plucked several hours earlier. I leafed through a translation of the Quran. I found my favourite verse about God's light being the light from a lamp that hangs like a star from a blessed olive tree, an olive neither of the East nor the West, like the glowing lamp of love in the human soul:

The similitude of Her light is as a niche wherein is a lamp.
The lamp is in a glass. The glass is as it were a shining star.
(This lamp is) kindled from a blessed tree, an olive neither of
the East nor of the West, whose oil would almost glow forth

(of itself) though no fire touched it. Light upon light. Allah guideth unto Her light whom She will.[8]

~

The windows were open to the night. My eyes were tired after the long, hot day. The room had acquired a dreamy, drowsy softness in the light from my reading lamp. I must have dozed off but I woke up some minutes later, with a vivid memory of a vision-like dream. I was in the company of my favourite singers. It was a women's music festival. ·There were a group of women Sufi singers, Abida Parveen prominent among them. She was sitting up on a divan and her other devotees and I were leaning against cushions on the rich, red rug spread on the floor. There was the light from many candles illuminating our radiant faces and much light-hearted banter among us. Abida leaned over and said something to me. I was pleased. Much laughter followed. I was in a joyous mood, peace and ecstasy were unmistakably present, and new worlds were unfolding through the women's music-making and laughter.

---

[8]Adapted from Marmaduke Pickthall's translation of the Quran, *Sura An-Noor: The Light, 24:35*. Pickthall, M.M. The meaning of the glorious Quran. http://www.sacred-texts.com/isl/pick/024.htm

6

Love Is a Spiritual Experience

Firdaus at work

Maulana Ashraf Ali Thanvi on the dangers of teaching women to write:

> As for writing, if there are indications that there is no shamelessness or boldness in her nature, there will be no harm in learning to write. In order to carry out household necessities, there is also a need to know how to write. But if one foresees harm, then instead of trying to learn unnecessary (not wajib) things, it would be better to save one's self from evils. In such circumstances, she should not be taught to write, nor should she learn by herself. This is the verdict of the wise on the issue of women learning to write.

—From *Behashti Zevar* (Heavenly Ornaments) by Maulana Ashraf Ali Thanvi, Deobandi scholar (1863-1943)[1]

Excerpt from Firdaus Haider's autobiographical essay, 'Saray Manzar doob gayey (All Vistas Drowned)':

Wanderlust and a love of literature was my gift from my father. He wrote poetry in Urdu and Persian and

---

[1]English translation of *Heavenly Ornaments* from http://www.jamiaashrafia.org/bahishti_zwear/bahishti_zwear_content.php.

was a fan of Faiz Ahmed Faiz. When Faiz was jailed and other political dissidents were arrested in Gujranwala, my mother burnt all the Leftist literature lying about our house. Abbaji wasn't so distressed about the loss of his political pamphlets and books, as he was about the loss of his divan.[2] My mother hated all poets and all politicians. She thought they were liars and irresponsible people, who tried to escape life's tougher realities. I learned to hide my writing from my mother because she was not in the least interested in it. When my first novel was published from Lahore and my father heard about it, he said: 'Keep writing. You'll save yourself a lot of suffering.' He was grieving the death of the poet in himself, yet celebrating the birth of the writer in me.

Her father's thwarted literary ambitions may have sparked Firdaus Haider's own. The tortuous path to self-expression brought in its wake other creative expressions: reiki and painting. Short stories, TV scripts, novels, plays, travelogues and literary criticism—she explored all these genres in her writing. Punjabi and Urdu she grew up with. And English, Persian, Pashto, Turkish and Thai, she added to her linguistic repertoire later.

I had met Firdaus as a writer of Urdu fiction many years ago. We had kept in touch over email sporadically during the years I was away in the US and India. When QT

---

[2]Divan: a poet's collected verse.

mentioned her name as the woman who wrote the TV play about three single women sharing a flat, I realized it was the Firdaus I already knew. There's no randomness about coincidences. That is, there are no meaningless coincidences. I was meant to meet Firdaus. And she was meant to share her story with me. I didn't have her current phone number but I did have an email address. I emailed and asked if I could meet her and perhaps include her story in my book. She replied immediately:

'Nighat, I was thrilled to read your mail. U r great. U have found the purpose of ur soul. i love ur courage. i am now a reiki master, teacher, counselling, healing and attuning people to reiki. It is wonderful to help others. Am busy on Saturday—it's my healing day. I see reiki clients and students. Come and see me on Sunday. We will talk.'

I arrived at her apartment on Sunday morning with a box of pastries. She hugged me and said I had greyed but looked more at peace since she last saw me. A decade had elapsed since we had met. She looked more magnificent at seventy than I remembered her at sixty! Vivacious, carefree, cheerful and completely at ease. At peace like an edifice that knows its place and sits aloof from the rippling tide of time.

Her kitchen cabinets had been ripped out. Cups, dishes, jars of spices and daals were stacked on the floor. A bearded carpenter was busy hammering away in the kitchen. I was taken aback to see someone else in her flat. I had reasons to feel frightened of men who looked like maulvis. Earlier that morning I had been robbed by a motorcycle-riding maulvi and his burqa-clad companion on my morning walk. I was still suffering the aftershocks of the incident. The bearded one's veiled female assistant had asked me what time it was, and as I glanced at my watch, she had jumped off the bike, grabbed me by my neck and yanked off my gold chain.

Meanwhile, the maulvi seated on the bike, had hissed: 'Give me your mobile!'

'Nooooo!' I groaned. 'Not my mobile.'

'Give it, *saali*, or I'll shoot you!' I saw it in his eyes. He meant it. They were narrow with deep hatred. What business did women have walking outside their home? Walking alone? They deserved to be robbed.

'Look!' I swallowed and waved my chunky grey phone before he could pull out whatever he threatened to shoot me with. All the contacts I hadn't saved to my laptop sniggered, as my wildly thumping heart contemplated what it would mean to lose all those numbers. 'You've got the gold chain. This phone's just an old phone. No camera. No radio. It's worth nothing. The chain's worth a lot more.'

'*Chalo, chalo,*' his veiled accomplice counselled him. 'We got the chain.' She spoke in a very unfeminine voice from under the naqaab. 'Let's go, let's go,' she pleaded, as if worried they might be seen by other passers-by. I prayed for such a passer-by to appear but none did. It was still early on a Sunday morning. I saw them whoosh down the deserted street on their bike. Was that a real maulvi and was that a real woman? Cross-dressers? The chain they robbed me of went to them with a prayer—— my grandmother had given it to me many years ago and it was meant to protect me from the evil eye.

'What I make of this is prayers shouldn't be engraved and worn on gold chains,' I told Firdaus, biting contentedly into a lemon tart. The trauma of the morning incident was beginning to recede with the infusion of sugar into the bloodstream and the impact of delicately-flavoured lemony-custard on my taste buds.

'I don't think that was a woman in the burqa,' Firdaus said.

'She didn't sound like a woman when she spoke,' I said.

'I don't know why they don't ban burqas!' Firdaus said. She sounded more amused than alarmed with the state of things in the city.

A city-wide ban was on, but certainly not for burqas. After the previous week's suicide bomb attack on an apartment building in Peshawar, there was a 'double sawari' ban in Karachi. That meant two men couldn't ride together on a motorbike. But a male and a female could. So a male and a male veiled as a female also could.

Firdaus somehow managed, despite the carpenter's presence, to enter her kitchen and return with two mugs of invigorating mint tea. 'I hope you don't mind the tea leaves floating,' she said. 'I didn't strain it. But it's better than using tea bags!'

After the tea and lemon tarts, we moved from the living room to Firdaus's bedroom, and I sank down even more contentedly on the faded rug on the floor. I glanced at her paintings. I didn't recall her inviting me into her room on my previous visits, but that was more than ten years back. I was younger and more unrefined then, and in doubt about calling myself a writer. Firdaus had been friendly then too, but this time I sensed a difference in her welcome. We had both travelled paths unknown to each other over the last decade, and the paths had transformed us; we could both sense it in each other. And it showed in the way we spoke to each other, and in the way we kept quiet about what we had gleaned from those travels. What we couldn't express in words, was in our eyes, our bodies, our speech, our silences. As fellow travellers we could tell we had both been on a difficult voyage and so the details weren't necessary to spell out.

The light falling on the wall was clear but not harsh, the fan above us was whipping the dry air mechanically, the carpenter's hammering kept me from feeling completely at ease, but Firdaus's paintings and her presence were there to counter it. I began to relax gradually. There was a large, stuffed cushion against the wall and another on the floor. A small table next to them was piled with books, notepads and pencils.

'This is my throne, she said, settling down on the cushions. This is where I sit and write. I'm working on a script for a TV serial, and I've just finished the last episode. So I'm a little more relaxed today. I'm sorry about the noise. Let's shut the door,' she said. 'My entire kitchen is termite-ridden. One of my sisters is an interior designer and it's a blessing she sent her carpenter.'

'How do you work with him hammering away all day?'

'I listen to music and meditate while he pounds the walls,' she said. 'I don't try to write when he's here.'

'Tell me what music means to you,' I said. 'I know I can't write until I have the right music on. Music taps into some mysterious part of my mind.'

'Of course it does! It does that to me too. Music is the very soul of creativity and spirituality. I grew up in a family steeped in Sufism. I used to drive my uncle to mehfil-e-sama, musical gatherings. There were many such gatherings in those days in Lahore. When I was alone, I'd dance to the music as I listened to the poetry of Bulleh Shah. But in the gatherings, I learned to go into a trance quietly. I learned that there was such a thing as being one with music without showing any outward change. I recently did a series of shows on FM 103 on spiritual healing. I played Sufi music and answered listeners' questions. The young RJs introduced me to Sufi rock singers like Mikaal Hasan, Shafqat Amanat. And Zeb and Haniya. Have you watched those two sing *Paimona Bideh*? They are amazing!'

Zeb and Haniya—the two-woman Pakistani band—yes, I'd heard their most popular song, *Paimona Bideh* (Bring the chalice), a hauntingly beautiful paean to love—based on Omar Khayyam's mystical rubais. What is it in that ethereal quality, verging on silence in their voice, the silence behind their words or the music that sinks your conscious mind into some hallowed space? I was with Laila in Oghi just a few weeks before meeting Firdaus and the Pashto-Persian words of *Paimona Bideh* rekindled those quiescent blue mornings drinking tea, watching the day break over blue hills.

'Sometime back I read in *Jang* that all kinds of music are haraam for Muslims,' I said, holding back a smile.

'Nonsense! If music is haraam (forbidden), what is halaal (permissible)? We might as well dig our graves. These mullahs pollute our minds with the horrors of life after death—if we listen to music, we go to hell, they say in their sermons. But I want to think of death as a beautiful event, a much-awaited transition. It's in the nature of the drop to seek union with the ocean. So when they speak of death, I laugh at them.'

We chatted until lunch, a simple daal-roti fare with a gigantic bowl of colourful salad. We ate on the floor, the food laid out on a table cloth. There was silence, there was order, there was peace. And I began to feel healed from the anger, the failure from the frantic, violent clash with the fraudulent maulvi who had robbed me. But the healing that began that morning would in the months to come, heal me at even deeper levels. Those frenzied, violent uprisings of the soul, the constant nagging pull of not achieving goals, not amounting to much, not living as purposefully, as joyfully, as famously—as if goals, purpose, joy, fame were birthrights—those preoccupations would begin to lose their iron grip on me. In the months after my meeting with Firdaus, in unexpected moments during the days and nights when I thrashed about berating myself for making idiotic life choices that had trapped me, I began to see another me, the me who felt more like me, the one I was not ready to accept—and what I saw surprised and relieved me. I had to admit I wasn't worthless. Not the greatest achiever, but—as a person, a writer, a mother, a daughter, a sister, a friend—I was doing the best I could. At the end of the day, I was only human and like all humans, I had blundered, I had fallen, but I had picked myself up, and was doing my best to walk again, to reinvent myself despite the limitations of time and age.

Love, then

'What I really came to talk to you about,' I said to Firdaus, 'is love. Can we talk about love? About what love means to you?'

Firdaus had brought in two more mugs of tea after lunch. This time it was lemon tea. The carpenter had finally left.

'*Zaroor*! Love is first of all, a spiritual experience. We came to earth to experience God's love for us, and because God wanted to experience being loved by us. The spiritual in us is God. Our soul is an expression of God's love for us.'

'And what about earthly, romantic love?' I asked, inhaling the lemony aroma from the mug and leaning back against her bed. 'I remember reading a short story of yours. It shocked me at the time. It was such an open admission of desire for physical intimacy by a woman.'

'You're talking of "Gaey". Yes, it was called obscene by the literary establishment. But I was clever. I wrote it as a symbolic story about a cow! So the critics couldn't pinpoint what exactly was obscene or immoral about the story. And some of the more sympathetic male critics sanitized the story by construing the desire I wrote about as a woman's desire for motherhood! Anything but sexual desire! As if women can't experience anything other than maternal instincts! As for the question of romantic love, I felt that intensely for my second husband. Sexual union was a spiritual union with him. But later our life paths diverged. That too was part of my journey. I had to keep educating myself, we kept growing apart as he kept getting into dalliances with younger women. He didn't like reading or sitting in libraries like me. There's always one person who outgrows a relationship. I think I outgrew him. But through him I met a wonderful woman. His mother! I never write saas-bahu serials for TV because both my mothers-in-law were caring women with whom I had really good relationships.'

'Oh, I didn't know you had two!'

'Yes, I had two husbands and two mothers-in-law.'

'And so you really loved your second husband. And after him?'

'After him other men did come into my life. But when they got close I found they still had a lot of growing-up to do! And they needed my help to do it. I wasn't ready to play Mom to them. I wanted to grow myself. God finally granted me the kind of freedom I had prayed for. I managed to earn enough money to keep my simple lifestyle going. My spirituality became my ecstasy. When my artist friends offered me a joint or a drink at parties, I told them, "But I don't need these props. I'm always in a state of self-achieved ecstasy!"

The restlessness of her soul grew more intense. Like the flute separated from its reed bed, she found solace in the cries of her own music. Only when the pain crossed its limits, the moment she was waiting for would arrive, she knew. This faith kept lamps of hope lit within her. It was this belief that finally made her victorious, and assuaged her longing.[3]

'You wanted my love story. Let me start with my first marriage. I haven't told too many people about it. My mother arranged this match. I agreed to it because of my love for learning. I had admission in a college in Lahore but my father didn't have the means to send me to Lahore. So when my mother suggested I say yes to a marriage proposal from a man in Lahore, I agreed. I was seventeen. I didn't know of a better way to get to college.'

He stood there with his body, strident, with certitude, but though present, he was absent. And in spite of belief in him, she lacked belief. She lowered her eyes. Desire had been trammelled from its zenith into an abyss. She had to surrender to him though he was not the mate of her choice. Her family had chosen him and she was forced to accept their choice. She wanted to accept everything, wanted to believe in everything, and yet her lowered gaze trembled. Night's maternal, nurturing spirit was being smothered. The moments waiting to spring from night's womb were stifled.

'In the beginning everything was fine. I was going to college. He even allowed me to ride my bicycle to college. I got pregnant soon after the marriage. I remember going to take

---

[3] All excerpts from Firdaus's short story, 'Gaaey (The Cow)' from her 1982 collection *Raaste Mein Shaam* (Twilight on the Path). Out of Print [http://outofprintmagazine.co.in/archive/sept_2011_issue/Nighat_Gandhi.html]

my exams with a big tummy. When my son was born, we
went to visit my husband's family in his village. There I
heard his mother tell him: "Either you stop educating her or
you stop messing around. She's a smart girl. She'll figure
you out soon." I panicked. What did she mean by saying
that? Was he messing around? With whom?'

> She remained tethered to the post. Her body burned
> slowly. She was compelled to lead a conscienceless
> life. Her inner eye opened deeper even as the lava of
> her essence kept melting away. Only then did her
> soul hear a voice which drowned all other voices, a
> voice that propelled her as the drop is propelled
> towards the ocean.

'"Ismat, please tell me the truth about your brother," I said
in a state of panic to my sister-in-law. Ismat and I had
become friends because we were almost the same age and I
spent most of my time with her in my in-laws' home.

'"He was married before he married you," Ismat revealed.
I stared at her. "I don't know how he convinced your family
to give him your hand. His first wife was sick of him
carrying on with all the village girls. She would fight with
him. He locked her up one night but she escaped somehow.
She took the two kids with him. She was pregnant with his
third child at the time.'

> She raised her hennaed hands and inhaled the perfume
> of jasmine garlands on her wrist; she fingered the
> silver dust in the parting of her hair. The silver dust

and the flame-coloured henna, and the embrace-famished fragrance of the jasmine made her restless. The henna glowed impatiently, the silver dust longed for the dampness of kisses, and the half-open buds of her lips ached to bloom.

'I was trying to make sense of what Ismat was telling me. As she told me more and more about her brother's philandering, in a flash of insight I knew I had landed the wrong role in the wrong play. The timing for this revelation couldn't have been more right. "You have to help me," I said to Ismat. I was holding my baby in my lap. I looked at his evenly heaving chest, his closed eyes. *Don't, don't let him pull you back. He'll come to you when he's ready.* I lifted his soft, just-nursed body from my lap into Ismat's. "I'm going to leave him with you," I said. "Tell him his mother had no choice but to leave.'

She, a mere droplet became the ocean of oceans; a rare pearl too invaluable to be bought or sold; she became earth and time and space. The flute's lament became sharper, its melody and her anguish becoming one. When dignity and desire embraced, earth and sky lowered themselves before her. She knew the much-awaited moment had arrived for which her Self had smouldered in the cauldron of anguish. She rose and tore off her golden veils and her iron chains.

'Next day, Ismat and I went out for a stroll, concealed under our chadars. She returned from the edge of the village and I stayed back, waiting for the next bus back to Lahore. From Lahore, I got on a bus to Rawalpindi. I wanted to go there because my husband's brother lived there.

"'Call your brother. Tell him I want him to divorce me," I demanded of my brother-in-law in Rawalpindi. "You're a lawyer. You know what needs to be done."

'I remember getting my statement typed by the munshi in the court. I said I was foregoing the mehr, the bride-price agreed on by both our families before the marriage. I laid no claims to my husband's money, any of his property or his child. I was dictating the statement to the munshi. The munshi looked at me, shocked: "Are you sure you want to word it like this?"

"'Yes, that's exactly how I want to word it," I said. All I wanted at that moment was to be free of that man.'

People tried to snatch that moment of self-knowledge from her. They were ignorant of the nature of that pain from which springs an ascetic's ecstasy. Her oppressors tried to stone her to death but the chains imprisoning her had already snapped. She had set herself free. Towards her goal she now walked and even ran, though her detractors did everything to hold her back.

'My husband was summoned by his lawyer brother. He arrived. He tried to make up all sorts of stories, blaming me instead of himself. Making up stories that I wanted to leave him because I was interested in some other man. I stayed firm with my demand for divorce. Finally, with the divorce papers in hand, I boarded another bus. I was nineteen years old, divorced, and penniless. I was a mother, but destined to live without my child. I reached my parents' house the next morning. I expected some sympathy but all my mother could say was: "A woman even loves the worthless junk of her house. And you left behind everything, your son, your jewellery, and came away with nothing?"

"'My life's been ruined, Ma!" I couldn't believe her. "And all you can think of is what I should've brought with me?"

'That same night, I took another bus. There was no place for me at my parents' home. I headed back to Lahore. There I went and collapsed at the feet of my Persian teacher from college, Professor Sufi Tabassum. I finally allowed myself to break down in his presence.

"'Who says your life has been ruined?" Sufi Tabassum Sahib said. "Just because you got a divorce, is life over?" he said. "You have to tell me what is it you want to do with your life? You were always good at sports, weren't you? Okay, so let's get you a physical education diploma. Let's get you a job after that."

She had become so powerful she wanted to merge with another power—to create, to give birth; a deed that seemed most natural, most elemental. Her suffering had reached its zenith. That moment of conception known as the Mother moment—who can deny the reality of the Mother moment? It needs no confessions or proclamations. All stand subdued before its power.

'I got in touch with my father only after I moved into the hostel and started classes for the Phys Ed diploma. "Can you loan me a hundred rupees a month for a year?" I wrote him. This was the early 60s. You could get by with a hundred rupees a month if you lived very simply.

'He wrote back a long letter. "My dear daughter," he wrote, "you were not a burden on us. You should've given me time to think. I'm a lawyer. I would have seen to it that you got a proper divorce and that your husband paid for his lies."

'"I couldn't wait," I wrote back. "I didn't have the patience to get embroiled in a long drawn-out court battle. I wanted to get on with my life. So I did it the quickest way."

When those who wanted to stone her reached the place where she stood strong with the force of her determination, they beheld a light. The light was emanating, spreading, and flowing from her being. They saw her kneeling before a greater power that enveloped her, holding her safe. The temple bells of her heart rang to confess the supremacy of that power. People saw a canopy of light beneath which her being flowed like fluid silver.

'The diploma in Phys Ed enabled me to get a job at Home Economics College in Peshawar. This was 1961. I arrived as the Phys Ed teacher at a girls' college. But shortly, after I got there, I met my second husband. He was the brother of one of the wardens with whom I became friends. We got married a couple of years later, but I continued working at the college and I also started work on my Masters in Urdu literature. After eight years of teaching at the college, I got tired of this job. So when an opportunity to travel materialized, I agreed to move to Thailand with my husband. He had been transferred to Bangkok for a few years. By that time, I had two children with him. Soon after we moved to Bangkok, my neighbours started telling me women visited our apartment in my absence when I went to Pakistan to visit my son whom I had enrolled in a boarding school. In those days, I never trusted my intuition. Instead, I relied on logic. I asked myself why would my husband want to cheat on me? There was no logical reason for him to do that. I was doing everything I could to keep him happy. I continued to deceive myself until one day his Thai girlfriend called me.'

Night held its breath. Frightened, speaking in hushed whispers, it lay buried under the weight of its own anguish. This night had come after endless nights of waiting—it made her perfumed body yearn, turning it into an ear straining to hear the summons of love. Moments slipped away. Each moment turned into a century and many such centuries passed. And her silence, her loneliness, her restlessness only grew.

'"I just want the truth from you," I told him. "But the truth was only this: history was repeating itself. He admitted he was in love with her, and no longer in love with me. I went into a state of shock. I insisted on meeting her. And one day he took me to meet her. It was a harsh meeting, and I was unkind to her. She was young, she couldn't have been more than sixteen and she had a glowing face. I still remember her face. I felt bad for her but I felt bad for myself too.'

> She listened. She tried to follow his decree. But in lieu of food and shelter, she could not demean herself. Surrender takes place in the heart, and radiates out from one's being like rays of light. But inside her, all was emptiness, loneliness, and desolate, stretching from her outer to inner self. How could such a heart be persuaded to submit?

'My Thai friends told me to ignore my husband's philandering. And let him keep his girlfriend and just live my life. Many Thai women, it seemed, were resigned to their husbands having multiple relationships. But I couldn't do that. I was broken. I started seeing a psychiatrist. He put me on tranquillizers for several years. I wrote to my father. He wrote back telling me to be patient and handle the situation calmly and realize that my husband was from a respectable, upper-class nawabi family, and having extra-marital affairs was normal for such men. The problem was my husband needed women who were in some ways inferior to him to make him feel good about himself. He said he felt bad about what he had done to our relationship. But he didn't really apologize. All men do it, was his defence. If he did it, what's so wrong? I asked him for a divorce after trying to keep the marriage together for many years. My heart failed to accept his affairs that continued with different women. I can accept it all now. It was my karma to get married to both those men and it was my karma that they both turned out to be such weak men.

The world simply belittled her desires and her convictions as nothing more than mental agitation. But within herself, was growing an indefatigable strength. Her worldly lord, angered by her growing strength tightened his grip on her. He began forcing down her throat strong and bitter drugs.

'Despite my two bitter divorces, I never grew bitter towards men. I love men. Some of my most helpful friends have been men. The three most important men in my life, my father, my brother and my uncle were my staunchest supporters. I lost all three of them. Their deaths happened in the same year. That's when I hit ground zero.'

In such a state of ecstasy she realized that no hovel was too small, no castle too large. No diamond was too precious, no pebble utterly worthless. She knew that despots could become dejected, and lords could turn into helpless slaves. She saw before her a mountain like Mount Sanai. Then came the voice of revelation, and self-knowledge descended like lightening.

'But because I had grown up in a family steeped in Sufism, I accepted all hardships as challenges on the spiritual path. Without such challenges how would I grow? My relatives were ready to offer me shelter after my second divorce. But I preferred to live alone. They had a problem accepting me as an independent woman. They didn't think it safe for a woman to live alone. So I had to come across as extra-strong and stable to assert my choice of living alone. I never lost my self-esteem or played the Poor Me game.'

> Her lips no longer remained lips, the henna no longer henna, the flowers no longer flowers. Everything had become One. Beneath the canopy of light, and beyond it, in the far reaches of heavens, in the depths of the earth, in the vastness of space, in the waves of oceans— all traces of duality had disappeared. Only her being flowed, her being which had become fluid silver, submerging all in its wake. All of creation, every speck in it was flowing with her. She was no longer afraid of those who wanted to stone her . . .

Love, Now

'Do you know, my eldest son from my first marriage, the one I had left behind in the village with his grandparents finally got in touch with me after twenty years!' Firdaus said. 'He called me from the US. He was crying. He was going through a divorce. He said he needed to talk to me. He could hear God's voice telling him to get in touch with his mother. That was the year 9/11 happened. He was on his way back to the US but got stuck in Japan. He couldn't return to New York. So he flew down to Karachi to see me. And he brought his son, my grandson with him. And that little boy and I became friends instantly. He was so excited that we're both Scorpios! And for his sake I bought a computer and learned to use it so I could stay in touch with him!

'I don't know how you lived with the knowledge that your son was out there in the world, but was keeping himself away from you,' I said.

'I came to accept that too. He grew up an angry man. He grew up believing that his mother had abandoned him. His grandparents and my ex-husband told him I had left his father for another man. And he was justified in what he believed. But now we're the best of friends. He calls me to get advice on all kinds of problems. He trusts me. Time has healed us.'

'In the afternoons I have tea with milk,' Firdaus informed me. 'I have fixed times for different kinds of tea.' She took out the lone remaining lemon tart from the box, placed it on a plate and sliced it into precise halves. What awed me about her was the disciplined way in which she practised her simplicity. She didn't go out of her way to impress me with a fancy meal, nor did she change her morning mint and afternoon lemon, and late afternoon milk-tea routine. As I bit into my half of the tart, I realized the silence interspersing our speech was growing longer and we were both okay with it. There are very few people with whom I feel comfortable being silent.

Firdaus's phone rang.

'I have to take this. It's one of my clients,' she said, looking at the name on the screen. 'She's recovering from a serious surgery but it's slow.'

She moved to the rocking chair to send her healing and asked me to go wait in the living room.

From the couch, I caught a glimpse of Firdaus on the

rocking chair, eyes closed, deep in meditation. I switched my attention to the paintings gifted to her by her well-known artist friends. The walls of her small apartment were a miniature art gallery. In a few minutes, she called me back to the room.

'When a client calls asking for healing in distress, I never refuse. If my meditation can help a soul in pain, I feel privileged.'

'So you practise distance healing too?'

'Yes, distance makes no difference. Healing is about sending energy. And it depends on your intention. When the intention is pure, good energy can travel any distance.'

'I still have to grasp that. It just seems unreal—that I can send healing energy to another person.'

'Once you become initiated and start practising reiki, and you heal people, you won't find it strange. It's perfectly natural.'

'How did you start painting?' I asked, glancing at one of her paintings—two frightened-looking, wide-eyed women, holding each other in a tight embrace in a forest. Surrounded by green, dense foliage, they're clasping each other, nude, in their most natural state, nurturing and vulnerable, frail, and yet somehow self-sufficient.

'My painter friend Tasadduq Sohail inspired me to paint. He was at my flat one night, working on a book cover for one of my short story collections. And watching him paint, a strange desire came over me. I wanted to paint too, though I had never held a paintbrush in my life. Do you think I can? I asked him. "Why don't you find out yourself?" he said. He returned to London but left all his paints and brushes for me to mess around with. Sometimes I painted all night, and those were the best times. When I can paint like that, I forget myself. I forget time.'

'I wish I could write like that—forget time and self-judgment,' I said. 'Most of the time, I lack faith, I get depressed when I read what I've written. It seems no good. There are a few moments of joy sometimes. But they are rare. I don't understand how I can love something so much, think of it as a calling, and also dread doing it so much.'

'Write without revising, and say to yourself, I can always discard it if I don't like it later. When you wake up, after you freshen up, take a few minutes to meditate and connect with the divine source, or your higher self. Get your energy for the day from that divine source first thing in the morning. And consciously remember these six principles—live in gratitude, harbour no anger, no worry, love all living and non-living beings, live honestly and practise forgiveness towards all. After you do this meditation every day, sit down to write. And thank the divine source after you finish writing. Don't look at what you wrote any more that day. You can come back to it the next day and if you don't like what you wrote, you can rewrite.'

I jotted down those six principles in my notebook and they sounded so simple and wholesome, I could see myself getting up the next morning and adopting them as daily practice. She had offered me the best gift, the insight of connecting my creativity to my higher self. Consciously, I continued to build bridges between my creative and higher selves, learned to dodge the traps of insecurity laid by my ego, that gossamer web of doubt, self-censure, envy and fear that the ego weaves; I had a feeling I might free myself from my ego's traps. I had learned to enmesh my defenceless little self in the ego's enticing specious logic. And this tendency couldn't vanish overnight. But I slowly allowed that whatever emerged from me was the purest, most authentic expression of self, shining despite fears and doubts.

'Will my fears about not being good enough leave me?' I asked Firdaus.

'Ask the Divine Source to remove the impurities of your soul. When the impurities are gone, your soul will shine like a sparkling mirror, and all your fears will leave you. All your wishes will be fulfilled without much anxious planning on your part or worrying.'

'You're inspiring me to take a five-year leave of absence from my kids and family,' I said, 'and go off on a journey I've been meaning to go on. I want to explore myself in complete solitude. I'm not sure how I can do it, or if I can afford it moneywise, or where I'll go. Am not even sure what I'm looking for.'

'Do it!' Firdaus said with the self-assurance of a master. 'Don't wait. Go out. Become a citizen of the cosmos. Find your path. If you knew what you were looking for, why would you go looking for it?'

'Right! If I knew what I was looking for, why would I go looking?' I smiled at her simple logic. And vaguely recalled reading couplets by Ghalib exulting in aimless exploration:

So why talk of finishing the journey?
At the sound of the camel-bell
Lose thy balance, and dance.
Ghalib, with this exultant joy,
To whom art thou bound?
Wax great in thyself alone
And with the shackles of disaster dance![4]

'It feels like you're saying it's okay to be as lost and unclear as I am at present.'

'There's an internal logic to your search but it won't get expressed in language. Not at first.'

Her words didn't make rational sense and yet, they *felt* profoundly true, and just what I needed to hear then. Truth isn't always rational. I thought of my travels in the past year, both near and far from home, and my meetings with Nusrat and QT, and Nisho, and Laila, and Nahid. And in the course of that year, how the idea of home was losing its stranglehold, its fixedness for me. I no longer needed an address google maps could zoom into. I was expressing a desire for freedom and solitude but what I didn't realize was that I was already fulfilling that desire. I was already walking the path I thought I wanted to embark on! The path and I had merged and I hadn't realized till this moment that I was already deep into the journey to meet my Self, walking away from space and time-bound limitations. But where was I

---

[4]*Mirza Ghalib: A Creative Biography* by Natalia Prigarina, OUP, Karachi, 2000.

going? Walking to where? Was it towards newer illusions or finally, towards more clarity?

You can't have all the answers right now, Firdaus's silence said.

'I feel more comfortable not knowing much about the future after talking to you,' I smiled as I started to carry the cups and plates into the kitchen.

'Don't wash the cups,' Firdaus thundered. 'I have my own way of washing them.'

Okay! I backed off, amused at how otherworldly she could be in one moment and how rooted in routine, how minutely finicky about doing her dishes her way in the next moment.

At the end of her autobiographical essay, 'All Vistas Drowned', she writes:

> The search for the divine is an ongoing human quest. But we can be deluded into thinking that finding divinity in this world means to make or become the centre of somebody's attention. To come free of such delusions is true contentment. I learnt this after much anguish and suffering. I now live in the present moment. I don't dread the future. Nor am I ashamed of my past. I'm immersed in the sound of my own internal music. Because all doors and windows open into my being and lead inwards, I don't become distracted by external noise. Once in a while I am asked, why do you live alone? My reply is: who can live with me? My life has never been lived bound even by my Self.

As I left her apartment that Sunday afternoon, I felt she had given me a gift for many lifetimes—I carried away in my heart a slice of the fierce wisdom I had received from this fearlessly free and compassionate woman. It was mine to take with me on future quests I was all set to begin.

7

Rakhi Sawant of Sind

*Shah's Faqirs tune their tamburas for nightly performance at
Shah Abdul Latif Bhitai's shrine*

Where the people of the Heart dwell
There reigns supreme the God of Love
Who knows the depths of that whirlpool
That holds God's grandeur at its centre?
What need to offer Him praise or reverence
When wrapped in His perpetual rapture?

—Shah Abdul Latif Bhitai,
poet saint of Sind (1689-1752)

As I step into the 7 a.m., air-conditioned Daewoo coach to Hyderabad, and accept the boxed snack, a glass of cola and newspaper the hostess hands out, surprised at the cordial service for a mere two-hour, three-hundred-rupee ride, I congratulate myself. Karachi has been a grim, unsafe place; to steer out in this urban maelstrom seemed risky and I almost didn't come. Reading the papers has been akin to attending an execution every day, not knowing who the real criminals are or what the true crime is. I mustn't, I mustn't read the papers every day, I tell myself, but it's the addiction of the well-informed. Who's responsible for the sudden outbreaks of violence? Nobody knows. Nobody is meant to know is more like it. Deliberately confusing conspiracy theories abound on the many cable news channels. The shoot-out in Karachi's Shershah scrap metal market has left sixty dead. Violence is becoming an everyday affair. Violence of all kinds keeps erupting regularly: kidnappings for ransom, murders, ethnic and sectarian clashes.

Nature seems to have grown furious too—the worst ever floods of the 2010 monsoon and the making of twenty million climate refugees; the ancient Indus and its tributaries have carried away in their frenzied waters cattle, homes, people. A dengue epidemic is raging in rural Sind. Hospitals in Sind don't have enough platelet kits for the influx of patients. And the real dictators of Pakistan, the IMF and World Bank, are impatient with the slow rate of taxation, the slow pace of what they call structural reforms: the IMF wants faster hikes in petroleum and power tariffs, which the beleaguered Pakistani government is inflicting at a glacial rate of only 2 percent every month. Was energy being doled out free earlier, was the hapless populace getting spoilt with cheap and abundant power? What did the majority of sixteen million Karachiites hope to wake up to each day, I wondered?

The early November sun from my bus window is an innocent, untainted ball of orange, resting just above the horizon in its marmalade-coloured halo, so large and perfect, it seems fake like a child's poster sun.

I had been texting and trying to call Nisho to find out if she was okay after the floods. She finally replied to one sms. 'Thanks, sister, Mirpur Khas *main koi problem nahi hai.*' No problems in Mirpur Khas.

After this, I made several more calls to her, and finally she answered. 'I want to come and see you,' I said. 'How is the law and order situation there? Things are quite bad in Karachi.'

She was attending an urs celebration at a saint's shrine in a remote village so her phone was out of range, she said. I didn't know if she was making an excuse for not taking my calls. May be she didn't want me to visit?

'It's peaceful here,' Nisho said. 'This is not Karachi. I couldn't attend my best friend's birthday party in Karachi. My boyfriend didn't let me go. He said Karachi isn't safe these days. I had my special outfit all ready for the party. I had gone to so many pains to match everything. What else do we live for? We don't have kids so we can't spend on them. We spend on clothes and jewellery and make-up. I want to get my hair streaked, so I'm saving up for that now. Yes, Mirpur Khas is safe. It's a small place, and people look out for one another here.'

No shootings? No bombings?

'No! No! I told you—this isn't Karachi.'

And dengue fever?

'Dengue?' Nisho sounded mystified.

Death by dengue, extinction by religious extremists, sniper fire, targeted killings, suicide bombers, gang rape, floods, rising inflation? Which of these was likely to get me if I took the bus to MPK? Half my problem, I told myself in one of my self-deprecating brooding spells as I debated to go or not to go to Mirpur Khas, sitting hunched at my laptop in the guest room in the plush, hushed house of my relatives was that the mere contemplation of any remotely rash action was circumscribed by the knowledge: I'm a woman. If I were a man, I would've boarded the bus to Mirpur Khas without a thought, and then if I couldn't locate Nisho's house, or she didn't let me in, I would go sit at a chaikhana and figure out what to do next over a cup of tea. But this gripping anxiety about safety, about not having chalked out a proper travel plan—itineraries, tickets, accommodation— the total absence of planning! The fear of some unknown tragedy was always a quivering presence in me. Fear of what-ifs—the legacy of my good, sound, upbringing. A woman's cautious consciousness. So insidious—it feels an integral part of being a woman. My outward fearlessness and go-with-the-flow bravado getting mocked by little, fretful fears milling inside me. The hemmed in, depressed by real and imagined fears, the unable-to-act me.

But my self-imposed fearfulness was meant to end that morning. Another one of those meaningful coincidences. A nudge from Beyond. In my inbox, the just arrived Nov-Dec 2010 issue of the *Muse India* magazine begs a reading, with its special issue on Bhakti literature. I'm browsing through Abha Iyengar's article on the Bhakti movement, and through the links in the article, I end up at Ahmad Salim's essay on Bhakti saints and their role in the cultural-spiritual transformation of the subcontinent. Slowly, as I read these revelatory lines from Ahmad Salim's excellent essay, I am delivered from my pre-travel jitters. Did Ahmad Salim write this passage to inspire me?

> The women saints in medieval Indian society emerged in an atmosphere of discrimination and suppression, but blossomed into thinkers, scholars and spiritually advanced and emancipated beings. Their lives and works constitute the supreme forms of self-expression. Sharply breaking away from the traditional role assigned to a woman as wife, daughter or mother, these women saints consciously or unconsciously departed from the established norms of social behaviour and spurned the limitations imposed on them by their families and society. Not only did their compositions carry the overtones of protest, their emergence was in itself a social revolt.

If the sixteenth century Meera could don anklets, sing love-intoxicated paens for her Krishna—'*Aye ri main to prem diwani* . . . I am lost in love . . .' and wander the deserts of Rajasthan, and fourteenth century Lalla Arifa compose vaks, and roam the valleys of Kashmir naked, what was Nighat, in the twenty-first century afraid of? Boarding a bus? That same dispassionate divinity that prompted Meera and Lalla Arifa to renounce their prescribed roles, heard my pleas. She responded in a strange way. She made me stop pitying my limitations as a woman, and my entrapment, to borrow Ahmed Salim's phrase, 'in an atmosphere of discrimination and suppression'.

I checked the Daewoo bus website for departure times and called the depot to make a reservation for next morning's bus to Hyderabad. I'd tell my relatives I was taking off for an NGO workshop in Hyderabad—a far more palatable explanation of my absence than telling them I was traipsing into the interior of Sind to meet a TG. Then explain what a TG or transgender is. And finally resort to using the derogatory term hijra. NGO workshop it would be. From Hyderabad I'd take a taxi or find another bus to MPK. I didn't bother to call Nisho to inform her I was coming because I feared she would tell me she wouldn't see me, but maybe, my heart whispered, just maybe, she'd go out of her way to welcome me and play the part of a glad host?

~

Next morning.

I'm sitting next to a young woman on the bus to Hyderabad.

She smiles and points to the book I'm reading. 'That's my grandfather's translation.'

I stare at her in disbelief. 'You mean Shaikh Ayaz is your grandfather?'

She nods, her smile deepening. 'Yes. He was my nana.'

I'm mostly a rational person. But the frequency of serendipitous events happening in the last couple of days is getting to be too frequent to appear as purely unplanned, random coincidences. I'm sitting on a bus heading to Hyderabad against my better rational judgement. On the bus I'm reading the Urdu translation of the poetry of Sind's most revered Sufi saint and poet, Shah Abdul Latif Bhitai, and my co-passenger turns out to be the granddaughter of the translator, the man who rendered Bhitai's *Risalo* into rhymed Urdu verse?

I started to tell Shaikh Ayaz's granddaughter, a college student in Karachi, returning to her home in Hyderabad for the weekend, about my book on Muslim women.

She offers: 'Come to my house. You can meet my mother. Shaikh Ayaz's daughter!'

~

The short, two-hour ride passes amicably. She talks, I listen mostly, but when silence falls between us, I stare out at the unvarying, brown and grey-green scrub of Sind's deserts. The bus glides on the smooth, faultlessly paved four-lane divided highway, and trucks, buses and cars swish past us like fluid images on a screen. The trance-like monotony of the desert landscape and smoothness of the ride makes the journey appear dream-like. I wonder fleetingly how a poor country, an economically downtrodden country, a 'failed state' as the international media has labelled Pakistan, manages to have such clean, no jerks or jolts, no pothole-ridden highways?

We pass small towns, and large, easy-to-read wall-painted ads addressing men's sexual fears start running like ticker tape along the highway. Sorcerer-scholar Juned Bangali, expert in black magic, charms and amulets, promises to resolve all amorous and sexual problems in just one sitting! I've seen variations of such painted wall ads all over Pakistan. A prudish society tolerates such crude displays regarding men's fear about sexual performance? But of course, it's men's performance, and men's fears about not being manly enough that's being addressed. I remember the excerpts from the chapter on successful copulation I translated from Dr Shah's *Islamic Etiquettes of Sex*. The nation's nationhood rests squarely upon its men's ability to sire sons. Even Nisho holds it as her one cardinal failure that makes her less than an ideal companion: she can't have children for her lover.

Shaikh Ayaz's granddaughter tells me how Shaikh Ayaz put his foot down when his sons wanted to put their sister, her mother, in purdah. 'My daughter will not wear a burqa. You put your wives in burqa, but not my daughter, my nana told his sons.' She chats animatedly about her career plans, tells me about her engineer and dentist sisters. I didn't hear anything about her tying the knot.

'Any marriage plans?' I ask.

'If it happens, it happens.'

'And love?'

'If it happens, it happens.'

I'm impressed by her self-assuredness.

'I'm not saying no to marriage. But career also matters.'

'Can you have it all? Marriage and career and kids?'

'Why not?' she says as if my question is outdated.

'I like the confidence of your generation! We were less sure.'

'Tell me about your book,' she says.

'Well, it's about women and love. And I wanted to visit Shah Abdul Latif's Sind because women were the true heroes in his poetry. He made them fearless love warriors. And he wandered all over Sind with yogis,' I say, suddenly wanting to proclaim this saint-poet as my protector, his all-embracing humanism as the heritage of a world that knows him very little, his spiritual message as an alternative to the soul-deadness I see everywhere. 'His poetry is replete with references to yogis and sanyasis and their ash-streaked foreheads, their ascetic ways, their singing and their blowing on conches. Sind worked her magic on him, and he on Sind.'

'Sind is still like that,' she says proudly. 'We have a very tolerant, faqiri culture.'

Her closest childhood friend, she tells me, is a Hindu, with whom she celebrates Holi and Diwali.

'Thank God Sind is still like that!' I say in gratitude.

She probably can't gauge how deeply indebted I am to Sind and Sindhis for having retained their liberal faqiri ethos. If I go by what I've read in the news, all I've read about Sind is it's poverty, its salinity, its feudal landlords, their indentured slaves, the *karokari* murders, and forced marriages of women to the Quran.

A little after nine, we pull in to the Daewoo depot in Hyderabad. Hyderabad seems peaceful and asleep. Shutters are down over shop fronts. As we cross the bridge over the Indus into the city, I'm shocked to see how the mighty Indus, which just a couple of months back had wreaked such havoc across the country, has whittled down to a tame and lazy, silvery trickle. Benazir Bhutto's smiling face beams down at me from a huge billboard announcing a Pakistan People's Party campaign for the local elections.

I say goodbye to Shaikh Ayaz's granddaughter as she gets into her waiting car.

The single lane highway to Mirpur Khas is lined with a green, tunnel-like canopy of lovely trees. My taxi driver, courtesy of a Hyderabad friend, is Pappu Chandiyo from Chandiyo village.

'We'll get there in one hour, Adi,' Pappu assures me optimistically. Both he and I know the seventy-five-kilometre ride is not doable in an hour but the sun is shining amiably, the traffic on the highway isn't choking our progress, so it's a good time to be optimistic. Preoccupation with punctuality seems to be unimportant. In fact, not much seems to be of importance here except the hospitable impression Sindhis want to make on outsiders and their desire to be treated with respect. In contrast to the desert vegetation on the way to Hyderabad, the highway going east to MPK passes through a lush, irrigated belt. Beyond the line of trees lie stubbled fields of just-harvested sugarcane and fruit orchards—mango, guava, banana. I ask Pappu to pull up so I can buy lime-green, orchard-sweet guavas for breakfast from a roadside seller.

A flurry of winged white birds alight in the fields. It's the season of migration and these avian visitors have travelled to spend the winter in coastal Sind all the way from the Siberian steppes.

Unlike the smooth-as-cream motorway from Karachi to Hyderabad, the highway to Mirpur Khas lives up to my expectations of jerks and jolts and potholed subcontinental roads. We enter MPK two hours after leaving Hyderabad, bones rattled and faces coated with dust. A smiling, seductive Katrina Kaif waves at me as I brush my dust-caked hair out of gritty eyes.

Katrina is beckoning prospective home buyers with the promise of owning 'your own home, your own peaceful heaven' if they invest in Zubeida Heights—a multi-storey apartment complex in MPK with all the amenities one expects in a modern urban home. Later, when I recalled the town, what I remembered most of MPK was Katrina's smile against the town's brownness; the brown of its dust, of overly sweet tea at a roadside stall, of unpainted, incomplete-looking homes, the brown of its narrow unpaved lanes, uncollected garbage, and the brown midday feel of its grimy bazaars.

We snake our way through the town's narrow, crowded streets and reach the mohalla where I remember Nisho had told me she lived. There we ask about the *moorten* (local lingo for transgenders). A man selling a mountain of blood-red, toxic-looking jalebis points to a gali tightly packed with squat houses behind his cart. The moorten live in houses on the right, he says, eyeing me questioningly as I thank him, and tell Pappu to go have lunch and wait for me in the taxi.

There's an open gutter running alongside the houses of the lane. I stop at a door on the right at random and knock. After a few dreadful moments, somebody with wide, kohl-lined eyes and frizzed hair opens the door a crack.

'*Kis se milna hai?*' The tone is abrupt, suspicious.

'I'm looking for Nisho. Do you know where she lives?'

She looks at me suspiciously. 'Nisho? How do you know her?'

'I'm a friend. I've come from Karachi.'

'Nisho's house is two doors down,' she says, moving the thick curtain of curls to her left, rolling her theatrically blackened eyes as she shuts the door on me.

'Shukriya', I say to the shut door.

I walk to the door she had pointed out. There are many doors like it in the wall and they all seem identical. I'm repelled by the cloying stench from the scum swirling in the open drain running along the lane, and yet I'm drawn to it. I can't take my eyes off the greasy-grey, frothy effluent flowing in it, flowing out towards the main street where the bazaar is. I imagine the filth reaching some fetid pool, the home of dengue mosquitoes. I recall Katrina's winsome smile and the salubrious promises of the clean, horizon-kissing lines of Zubeda Heights as I stand on the threshold of what could be Nisho's residence.

It turns out it is! The door opens a wedge and Nisho's hazel eyes peep out, recognize me, and then the door opens wider.

'*Asalamalaikum*. Sister, *aap yahan*?'

'*Walaikumsalam*. I hope you're not going to turn me away,' I say apprehensively. 'I wanted to surprise you.'

'No, no, sister, come in,' Nisho steps back. She might have been put off by my sudden appearance but it's too late to send me away, or she's too polite to tell me to get lost.

I step across the threshold into a tiny opening, steering clear of the two bricks placed to bridge the drain. I am standing in a narrow aangan. Nisho closes the door, shutting out the putrid smell from the drain. Sweet basil and pink roses are planted along one wall, and a small burlap sack hangs over a doorway to the right. That must be the toilet. There's a stove in one corner and near it, a large, wire cage with two brown and white pigeons. Behind the cage, a door leads to a room, the room that turns out to be the only room there is.

I could sense several pairs of eyes directed towards me as we enter this dark, windowless room. It seems darker at first but soon my eyes grow accustomed to the muted light inside. A few people are sitting on the chatai-covered floor. All of them are staring at me as if I'm some abnormal creature.

I give Nisho a hug. 'Sorry, I didn't call you. I wanted to surprise you!' I repeat as I hand her the gifts I've brought for her, a pair of earrings and a stole.

'Nisho, *yeh to bata*, who's this baji?' One of the moorten

finally speaks up. Hers is a shrill, mannish voice, and yet it's not quite a man's voice.

I squeeze myself on the floor in the space they've created for me in their circle, removing the protective dupatta I had wrapped around my head for the journey. Nisho brings me a glass of water. I think of the water bottle in my backpack and of jaundice and cholera as I accept the glass from her. I recite a silent prayer to boost my immune system. Nisho is watching me.

'This is Nighat baji. She has come from Karachi,' Nisho says to her friends, satisfied after I hand her the emptied glass. 'She's writing a book about women. She thinks we *khadras* are women. I met her last year at that workshop where they told us about AIDS and condoms and all that *bakwas*. Baji, these are my friends,' she turns to me and introduces them. 'Rubina, Gulnar, Bandook and Mashook.'

Suddenly, the darkness and stuffiness in the room lifts. The load-shedding hour has ended and the fan and light come on. Rubina and Gulnar stare at me more defiantly in the new light, as though they are trying to figure me out, to gauge if I could be genuinely interested in them as women. They have youthful figures, and are slim and attractive, probably in their twenties. Their mouths move meditatively, working the paan or gutka which they never stop chewing, and their eyes are sharp and lined with kajal, giving them a worldly-wise and piercing gaze. They are dressed in simple, yet fashionable and tight-fitting clothing. But the two men with rhyming names, Bandook (Rifle) and Mashook (Beloved) appear shy and retiring, dressed in loose and dark men's shalwar-kurtas. Mashook has pencilled brows and a torn, flowery dupatta wrapped around his neck. Both avoid looking at me and stare at the pattern in the chatai as if wishing either me or themselves gone. I can tell they are embarrassed by my presence, especially these two. They look like men, but they sit demurely, barely speaking, like shy women, whereas the other two, Rubina and Gulnar, who look like women, are more outspoken. They are ready to take me on.

'Are those your real names?' I ask Bandook and Mashook after we are introduced.

'No,' they smile coyly, shrinking even more towards the floor. *'Pyaar ke naam hain*. These are nicknames.'

Nisho on Calling Herself Nisho

We have two names. One that our parents give us and one which we are given when we enter this field. The names our parents give us are boys' names. But we live like women after leaving home, so we can't have masculine names. You are given a feminine name by your guru, a name that goes with your personality. So I chose to call myself Nisho. I didn't take the name my guru suggested. I liked the name Nisho so I told my guru I would call myself that. Nisho was an actress and when I am dressed up, people tell me I look like her. But if I could change my name now, I would call myself Rakhi Sawant. I think I resemble her more.

Nisho on Falling in Love

Who hasn't been in love? At least once in their lifetime? I mean, if you haven't loved, life is absolutely worthless. There's no point in living without love. We'd just come to life, live like animals and die. People think only a man and a woman can make a couple. They say that is how nature intended it. But, the truth is, anybody can fall in love with anybody. A man can fall in love with a man, a woman can fall in love with a woman. But society doesn't accept such love.

The story of my love? Why do you ask? I feel very shy about telling you. I've been in love with the same man for seven or eight years. I met him at one of my dance performances. He's four or five years older than me, but he's a complete man—tall and wide-shouldered. I was instantly attracted to him. We exchanged phone numbers. You think my eyes are like Aishwarya Rai's? He says that too. He saw that I was very sophisticated even though I was not educated. I was only seventeen or eighteen when I met him.

When I fell in love with him, I began to question why God made me the way I am. Why didn't He make me into a complete woman? Is there any difference between us and real women? No, it's just that we aren't accepted as women by society. If I were a real woman, I could've gotten married, had kids, made some man happy. But this way, the way I am, I can't. I don't fit into any role. I'm told I'm engaging in a najaiz (sinful) relationship. But I don't think my relationship is sinful. Maybe the world thinks I'm committing a sin. It would be sinful if I were to cheat on my lover, if I got into another relationship behind his back. But I follow my heart's bidding, and love him, where's the sin in that? I've always listened to my heart.

Nisho on Lovers' Quarrels

My boyfriend and I fight a lot. Like if he comes a few minutes late, or doesn't bring me something I asked him to bring, I let him know—you're a henpecked husband, I say. You just follow your wife's orders. You deserve the award for the best enslaved husband. Sometimes he also gets mad at me and sometimes he even slaps me when I talk back to him. He hits me to bring me back to my senses. If somebody else uses abusive language, or gives me a gaali, I can't take it. But my lover can curse me hundreds of times, and I can say a hundred mean things to him, but afterwards, when we make up, I forget all that.

How do we make up after a fight? Simple. I give him a missed call. The longest we've stayed away from each other is fifteen days. That's a world record. When he showed up at my door after two weeks, I didn't let him in. I said to him, why are you coming back to me now? What can I give you? Go back to your wife. But after fifteen days, I forgot we'd ever fought. That's love. Love is like cream in milk. The cream always rises to the top.

Nisho on Marriage

I can't marry him. I can't marry a man and give him children.

All I can have is this unrealistic, romantic, filmy relationship. Like in a song in a film where the hero and heroine come together, sing and dance, and then go back to live their real lives. I knew he wouldn't ever marry me. And yet it was so painful for me. We've been given men's bodies, but everything about us, our thoughts, our soul, the way we live, everything, everything, is like a woman's. You know, I wish I could go to Switzerland and have some surgery so I could become a real woman. But I know, even then I won't be able to get pregnant. And where will I find the lakhs of rupees I'd need to go to Thailand or Switzerland? By the time this technology (for sex change) comes to Pakistan, I'd be too old. Pakistan, as you know, is a very slow country!

It was just last year that he got married. But he still cares for me. He still visits me every day. He never lets me want for anything. And he says he loves me. Here, let me show you his picture. We went to a studio to have this one taken. Don't we make an enviable couple? What more can I ask for? He didn't want to get married but his family forced him to. His mother was the one who wanted him to get married. She knew he was in love with me. But his family used insulting words like hijra for me. He belongs to a very prominent, respectable family so our relationship was kept all hushed up by his family. And now he has a wife and a five-month-old son. If I didn't love him, I would've left him after his marriage. I could've said, I'll also find another lover. But I love him.

Nisho on the Future of Her Love

I know this love isn't going to last. He'll grow tired of me. He'll become preoccupied with his family responsibilities. In a few years he'll have two or three kids, and when they grow up, he'll be even more tied down, worrying about their education, their marriage. He'll forget me by and by.

For him I need to keep myself in shape. I went on a diet and lost four kilos in one month. I had to. I was getting heavy. In our profession, you need to maintain your figure. My paunch was beginning to show. People don't like it if a dancer is flabby. I started taking this powder with green tea to kill my hunger. I'm a big chatori, a glutton. I like to eat whatever takes my fancy. If the dahibada wala goes calling, I send some child with money and ask him to bring me dahibada. Now I've stopped eating like that. You can't dance well if you put on too much weight.

But in the end, our lives end badly. There's nobody for us once we're old and we can't earn from singing and dancing. Only those who have put aside savings, can hope to have a somewhat comfortable old age. But those who don't have any savings, they get kicked about in old age.

But when the married ladies in my mohalla tell me stories of how cruelly their husbands or their in-laws treat them, when they cry about their mothers-in-law—she did this to me, she did that, my husband is so mean to me—then I wonder why women who can give men children, why are they subjected to such cruelty? Then I thank God that there's no husband or mother-in-law shouting orders at me like a blood-sucking vampire or the angel of death threatening to strangulate me. Those married women can't do much of what they wish to, they can't follow the desires of their hearts. I suppose our life isn't much better than theirs. Like if I'm in love with somebody, I don't feel like having sex with anybody else. There comes a time even in the life of a hijra, when she wants to settle down and give up her old way of life.

Nisho on Jealousy

I think of his wife as my saukan (rival). I'm very jealous of her. I hate her most of the time. But I also feel sorry for her because she puts up with my presence in his life. I wouldn't have been as generous if I'd been his wife. I wouldn't let him go to another woman. She's not happy about our relationship. She found out about me the very next day after the wedding. She found a photograph of us—a New Year's party picture. I always celebrate New Year's and Valentine's Day. But she has no reason to fear me. She knows I can never challenge her legal status. He won't ever marry me, even if he could. I could never give him children like she can. She just has to put up with him visiting me sometimes. So I'm not much of a threat, you see. She knows I'm not like a real mistress, like a real woman could be. If he had another woman, she could make demands. She could demand to become his second wife. Not me. So his wife can be jealous of me but she knows her own position is safe with me in his life.

Nisho on Morality

I don't know why the world thinks of us as immoral. The world's full of hardcore criminals, alcoholics, drug addicts, adulterers, gamblers, murderers, terrorists. Do we plant bombs? Are we murdering people? Do we take bribes? What kind of threat do we pose to society? We keep to ourselves. Then why does the world shun us? Treat us like criminals? Some call us dozakhi (destined to go to hell). I say to those people, we too are desirous of going to heaven, just as you are. If I commit sins, I will be held responsible for my sins on the Day of Judgment. Nobody has a right to tell me I am committing a sin and send me to hell except Allah.

Nisho on Rights

People keep talking about rights. But who gives you your rights? Nobody. Our small town has many Khawaja Sara[1] and they have small minds. They're not clever like educated, city people. And they're afraid of harassment, so they keep to themselves. They'll never give an interview or talk to an outsider. They don't trust people, they don't like people asking them questions about their lives. They're always worried about consequences.

My guru was telling me about a new law for us, the Khawaja Sara. Workers from the NADRA (National Database and Registration Authority) office came to my

---

[1]Khawaja Sara: the non-derogatory term for transgenders in Pakistan.

guru and told her we could now get NIC (National Identity Cards) for all the Khawaja Sara. But what are we supposed to say on the application, I asked. Do we write men or women? They said we can put ourselves into a third category, that of Khwaja Sara. Some of us would say we're women, some would say we're men. But if we want to say we're women, shouldn't we have the rights that belong to women? Like the right to marry? And if we say we're male, shouldn't we get the rights that belong to men? But we'll get neither the rights of men nor of women. They'll just create a Khawaja Sara category for us but give us no respect or rights.

I've seen that excellent film about Shabnam mausi of India. She went into the field, and campaigned for her right to contest elections. She was right, when she said, people from our community need to be elected to fight for our rights. You know, in the film, they show a man fell in love with her. And then somebody in the film passes an insensitive remark about her. They ask the man how he could possibly fall in love with a hijra? And Shabnam mausi cries. She's so upset. Can't a man fall in love with us?

Nisho on Respect

In my mohalla, all the children respect and love me. Whenever they see me, they greet me, Nisho baji, Nisho baji, *asalamalaikum*. I also chat with the ladies in my neighbourhood. We exchange recipes. Their husbands know me and trust me. They've never stopped me from going into their homes, or meeting their wives. But outside my mohalla, where people don't know me, they taunt and tease me, they call me names—chakka, hijra, zenana. They make fun of me by trying to imitate the khadra's clap. But you know, we don't go clapping all the time. To clap for no reason is completely against the behaviour code of our community. But for most people, a khadra's trademark is their clap, so whenever they see us, they clap to imitate us. In our community, we clap only to signal disagreements among us, or when we want to end an argument. Or if we go for badhai to a house where there's been a birth, then we clap.

More than anything else, I want respect. I want the world to accept me, and respect me for who I am. That's all. Other than that, life is fine. God provides for all his beings, even a worm living under rocks finds food and shelter, and I'm a human being. I shall be provided for by Allah. But love and respect, that's something else. Sensitive people treat us well but the insensitive ones, they don't realize how their taunts hurt us and how we go home and sob, remembering their insensitivity. Sometimes I ask Allah, why have you given us this kind of life? Why is it that we aren't valued like other people in this world? Even if I work hard all my life to build a respectable image of myself, I don't think I can succeed.

You can offer any man on the street twenty or even thirty thousand rupees, and ask him if he'll agree to wearing sandals like these and a flowery shalwar-kameez, and put on lipstick, and go dancing thumak-thumak in a bazaar. Do you think he'd agree to do it? Why is it that people don't understand why we live the way we do? Do they think we adopt this lifestyle for fun, or because it makes us rich? We make less money than most people. In every way, we are considered inferior to the average man or woman. So there must be some other reason, right, why we still dress and live the way we do?

Nisho on Family Relationships

If there are two friends in our community, and if they are very affectionate towards one another, they can decide to become a mother-daughter pair, or they can become sisters. There'll be a ceremony where the relationship they choose is announced to all. They'll exchange gifts with each other, like new dupattas and bangles, distribute sweets, sing and dance. You know, the way people celebrate a wedding, we celebrate our new relationships. My guru's guru is quite old. I call her dadi. This is how we define kinship in our community. My guru considers me her daughter-in-law. It's up to us how we want to define our relationships. Everybody loves their brothers and sisters, father and mother. But real love and family is the kind we develop with one another.

I left my family when I was about ten. I only studied up to class four. We were eight of us—four brothers and four sisters. Well, four and a half sisters, I should say! I always liked being a girl. I dressed like a girl. I never played cricket or football or gulli danda—all those are boys' games. I played with dolls, and kho-kho. I used to watch my sisters and from them, I learned to cook. My brothers used to love me until my father passed away. Whenever I went out, and saw others like myself—and saw how they dressed up like women and how freely they moved about, I wanted to join them. So I ran away from home and joined the Khawaja Sara's gharana. I stayed away from my family for two or three years. My family didn't like my entering my guru's community. Once when I went home to see my mother, my brothers chopped off all my hair, which I had taken so long to grow, and with so much effort. So after that, I stopped going home. Nowadays, I go home to meet my mother and sister but I don't stay. I was never close to my brothers. But since they are the heads of the family after my father, I have to show them some respect.

Nisho on Spirituality and Faqiri Culture of Sind

You know the kind of acceptance I've found in Sind, I don't think I could find that anywhere else. Not just in Pakistan, I mean anywhere in the world. Sind is the land of Sufis and faqirs. And the poor people of Sind are much more tolerant than the rich people. Why? Because the poor have nothing to lose in loving us.

You know in that film, when she's really hurt, Shabnam mausi goes and prays at the shrine of a saint. She wants the saint to protect her. I do the same. When I'm really worried or tense, I just take a rickshaw and go to a dargah. I go and sit at some shrine and pray. And somehow by doing that my heart feels lighter. I feel refreshed. I go to Bhitshah with my friends for the urs. And during the urs, we do dhamaal there. You know, God's holy men, I believe, never discriminated against people who were different. It's ordinary

people who've set up these boundaries. We're like faqirs—
we are happy within ourselves. We don't involve ourselves
in the affairs of the world. We just live, accepting the way
Allah has made us. Probably Allah didn't want us to get
embroiled in the intrigues and corruption of the world so
He spared us all that by making us different.

~

Tea in a blue enamel pot is delivered by a boy from the
bazaar. Nisho pours it out and passes it around with biscuits.

Nisho tells her friends they have to dance and sing for
me. The first to perform is, surprisingly, Bandook. He sings
a Sindhi song and the others join in a chorus. Throughout
the song, he sits and looks steadfastly at the chatai, never
meeting my eye. He smiles when I praise his singing, the
words of which I haven't followed fully, but his voice had a
poignant sadness, even though he was singing a flirtatious
love song. Mashook says he can't sing or dance and sits
stiffly in his corner. Nisho gets up and turns on the CD
player. The music is loud, and most neighbours can hear it,
I'm sure. But nobody seems to care. Gulnar and Rubina
shake out their hair, tie their dupattas around their waist,
and wait for their song to come on.

Their gyrating, twisting, heaving bodies leave me awed
and envious. The way they thrust out their padded bosoms,
widen and roll their eyes, smile seductively, come near and
suddenly spin away with a swish as if I'm a man in the
audience ready to lunge at them, leaves me amused. As they
lip sync to Noorjehan's Punjabi songs and Lata's Hindi

songs, I wonder who teaches them to dance so professionally. Their steps are practised and their bodies supple but their movements somehow lack finesse and feminine grace. But they could fool anyone into thinking they were women. The perennial themes of unrequited love are what their songs are about: the ways of the beloved are cruel and the hapless lover must incur risks to life and reputation to meet the beloved at the village well, in the fields, in the world. The last performance is Nisho's and she dances to another Noorjehan song. Everybody's watching appreciatively and seriously, like artists who regularly critique one another's work.

Nisho is out of breath after her dance.

'You were great,' I tell her. 'Where did you learn to dance like that?'

'On my own. And by watching other khadras, and from films,' she says. 'You must be tired and hungry,' she says, playing host as I had hoped she would.

She tells her friends to leave us alone for a while and they file out obediently. She orders lunch on the phone and gives Mashook money to go pick up the order from the bazaar.

'Bring salad too,' she shouts after him.

In a few minutes hot-off-the-tandoor naan and chicken—spicy, shredded and floating in lots of deep red grease, arrives. By that time, I'm so hungry I don't care about the grease factor.

'Where's the salad?' Nisho asks, opening a paper package that has only sliced onions and two wedges of lemon. There's no salad!' she turns to Mashook.

'I told him, but he said, tomatoes are selling at hundred rupees a kilo, cucumbers at eighty. What do you expect to see in your salad?' Mashook says sourly.

'Look at that! We can't have tomatoes or cucumber in salad now! Only onions,' Nisho says, laying out a plate and spoon for me on the chatai. 'What's this country coming to?'

Mashook leaves as Nisho and I sit down to eat. I tear off large chunks of naan and scoop up as much as I can of the gravy and chicken without the grease. Nisho doesn't eat much.

'Why aren't you eating? This is delicious.' I know she's a serious figure watcher.

'It's jhalar chicken, a local specialty. I had a big breakfast. I won't eat lunch. I'll just drink a glass of milk at dinner time.'

'Nisho, I want to ask you a favour,' I say, when the jhalar chicken and naan have disappeared and entered my bloated stomach. The meeting with Bhitai's translator's granddaughter on the bus wasn't simply a coincidence, I'm convinced. Nisho is like one of Bhitai's seven queens, one of the seven heroines of his *Risalo*, all of them love-warriors, who chose to die for love. 'Can we go to Bhitshah?'

'You want *me* to go to Bhitshah with you?' Nisho looks at me, a little puzzled.

'Yes, very much,' I say, before stretching out on the chatai for the world's most sated nap, losing momentarily my never-ending restlessness. My questions about women, about love, about transgendered women, some answered, most still veiled in mystery, disappear into the softness of the pillow Nisho hands me.

When I wake up, Nisho is sitting by the stove on the floor of the covered verandah, making tea. I sit up and watch her and the two pigeons in the cage. One of them seems to be sitting on eggs.

'I haven't seen brown pigeons before,' I say. 'Only grey ones. Are these two a couple?'

'Yes, and all they ever do is make love and have babies,' Nisho replies, pouring out the tea. 'Look, the male is sitting on the eggs now. They both take turns to sit and feed their chicks. Aah, what a useless creature I am compared to them!' She strikes her forehead with her palm in an exaggerated gesture of regret. 'My friends tell me: "Nisho, these two caged pigeons are better than you. They've given birth to a whole harem full of pigeons. What have you produced? Nothing!"'

I laugh as she puts down the cup before me on the chatai. It is almost five.

'Are you coming? I want to spend the night at Bhitshah listening to Shah's faqirs sing.'

'You're really serious about going there?' Nisho looks at me. '*Theek hai*, I'll come with you.'

~

Nisho slides a fresh basin of water and grain for her pigeons into the cage. And then puts on her black burqa as I wrap my dupatta around me. Only her lovely, pool-deep, hazel eyes are staring out of the burqa's blackness. She snaps her flimsy front door shut with an equally flimsy padlock. She knocks on her neighbour's door. Mashook comes out. He and the others have been sitting there after they left Nisho's room. Nisho tells them we're taking off for Bhitshah.

Ghazala shouts: '*Arrey Nisho, wah! Kya zabardast lag rahi hai tu burqey mein*! You look splendid! Lend me two hundred before you go. I'll pay you back tomorrow.'

Nisho fumbles in her purse and produces two crumpled hundred rupee notes.

'*Shukriya*, sister!' Ghazala blesses her. 'May your fair skin become even fairer!'

As we walk to the taxi, I ask Nisho: 'Will she pay you back?'

'She will. We help one another out. She'd do the same for me. You have to look out for one another in our community.'

That's what it means to live on the margins. No bank loans or monthly incomes or pension cheques.

In the taxi, Pappu is surprised by my burqa-clad companion, but he doesn't say anything.

'Plans have changed slightly,' I tell him. 'I'm not returning to Hyderabad this evening. Instead, please drive us to Bhitshah.'

The sun is a fuzzy, soft round disc in the top left corner of the windshield, fuzzying the brownness of MPK and its environs with a sad, dusty sheen. Nisho doesn't say much on the way, probably because she's concerned that the driver might think her deep, masculine-verging-on-feminine voice strange.

When we arrive at Bhitshah, it's dark but the street lamps leading up to the dargah have come on, and brightly lit shops selling dry fruits, sweets, Sindhi ajraks, caps, are open. I pay and let Pappu go. He asks if we'd be okay on our own and I say, '*Bilkul!*'

Nisho and I enter the wide open expanse of the dargah complex and walk up to the mausoleum's entrance. Nobody stops us. There are no signs restricting women's access here. This is my first visit to Bhitshah and I feel small and safe and special surrounded by the serene blue and white tilework, and crowds of mostly poor villagers. There are booksellers and little boys running around taking orders for tea. Men, women and children throng the vast open courtyards and the arched domed verandah whose walls and vaulted ceilings are also covered with painted Hala tiles that tell a bewitching, infinitely repeating tale. The patterns on the tiles create a trance-like effect, and if I stare long enough at them, patterns within patterns begin to emerge.

Soon after we settle down on the floor, the faqirs arrive. They are a dignified group of eight, young and old men dressed in sombre black. Some have beards, some have moustaches, some have both and some are clean-shaven. They sit on cushions in a semi-circle facing the entrance to the mausoleum. They begin slowly and continue to sing and string their tamburas into the night. And the gift of peace descends on me with their voice mixed with the cool night air, like balm for my weary traveller's soul. Their singing is hypnotic and perhaps because I don't understand the Sindhi words, the mind settles into a feelings-only, no-cognition zone. The tamburas add softness and charm to the dignity of the night.

~

A group of women in colourful long skirts and white plastic bangles all the way up to their shoulders comes in singing and beating a drum. They go inside the mausoleum to offer the chadar they've brought for the tomb of their beloved saint. And as they file out into the courtyard, I get up and follow them. They start singing, and some of them begin to dance. My God, where am I? This is some charmed world where women are free to move and dance. I feel whole and healed here after the way I felt diminished by the way women were seated outside Nizamuddin's dargah in Delhi.

It's almost midnight when the faqirs stop singing. The shrine's caretakers lock up the heavy carved door to the tomb. Peace, just plain, unpretentious peace, reigns as the most enduring aspect of the night. A man next to me has fallen asleep on the floor, his body covered with his colourful patchwork ralli. A cat sits next to him in sage-like reverie, poised and unruffled.

Several women and their children have settled down for the night all over the large courtyard.

Nisho and I also spread out the chadar she brought and place our bags under our heads as pillows. I rub some mosquito repellant on my arms, feet and face, still worrying about dengue fever but Nisho says her burqa is protection enough against men and mosquitoes.

'I've never slept at a shrine before!' I say.

'It's a good thing you made me come,' Nisho says before turning in. 'Or this evening would've been like every other evening. I'd go out to buy milk, bring it back, boil it, drink it, watch TV, and go to sleep. This is how every day ends except when I have a night dance programme.'

The next morning, we wake up early. The dargah complex is quiet except for the swish of the cleaners' brooms and the chatter of birds. The blue-tiled splendour of the domes and pillars holds my eyes in a magical, mystical trance. Many of the people we spent the night with are still asleep but some are beginning to stir. Nisho and I are hungry, very hungry. We freshen up in the women's toilets outside the shrine, and walk out. Only one or two roadside restaurants have opened. We settle down on the not-so-clean charpais laid out inside New Shah Abdul Latif hotel. I'm not sure why this hole-in-the-wall place is called a 'hotel'. Abida Parveen's Sufi songs are playing, and I sit as though in a dream, the spirit glad at nothing in particular, contentedly waiting for tea and fried eggs and curried chole and parathas to arrive.

I tell Nisho: 'It was an amazing night. I can't believe how beautifully the faqirs sang. And I felt so safe and at peace at the shrine. Really safe.'

'Did you hear the firecrackers go off last night?' Nisho asks.

'Yes, I did,' I say, somewhat hazily. 'What were they for?'

We ask our server about the firecrackers. He's a gracious man who serves us an extra helping of chole at no extra cost to help us finish the last few bites of paratha. 'It was the New Year of the Hindus,' he informs us.

'Oh, so we celebrated Diwali at Bhitai's dargah!' I remembered the group of drum-beating, singing, white-bangled Thar women who had come with the chadar.

'Those were Hindu women!' I tell Nisho in an excited voice.

She nods as if not sure what I'm so excited about.

~

Once more, I've come upon hope and love in one of the most unexplored corners of the world, at a remote shrine in Sind. In a corner of my heart, the blood is beating against the heart's walls in anticipation and ecstasy. Love and her partner peace, still have a chance in places like Bhitshah. As I board the bus back to Hyderabad and Nisho takes one back to her hometown, we both sort of carry the knowledge about last night, Diwali night, as a sacred glimpse into that possibility. My coming to meet Nisho, following my hunch, and my decision to come to Bhitshah, because I was carrying a copy of *Shah jo Risalo* with me on the bus, and happened to meet the granddaughter of Shaikh Ayaz, none of this could be dismissed as purely accidental. Had the universe in some way conspired to bring me here?

8

Love Means Selfishness

Khusro Bagh, Allahabad

Muddaten guzreen teri yaad bhi ayee na hamen
aur ham bhool gaye hon tujhe aisa bhi nahi

Ages have passed, erasing memories of you
And yet, I can't say I have forgotten you

—Firaq Gorakhpuri (1896-1982)

After I returned to India from Pakistan, I spent a few months in Allahabad writing up the Pakistan chapters. But my thoughts kept turning to a young friend, a Muslim woman of Allahabad whom I wanted to include in the book, Nahid. But there were doubts. She was young. Was she, at nineteen, experienced enough to have meaningful insights about love? Would her views be weighty enough to become a part of this book? I chided myself for my biases and finally called her up. I told her about the book and she was excited. It was about time, her tone seemed to say, that somebody wrote about her skirmishes with love.

'Didi, come to the railway station on Thursday afternoon and I'll meet you there after work and take you to my house. And would you also like to see a demo of the electric flour mill?'

Nahid's latest job was in telemarketing. She called up people to get them interested in the water purifiers or electric flour mills her company was marketing. She would try and convince them to give their addresses. A salesman would then visit those who did and give a demo of the products. She asked me if she could sign me up for a demo.

'What?' I laughed. 'You expect me to grind my own grain? And give up the convenience of buying packaged, adulterated flour from the store? And feed my family rotis made with pure, home-ground atta? I'm not that devoted a housewife!'

On Thursday afternoon, I waited for Nahid for almost half an hour in the parking lot at the station, trying to cultivate detachment by listening to Abida Parveen's *jo ho so ho* on my CD player. Punctuality is not an Allahabadi trait so I had to school myself not to get impatient. But guilt about wasting fuel by keeping the air-conditioning in the car running was making me irritable. Finally, an sms beeped on my mobile.

'Didi, am looking for you. Where are you?' A minute after I sent off my somewhat exasperated reply, a smiling, lanky and apologetic Nahid appeared next to the car window. I stepped out. She had on a tight shirt and jeans, a backpack, and her girlish cleavage was peeping out from the shirt's neckline.

I decided not to complain to her about making me wait. We crossed the railway overhead bridge and walked out of the station on the other side, leading towards Khusro Bagh. It was a clammy July day and I had unwillingly relinquished the semi-darkness of my cocoon-like air-conditioned bedroom to come out and meet Nahid. Sweat started pouring down my inflamed face as soon as we started walking. Another hot flash or was it the price for being out on a summer afternoon when I would've been better off napping? I bought two orange lollies from the ice cream man at the entrance to Khusro Bagh and we went in. Nahid found a bench under a grove of mango trees where we could be out of the sun.

'You asked me what I think of love. The more I think, I

think nothing of it,' she said. 'There's no selfless love. Even parents love their children selfishly. I think my father, not this father, I mean my real father, did love me. Once when he came home without any sweets, I made such a fuss he went back and brought all the jalebis he could find in the mithai shop! Eat, eat as much as you want to. Let's see how much you can eat? he said. When he left for Mumbai, I don't know why he never came back to us. Some say he got killed there. Some say he went mad. All I see in people is selfishness—everywhere I turn,' Nahid said, 'I see men just after one thing—women's bodies. For two minutes of pleasure, they're ready to give two hundred, even five hundred rupees.'

A man in a dirty, torn shirt lay curled up like a dog under another tree. Two more were sitting on a nearby bench, staring at us. We were the only women around. The sticky, orange sweetness of the lolly trickled down like chilled honey into my throat. I tried to focus on how divine this five-rupee ice treat was. Nahid licked hers distractedly.

'Look, how they're staring at us,' Nahid said.

I looked. The men on the bench were trying to figure out who I was, who she was.

'No girl can come here alone—it's not safe, not even in the daytime,' she said. 'Once I came here with my cousin. The police are always after couples they find in the park. They thought I was doing dhanda, that I was a prostitute. They took us to the police station. They told me if you spend a night with us, we'll let you go. I yelled at them and escaped somehow, but my cousin couldn't get out until the next day. He had to bribe them before they let him go.'

'We had better leave then,' I said. The men's stares were making me uncomfortable. We walked out of the mango grove, and strode along the path leading to the tombs. On one side were the guava orchards, and beyond them, the magnificent, weathered sandstone mausoleums. I'd lived in Allahabad for more than a decade but this was my first visit to Khusro Bagh. Khusro Bagh doesn't have the best of reputations as a safe park. These neglected tombs, one of which was Prince Khusro's—why was he buried in a place like Allahabad? So far from the Mughal capital? I knew next to nothing about this bit of Mughal history. The information board said Khusro was one of Emperor Jehangir's sons, banished into exile here, in this garden, for fomenting a rebellion against his father. Blinded by his father, and murdered by his brother, Shahjehan, who later ascended to the throne, Khusro lies buried in this beautiful garden alongside the tomb of his mother and sister. Man Bai, Khusro's mother, was a Hindu princess, who later came to be known as Shah Begum, a title conferred on her by her husband after her son's birth. 'She committed suicide at Allahabad with an overdose of opium as she had become heartbroken and distraught at the bitterness between father and son,' said the information board outside her mausoleum.

Three centuries later, lovers with no place to hang out, hookers, and the homeless seek refuge in this vastness, the unkempt greenness of Khusro Bagh, in the eternal resting place of a Mughal prince and his mother and sister. The seventeenth century tombs look grand and forlorn in the midst of a Mughal garden. Death was an event to be welcomed with flowers and fountains for the Mughals—a wistful reminder of a highly evolved aesthetics, but also of impermanence. All earthly grandeur must end. Princes lie forgotten. Paupers loiter and students prepare for competitive exams in Khusro Bagh's mausoleums, where Khusro, the prince-in-exile once strolled.

We climbed up the steps of Khusro's sister, Nisar Begum's tomb. Hers is the most beautiful and intricately designed tomb in the garden. I felt like crying, saddened at the state of neglect of our cultural heritage. All of humanity's history seemed at stake, right here. Two boys were sitting on the steps leading up to the tomb, and asked me if I'd take their picture. I was in a mean mood. No, I said. I moved away, and took photos of Nahid sitting with her legs hanging down from the high pink, sandstone platform of Nisar Begum's mausoleum. All the while I felt ready to burst into tears as if witnessing the death of a beloved. On the grass below, under a neem, a woman in a burqa looked away, embarrassed. The man she was with, stared at us, then leaned towards her and said something, and they laughed. We were not welcome.

We walked out into the filth of Khuldabad sabzi mandi through the massive wooden doors on the south side of Khusro park. This exit was even more shockingly rundown than the entrance through which we had entered. Something like an extended, continually rotting, never-emptied garbage container came into view—emaciated cows and unloved dogs slept in the heat-addled afternoon; a mountain of lemons gone bad, rust-coloured and slime-covered vegetables dumped on the street next to a sabziwala's cart. Yesterday's rain had slushed the unpaved shoulders of the street into a messy border of grey-black muck.

The stench all around was disturbing enough, but compared to the more assaultive presence of heat, sweating human bodies and vehicles, it was mild. We got into a rickshaw and got out at the end of a dark, narrow lane. We entered the courtyard of a house. A woman was scrubbing pots and pans in a corner. Thinner than Nahid, sallow-cheeked and not much older than her, it was hard to imagine this woman as Nahid's mother.

'You can sit out here,' she said, pointing to a cot in the courtyard.

'Why?' Nahid snapped. 'It's hot out here. Why can't we sit inside? Why don't you ask him to leave?'

Nahid's mother glared at her, almost ready to strike her. She peeped into the room and muttered something.

A bare-chested man, wearing only a checkered lungi, came out, and stood in the doorway. His grin was defiant and his teeth yellow. His hair was thick and black and he seemed conscious of its thickness and blackness. His brown chest was thrown out; it was hairless and sparkled with a mist-like film of sweat.

'Who's this?' I asked.

'This is my mother's husband,' Nahid said. He was displeased at the introduction and knit his brows. His grin disappeared.

'He's her father!' Nahid's mother snapped.

'You don't look old enough to be Nahid's father!' I tried to make light of the situation.

'I'm ninety-five!' Mr Slick Hair said.

'Really! You still have black hair and all your teeth at ninety-five?'

His eyes narrowed, a yellow-toothed grin appeared, and he leaned back self-consciously against the thatched wall of the hut. 'How old do you think I am?'

'You said you're ninety-five. So I'm assuming that's how old you are. Can't we sit inside the room?'

Slick Hair moved away from the doorway somewhat unwillingly.

Most of the room was occupied by the bed. A couple of trunks were stacked against the wall with a TV atop one of them. A wobbly fan whirred, suspended from a hook in the thatched ceiling. I didn't feel safe sitting under it. The walls of the room didn't come up all the way to the ceiling. Was that deliberate? For better ventilation?

Nahid's little brother and sister tumbled into the room. The little boy was holding a small aluminium pot and he removed its lid to show us a pair of just-hatched chicks. 'They fell out of their nest,' he pointed to a fuzz of straw in a corner of the thatched roof. Both he and his sister were in shorts. Their backs were bare and red with heat rash.

'She's come, she's come!' the little girl screamed excitedly as the mother sparrow flew in through the gap between the ceiling and the wall, carrying bits of rice in her beak. She fluttered around the room, looking for her babies. Nahid's mother had left for the store to get a cold drink. Nahid had gone out to wash glasses. Her stepfather hadn't come back in.

The little boy placed the pot on a shelf and the sparrow perched on its edge. The chicks squeaked weakly as she fed them. All three of us were silenced by this moving spectacle.

I had brought cake for the children. The little boy and girl took the box from me and started eating the cake with their hands.

'How's the cake?' I asked the boy.

He looked up shyly. There was icing around his mouth, on his nose, and fingers. 'It's sweet,' he pronounced after thinking for a minute.

The little girl scattered cake crumbs on the bed. She wasn't interested in eating it. She climbed down, brought a comb and stuck it into the icing.

Their mother entered with a bottle of Mango Maaza. She didn't notice the big cake mess on the bed. Or she chose to ignore it. Behind her, Nahid's married sister and a young man came in. She was the younger sister Nahid had told me about. The one who ran away to marry her lover. She looked like she was sixteen. Her husband didn't look much older than her. She was thin except for the protrusion around her midriff.

Her young husband sat down on the bed. Nahid's mother poured out the cold drink. She handed me one glass and one to her son-in-law. The Maaza was extremely cold and excessively sweet. I wasn't sure if I should focus on its welcome coldness or its unwelcome sweetness.

'Why are you standing? Sit down!' I said to Nahid's sister, the child-wife.

She perched uncomfortably at the edge of the bed between her husband and me.

'Tell me how does a little girl like you take care of a husband?'

She hesitated, trying to gauge the seriousness of my tone. 'I do whatever he asks me to. I cook for him, I wash his clothes.' A nose stud trembled faintly with each breath she took.

'And how does he take care of you?'

The young husband scowled as he sipped his Maaza.

'He gives me love,' she looked down into her lap. Her voice carried no conviction. The sallowness of her face, despite the golden gleam of the nose stud, gave it an expression of disappointment that sat oddly on a sixteen-year-old face. The young husband left as soon as he finished his drink. He sensed he was in bad company.

Nahid's mother started telling me how hard her life had been since she moved to Allahabad. Nahid's father, her first husband, had taken off for Mumbai to look for work many years ago, and left her and the two girls in the village. He never returned.

'Life must have been hard for you in the village,' I said.

'It was very hard. That's why I had to come to the city. I had to find work.'

'So how did you meet your second husband?' I asked her.

'In Allahabad. I started working at a nursing home. I met him on the night of the Eid moon. He was a driver for the nursing home. And the next day, on Eid day, we got married. I knew I could trust him the moment I met him.'

'Really? So fast?' I said.

'Yes, totally!' she said with certitude. 'He agreed to accept my daughters as his own. What more could I ask of a man?'

Nahid spoke up. 'He didn't do anything of the sort. We had to go out and work. I had to wash people's dishes. You have forgotten all that. Remember the thousands of kites we glued every day? He didn't feed us for free.'

Nahid's mother looked at her. 'Your ungrateful tongue will ruin you, you wretch.'

'My ungrateful tongue doesn't speak falsehoods like yours does,' Nahid snapped. She turned to me: 'Husband No. 2 never told her about the two wives he already had. She was so honest with him, she told him about her first husband. She found out about his two wives after she married him! And she still believes he did us a great favour!'

'Why did you marry him?' I asked her mother. 'You had a job at the nursing home. You didn't need him to feed you.'

'Don't you know what it's like to live alone in a city with two daughters?' she said drearily. 'If I had two sons, it would be different. Tongues wag when you are a woman. We needed a man in the house.'

I looked at her frail, fading attractiveness and thought what if, what if she allowed the daughter who wanted to be her son, become a son? I could sense Nahid's jealousy towards her stepfather. She wanted all the love her mother had wasted on him. Nahid could be the man of the house if that man went out of the picture. A rainbow of possibilities could erupt, Nahid's impatience seemed to say, if only her mother hadn't reduced herself to becoming a puppet, and handed over her strings to the man with yellow teeth.

A few drops of rain landed on my shoulder. I peeped up at the grey sky from the gap between the ceiling and the wall. 'Maybe we should go before it starts raining hard,' I said.

I could sense Nahid's mother's relief that I wasn't planning to stay longer. An imperious, uninvited guest, I'd been prying, lifting veils from well-concealed tales. She had every reason to wish me gone. I had questioned her about her life, and told her nothing about mine other than I was writing a book on Muslim women.

'Your sister looks sickly. She's anaemic,' I said to Nahid as we walked out of the lane into the street and waited for a rickshaw.

'She's sick in the head too. She's got herself pregnant! I had told her not to do this. It's all the sex he has with her, that's what making her sick. She fights with him, says she'll never go back to him, but the moment he comes for her, she starts making tea for him, and serves him like a servant. I don't understand it. Can you call this love?'

'Maybe not. But there must be something you can call love?' I said earnestly. How could somebody be so disillusioned so early in life, when others her age were just beginning their hopeful journey towards that unexplored territory called love?

'You saw what my mother and sister have landed themselves into in the name of love! Love or slavery? Two people should respect each other's freedoms, they shouldn't use each other. I don't need such love. I used to think real love was the kind of love that happens between a man and a woman. But look at my mother. Do you think her husband loves her? He beats her and abuses and she thinks he's a good man because he agreed to live with her and let her keep her two daughters. Do you think my sister and her husband love each other? Her husband uses her for sex. And that's it. Does my mother love me? When she needs money, I'm my mother's best daughter. As long as I'm paying her a thousand rupees every month, I'm welcome in this house. Is that love? *Pyaar ka matlab hai matlab ka pyaar.* The meaning of love is selfishness.'

Our rickshaw was inching past a row of low, white-washed houses, almost doll-like in their tininess.

'That's the sweepers' colony,' Nahid said.

I asked the rickshaw to stop. The drizzle hadn't turned into a downpour yet. But the thick, hazy heat had temporarily relaxed its stranglehold upon our lungs. I walked up in the soft rain, as if to some museum display. I paused in admiration at the clean lines and the smallness of scale of the houses, and the way the rain was carving well-defined, clear rivulets in the soft, clayey earth in front of the well-swept houses. The absolute absence of filth in this colony, a haven of sanitation in garbage-choked Khuldabad, in the sweepers' colony? It was as dignified and silent an announcement as a community could make about itself.

'The sweepers live here? Is that why they keep it so clean?'

'That's where Sawan used to live,' Nahid said, pointing out a house in the colony. 'But let's go. I don't want to be seen here by his family.'

We got back into the rickshaw and as it wove its way through the chaos of tempos, cars, pedestrians, and cattle, I wondered what it was about that colony other than its cleanliness that made Nahid point it out to me. Nahid drew my attention to a young man sitting outside a shop on a crate. I turned back to get a better look at him. He was smoking and staring at the street with a bored, vacant look.

'He was my next boyfriend. After Sawan,' she said. 'I broke up with him six months ago. I was sick of his trying to control me. Don't come back home so late. Don't meet this man. Don't talk to that one. I told him, listen, I'm a black belt in karate. I can take care of myself. I don't need you to tell me whom to meet and whom not to. I think I would've lasted two months if I married him. But Ammi loved him. He's Muslim, you see. Not Hindu like Sawan was. She thought I shouldn't refuse him. He used to bring her gifts to win her over so she would force me to marry him!'

When she came to my house a few days later, I asked her about Sawan.

'Sawan? He was different. He was the only one who truly loved me. And my father, of course. Sawan knew what love was,' Nahid said. She was sitting across from me, holding a cup of tea, and looking down into its depths, as if trying to fathom something in its opaqueness. 'He was the sweeper of my school,' she continued in a flat voice. 'He cleaned the classrooms and toilets. He used to bring roti and sabzi and make me eat it after school. While I ate, he would go about his work. Sometimes he sat next to me and fed me with his own hands. Every day he asked me what I would like to eat the next day. That was so funny! He fussed over me just like a mother! I must have been twelve then but I could tell his love was of a different kind altogether. He never wanted anything from me. He didn't try to touch me even once though we were together for four years. When I was about sixteen, he asked me to marry him. My stepfather said, "You're going to marry a sweeper? A mehtar? A Hindu?? You'll become a sweeper's wife? Are you crazy?" Sawan wanted me to run away with him. I was very young. And I was confused. I was scared of my stepfather. What would he do to my mother if I ran away with Sawan? He'd hit her even more than he normally did. But that was then. Now if Sawan came back and asked me, I would run in a minute.'

'So why hasn't he?'

'Sawan waited and waited for me to change my mind. But I kept saying I was scared. I couldn't run away. I was hoping my stepfather would say yes one day. So he got tired of waiting.' She paused but then related the ending of this tale as casually as if she were talking about the weather. 'One day he doused himself with kerosene and set himself on fire.'

I looked at her eyes. There was no trace of sadness or grief or regret. Prolonged mourning over dead lovers was not her style. Nahid's life was all about the necessity of moving on.

'His family blames me for his death. I never go to his house anymore,' she said, sipping the tea. 'But some nights I wake up and remember how he used to sit with me after school and wait till I ate the food he brought for me because he knew I came to school hungry,' she said in the same fuss-free voice. 'I think he was the only one who loved me. I've had boyfriends after him. But they're nothing compared to him.'

'Only the simple of heart have the courage to love so completely,' I said.

'And he was simple. A simple fool. He died for his love.' Nahid let out the slightest of sighs. She was looking past me at the tree outside the window. With what sounded like a buried, ambiguous longing, she added: 'I would've married him once I was older. If only he wasn't in such a hurry.' But the very next moment, the feisty Nahid took over. 'But maybe not, didi! Maybe I wouldn't have married him. He too would've wanted me to become a good wife and a good mother and take care of his children. And I just don't have it in me. My freedom means more than anything else to me. I have friends who are boys. I wouldn't give up seeing them after I became his wife. And which man would like his wife talking to other men?'

We got out of the rickshaw at the station. 'Show me the places where the CRPF men take their whores.'

'Okay!' Nahid said, and charged ahead of me, backpack swinging on her narrow, girlish shoulders. I hastened to keep pace with her. She took a detour, and marched on the path behind Platform 1. We were passing the railway residential quarters. I saw a few men watching us in the spongy darkness. Their eyes turned to follow our progress. Nahid was still wearing that deep-neck shirt but had thrown a flimsy dupatta over it. I wondered if the men were reaching some conclusions from her skin-hugging outfit.

'I'm tired of the idea of sex. What men call sex is nothing but grabbing and pushing,' Nahid said. 'When I ride my bicycle, the rickshawallas comment on my boobs. Some say, come with me for an hour. Some say, I'll give you five hundred for half an hour—or if I'm standing at the station, somebody will walk past me and ask me if I'm ready to go with them.' And immediately, as if to dispel any bad impression I might get of her, she added: 'But I know how to deal with them. I give them a few dirty galis and they back off!'

We picked our way, avoiding puddles and rubbish dumped everywhere. Nahid skipped over known territory while I trod carefully. Deep, thick stench rose from the garbage heaps in moist waves in the post-rain breeze. A man was urinating against a wall. A little girl was scrubbing pots at the side of more uncollected garbage in a vacant lot. Jaundiced street lamps had come on, and everything wore a sticky, tragic look. The drizzling had stopped and the air had returned to its earlier sultriness. Fresh stagnant water pools had emerged on the street's surface like sudden abscesses.

'Here. And over there,' Nahid pointed out gloom-filled corners—dark and dingy. Under staircases, bridges and overhead walkways.

'In these places? How?' I asked, baffled. 'There are no doors, walls, rooms, no privacy.'

'People watch out for one another. When I do it, you keep watch, when you do it, I'll keep watch. It's like that. They have an agreement. The CRPF (Central Reserve Police Force) men are good. They know they're not supposed to be doing all this while on duty. So they're quick and quiet about it.'

I didn't want more details of sordid soirees conducted in the dark by CRPF men. We turned around to go back to Platform 1. A woman was sitting on a flattened-out cardboard carton on the footpath. Even though it was dark, her rouged face and brightly painted lips gleamed.

Nahid seemed to know her. 'Where's your husband?' she asked.

'He's taken my son to the doctor. He's been sick for many days. Rain fever.'

We walked past her, and up the steps leading up to the platform. 'She's one of the regulars. She even has a husband and children!' Nahid said. 'I've walked around here so much, I know many people really well. The station's like a second home to me.'

We strolled up Platform 1 to the little shrine of Line Shah Baba at the far end. Nahid seemed at home everywhere except at home. 'I've spent so many nights sitting here at this dargah. Whenever my stepfather came home from one of his road trips, he'd get drunk, there'd be a fight, and he'd hit me or throw me out of the house. Then I had nowhere else but the railway station to come to. I would sit here all night.'

There was a crowd gathered outside the shrine on the platform. How could there be a saint's shrine in the middle of a railway platform? It was Thursday evening, and a qawwal was singing. As we drew closer, I couldn't catch his words, but the rhythmic clapping, the beats of the dhol and the sound of harmonium became audible. Nahid parted the thick wall of men, and pushed me to the front of the crowd, so I found myself standing only a few feet away from the qawwal. He was seated on the ground, a blind young man, in an embroidered cap and a bright green waistcoat. The bright lights from the shrine lit up the golden threads of embroidery in his cap. His eyes were glued shut like sealed lips, and he was singing away in a full-throated way, while two other men were beating dhols and two more were clapping. I imagnined Nahid sprawled out in a corner on one of those nights when she had no home to return to.

The qawwal repeated the same lines:

Bulaya hai gar aap ne sarkar chadar mein
To phir lazim hai dikha dijye deedar chadar mein

Oh, saint, if you invited us to visit you in your cloister
You must accord us a glimpse of your face in your cloister

Men were placing ten-rupee notes as donations on top of his harmonium. The air became rent with 'Wah! Wah!' The qawwal went on repeating the same lines, and raised his hand to his forehead to acknowledge the appreciation he was receiving.

Suddenly a stout woman got up and started whirling as if entering a trance.

'Ay, ay, don't do that. Sit down!' the shrine's caretakers reprimanded her. She slumped to the ground without protesting.

I asked Nahid to place our offering of money on the harmonium and we pushed our way out of the gathering.

There were garland and trinket sellers on the side of the platform. One man was selling rosaries and posters. I met

Katrina Kaif again, this time in her most incongruous avatar. Her face was wrapped in a virginal white dupatta, and next to her Salman Khan was smiling in a white topi. It was the holiest of smiles. In the space between their hallowed faces, there was the dome of some revered shrine and under it, the kalima was calligraphed in Arabic. Nahid and I burst out laughing. I paid ten rupees for the poster and tucking the rolled-up treasure under my arm, climbed up the overhead bridge leading out to the parking lot.

'I can't believe they use Katrina and Salman to sell religion,' I said.

'Why not?' Nahid said. 'Anything to make money! Didn't you get tempted yourself and buy it?'

We had reached the parking lot.

'Pray for my back,' I said to Nahid, getting into the car as I felt a fresh stab of pain in my lower back.

'God doesn't listen to my prayers so I've stopped praying. I've stopped believing in him,' Nahid said. 'I've sat in temples and dargahs and prayed to all sorts of gods. But none of them ever listened. But I'll pray for your back if you want me to. I have a better idea—I'll come and massage your back!'

'Okay! A massage is the answer to my prayers! And we have to go to your village soon,' I said. Nahid had promised to take me to Thikri, where her maternal uncle and aunt, her mamu and mami, lived, about 50 kilometres from Allahabad. I drove out of the parking lot and Nahid started back towards the overhead bridge. Where was she headed, I wondered with the prayerful anxiety of a mother for her. To a home where she wasn't welcome, or the dargah, or to one of those dark corners behind Platform 1?

~

It was winter before we could make it to Nahid's village.

I'd been anxious and up since 4 a.m. I got out of bed, made tea, sat in my favourite black arm-chair and wondered what was making me anxious. Would it be safe to drive out to the village? Nahid and I alone in the car? What if the car broke down? What if I had a flat tyre on the highway? What if I couldn't come back in time? The maid would leave at mid-day and Suroor, my fifteen-year-old daughter, would be alone at home.

'Don't go, Mamma,' Suroor grabbed my arm as I bent down to kiss her soft skin peeking out from under the quilt.

'I'll be back before you're fully awake,' I murmured.

It was Sunday and I knew she'd sleep till noon!

Nahid and I drove on the highway heading south to Thikri. We had left home a little after six. Lovely, indecisive mist hovered in the fields and the trees lining both sides of the highway. The sun was just beginning to climb up shyly above the trees. How long before they cut down these trees to widen the highway, I thought, trying to name the trees we passed—mango, mahua, neem, Ashok.

We stopped for tea. The man at the tea stall wasn't happy to see us, or maybe he had just woken up, and wasn't used to women pulling up at his shop, looking bright and happy, asking for very specific kind of tea—less sugar, more tea leaves, fresh ginger, and kullarhs please, no plastic cups—so soon after he raised the shutters. He had nothing 'hot' to eat. Everything was cold and looked stale, including the rasgullas. But he did make fresh tea according to my instructions. The damp clayey fragrance of the kullarh and the subtle sweet spiciness of ginger rising from steaming chai on a misty winter morning! Something as simple as that was enough to convince me our two-women extravaganza in rural Uttar Pradesh was no ordinary event.

'You know what's nice about going out with women?' Nahid said, relishing the tea. We were standing on the side of the road, and the highway was not yet crowded with trucks and buses, and there was an ethereal feel to the just waking-up life of a village beyond the road on a chilly December morning. It felt good to be outdoors when most people were still tucked under their razais. 'I feel free. There's laughter, simple laughter. If I were with boys now, they'd be sizing me up, and I just wouldn't feel the same. I'd be anxious but I would pretend to have a good time.'

We got back into the car, and drove on. We turned off the highway into Vishwanathganj. A beat-up tempo that reminded me of Kafka's man-become-insect from *Metamorphosis* was parked at the intersection.

'I can't believe this thing moves!' I said. 'Looks like it was abandoned long ago.'

'It moves all right! It may take two hours to fill up,' Nahid said. 'But it'll go only when it is full. There's no bus from the highway to our village. There are only these tempos. Or you walk.'

The paved smoothness of the highway ended and we

began our crawl over a rough, gravelly road to the village. The new road was being laid but other than the heaped gravel and stones and sand piles on the sides of the street, there were no workers in sight. It must have taken an hour to cover the few kilometres from the highway to Thikri, almost as long as it had taken us to drive the forty-five kilometres from Allahabad to the Vishwanathganj intersection.

I got tired of creeping on the gravelly road so when Nahid asked if I'd like to see Vishwanathganj railway station, I immediately agreed. We parked the car under a tree and walked towards the station. Vishwanathganj station had two platforms, one for trains arriving from Allahabad, one for trains departing to Allahabad. A beggar was squatting with his head tucked in a shawl, and a woman sat on the ground, selling packets of biscuits and candies. We entered the station master's room. It felt like we had entered the past. I was entranced by the control switches, black phones with receivers, and a big wooden box stacked with rows of tickets. I bought one to Pratabgarh for Rs 14 as a keepsake.

'That's the lowest fare from one place to another in India,' the station master's assistant informed me. 'We'll soon have computerized tickets,' he said proudly, and showed us the big generator and the boxes of computers lying in a corner which were soon to be installed. I was surprised why they trusted me so easily, why they didn't ask me to show my ID when I said I was a journalist doing a story on Vishwanathganj.

Only a few trains go through Vishwanathganj, and nobody

can tell when they'll arrive. Two shawl-wrapped ladies were chatting contentedly on a bench.

'Which train are you waiting for?'

'We're waiting for the 9.27 to Pratabgarh.' It was close to ten-thirty then. 'But it might not come before two in the afternoon,' one of them told me pragmatically and went back to chatting with her companion.

As we were walking back from the station towards the car, I found several men standing around, staring at the car.

'Who could they be?' I asked Nahid.

She shrugged.

When we got close, a man with a moustache, on a motorbike with a 'Press' sign on the front, came up to me.

'*Kya baat hai, bhayia*? Is there something wrong?' I asked him. The interest of the other men perked up and their eyes became fixed on us.

'Madam, we noticed this car has been left here for a long time. We are wondering whose car it is and why it has been left here unattended,' the man replied.

'It's my car,' I said, unlocking the door. 'And I left it here. And it hasn't been that long .'

'Is this your car?' he asked in disbelief. 'You left it here?'

'Yes, it's my car. And I left it here. Is there a problem?' I asked, getting in. I glanced at Nahid. She was trying to hide her smile. This reassured me. I was beginning to get a little uneasy with those questions and all those men staring at us.

As I backed the car out onto the road, the crowd continued staring at us, and some began to move away reluctantly. I felt irritated at the men who had stopped everything they had to do in the world, to find out whose car it was. Later we had a good laugh. We had caused a stir in the life of Vishwanathganj. Maybe one of the villagers had called the press guy who hurried to the site to scoop up an abandoned-car story. I imagined him doing his daily rounds, scouring the uneventful villages for a story. But we had turned out to be so disappointingly ordinary.

When we arrived at Nahid's uncle's house, he and his wife were leaving for the fields. The morning meal was over but they had saved food for us since Nahid had called them earlier. We were shown the hand pump, and while we washed, her pregnant cousin who looked like she could go into labour any minute, brought out rotis and potato sabzi and placed it on the wooden cot in the verandah. She took up a hand fan and fanned us to keep away the flies. I was hungry and the cold sabzi and rotis were welcome. After we ate, she brought us tea. She never took her eyes off Nahid. It must be her tight jeans, I thought.

'Didi, come, I'll show you the village,' Nahid said.

We walked out into the fields, and said hello to her uncle and his wife and sons who were busy weeding and hoeing. Yellow mustard was beginning to bloom and the winter sun's warmth was luring me into my naïve yearnings for a pastoral life. Then I remembered the cousin saying there was no electricity in the village since yesterday!

Nahid started pointing out familiar landmarks: the clump of bamboo where she and her sister hid whenever their mother came to see them from the city. In those days they hated her for having abandoned them in the village; the low, white madrasa where the maulvi beat her with his cane when she didn't learn her lessons; the canal she floated in, holding big bundles of firewood; the paths she walked on with her grandmother, carrying a basket of bangles on her head.

'Whenever villagers gave us food or sweets, we would sit down and eat it all up before returning home,' Nahid laughed. "Don't take it home, or your mami will give it to her kids," my nani used to say. We used to walk all over the village selling bangles. I used to love that. When nani died, I just wanted to be gone from this place. I didn't want to be here anymore.'

We walked past a field with the two graves. 'I used to hide behind these graves whenever I wanted to get away from my mamu. I still can't let go of a roti until it's a perfect circle,' she said. 'Mamu used to hit me on my hand if I didn't roll them out as perfectly as he wanted me to.'

Mamu was her mother's oldest brother, the man we met in the fields. Nahid and her sister lived in his house for several years when their mother left them to find work in Allahabad. He farmed his little bit of land, and on the side he worked as a baker, travelling to nearby villages, baking naans at wedding feasts. He didn't say much when Nahid said salaam and introduced me. He seemed suspicious.

'Didi wanted to meet my relatives in the village,' Nahid said to him.

Mamu set aside his sickle and lit up a bidi. '*Accha*?' he frowned. 'What's so special about us in the village?' His dark face was puckered like a raisin, and his sunken chest heaved as he inhaled from the bidi. It seemed a stretch of the imagination to see this wasted, shrunken man as the violent, stick-wielding taskmaster Nahid had depicted him to be.

His wife started to make reconciliatory gestures to make up for his rudeness, smiling, asking us if we had eaten enough, and why didn't we stay the night and go back the next day. She was trying hard to sweeten her husband's acerbity. 'I have a gift for you,' she said to Nahid. 'Come.'

We left him in the field, sitting on his haunches, puffing on his bidi.

In one of the rooms of the house, a mud and thatch affair, sectioned off by mud partitions into four tiny rooms, Nahid's aunt opened a tin trunk and fished out a folded bit of cloth. Nahid unfolded it and her face lit up. I had not seen such a wide smile on her face.

'You got this for me?' she asked her aunt. 'Where did you buy it?'

The aunt smiled. 'You think we can't buy these things in the village? Do you like it?'

'Yes! Yes! It's beautiful,' Nahid said, and showed me the gift.

I FEEL GOOD was lettered in large bright pink letters across a white stretch-cotton T-shirt. 'Nice!' I said, smiling at the aunt. 'You don't have any objections to her wearing a T-shirt?'

The aunt considered before replying. She adjusted her sari pallu on her head. 'Her mamu still doesn't like girls wearing these things. But times are changing. If I gave her a sari or a suit she wouldn't wear it, so I got her a T-shirt.'

I got a call at that moment from Suroor: 'Mamma, when are you coming back?'

'We have to go,' I told Nahid's aunt and her pregnant daughter who was wondering if we were going to stay overnight. 'My daughter's calling. She's alone.'

'Where's your husband?' the aunt wanted to know.

The same old questions no matter which village I went to!

'He's abroad.'

They went silent, imagining how a woman could survive without a husband at home, and leave behind a child to visit a village. But at the same time, I saw I had gained some respect in their eyes. I had a husband and a daughter, so I wasn't as footloose as they thought at first, even though I was gallivanting from city to village, leaving behind my child, and that too, in the absence of my husband.

'We embarked on our return yatra back to the main highway but somehow the crawl over the unpaved road seemed less tiresome because we knew how long it would take. At the intersection to the highway, the tempo seemed to have three passengers inside. It still looked like it would be a while before it filled and departed for Thikri.

~

As soon as we were out of Vishwanathganj and back on the highway, Nahid began to sing. She seemed at ease, singing loudly. Her friend from work called her on her cellphone. Nahid stopped singing to share the crowning success of the visit to the village.

'*Arre*, Zehra, you won't believe it. Today's my lucky day. Mamiji gave me a T-shirt! It's the first time she has ever given me anything. A T-shirt! You know what they had said when I went to see them wearing jeans last year? Don't come here wearing these things. I told them if you don't want me to come, I won't. But if I come, I'll wear what I feel like wearing. So they were fine today! Maybe they like me now.'

'Didi, have you been in love with anybody other than your husband?' she asked me after she ended the ecstatic conversation with Zehra.

'I had a boyfriend in college. I thought I was in love with him. We were to get married after college.'

'But you didn't love him?'

'I suppose I did. But before I could really find out, he left me for another woman.'

'Do you still feel sad when you think of him?'

'Not anymore. All this was a long time back. Now I thank him for leaving me. He forced me to grow up and move on.'

'Nobody's ever made me truly happy either,' Nahid confided. 'Except for Sawan. Happiness, I mean, not just the body's happiness. If a boyfriend doesn't understand my emotions, he can't make me emotionally happy. So how can I say he loves me? Love is about understanding the other person's feelings completely.'

'Yes, love is about knowing the other thoroughly.'

We stopped to buy guavas from a roadside cart in some small town. When I got back, Nahid was on the phone again. She seemed cheerful, almost flirtatious, the way she was giggling.

'It's Zehra again,' she said. 'She says she's bored at work without me. You know we have so much fun together, I wish I could live with her. The two of us could rent a place. But she wants to marry her boyfriend. He's an army man, totally boring, but he says he can build her a nice house. I can't build a house for her.'

'And she can have kids with him,' I said.

Nahid smiled as if she knew why so many women opted for marriage.

We were getting close to Allahabad and the traffic wasn't as sparse now. As we got close to the street where I had to let her off, she said:

'If I had a nice family I would've behaved like good girls do. Always scared. I wouldn't have come out like this with you. Or gone anywhere. Now I can roam anywhere, anytime. I'm not afraid. What's the worst that can happen?'

I nodded, keeping my eyes on the road. 'In a way, your unloving family made you what you are. They didn't intend to, but it happened!'

She didn't share what the worst was. I got the feeling the worst was old news for her. She'd already paid the price for fearlessness, for freedoms not meant for her. Not just once. Not just twice.

~

Over the next few months, Nahid met a woman who offered her a job and a place to stay . She was getting into fights with her stepfather regularly. During one episode he hit her with a rod. She left home that night. She managed to sweet-talk her way onto the train to Pondicherry without a ticket. I was on the train back from my retreat in Himachal when I got her sms in English

'Didi, am very happy here. Am learning English. Am teaching karate to women. I'm very very good and I miss you.'

And a couple of weeks later, this: 'I have a French boyfriend. Very sweet boy. He very afraid of snakes and scorpions. I hope you are very good. Many love and many hugs and many kisses.'

Of course, being the restless, not-one-to-settle-down, never-at-peace Nahid, she didn't stay too long with that boyfriend or in that town. When I last heard from her, she was exploring another town, another job, and perhaps another boyfriend. Love had always been too elusive, too pricey, too risky a thing to come by. Life had cheated her of love and she had learned not to pay too much importance to love's absence. She would tell me: 'Didi, I'm bindaas. I don't worry about the past or the future. I just try to be happy.' Though she said she was bindaas about love, I suspected it was the hope of finding it in its purest form that kept her flitting from place to place.

9

Love Me or Kill Me

Dollar Villa balcony where I spent my mornings with tea

'I am the mother of the pearl, I am an oyster,
In my heart is engendered a harvest of pearls.'

—Sufia Kamal, (1911-99)[1]

[1]*Mother of Pearls and Other Poems* by Sufia Kamal, Bangla Academy, Dhaka, 2001.

Januaray 2011

Benapole, Bangladesh border town

I was waiting in the Immigration hall to receive my passport. The officers at the upper level seemed in no hurry. Processed passports were being tossed down every few minutes. There was a long line and only two immigration counters were open on the ground floor, so the mezzanine-level officers had offered to help. I was counting on the coolie I had hired, a gnarled forty-something man, to get my luggage and load it onto the bus. He and I were both waiting, straining ourselves to track the progress of my passport.

'See, see, sir has your passport,' the coolie said soothingly.

'Which sir? Where?' I asked petulantly.

I could see passports passing from sir to sir on the mezzanine floor, but which of the sirs had mine? The atmosphere was chaotic yet casual, not unlike a bustling vegetable market. I sat on the unmoving luggage conveyor belt, keeping my anxious eyes trained on the sirs at the upper level. Reassurance was in short supply. I admired them for appearing so wholly stress-free, chatting, laughing, even shouting and joking with the impatient passengers in the hall below, and tossing out stamped passports into outstretched hands, with no trace of the hurry sickness that has beset the modern world.

The coolie finally caught mine. He waved it at me triumphantly and said in Bengali: 'Madam, Madam, look, I got your passport! Come this way.' He lifted my bags. I snatched my passport from him and stuffed it into my purse. It was more precious than life itself at that moment, and after receiving it, I was deeply relieved. I followed the coolie, bypassing some harried-looking passengers, and arrived at the head of a vague queue at the Customs counter. The customs officer pointed at my duffle bag, his phone sandwiched between his ear and shoulder. I unzipped it. The fat, leathery catalogue I had received from Seagull Books in Kolkata lay on top. He looked disappointed and waved me on impatiently, jabbering into his mobile.

Coolie and I celebrated our successful exit from Immigration and Customs with roasted cobs of corn. We still had to wait in a small office across the street where all Sohag Bus passengers were to reassemble before reboarding the bus. The Sohag's staff in Kolkata had reneged on yet another promise: that of assisting us with luggage transfer at the border. The driver and conductor said luggage transfer wasn't their responsibility when we pulled into the Immigration centre at Benapole.

Several coolies had assailed me as soon as I alighted from the bus: 'Madam, which country? Which passport?'

What relevance did my passport or my country have for them? Their job was to carry my bags through the maze of Immigration and Customs into to the Sohag waiting room on the Bangladeshi side of the border. I chose one man who seemed older, and less persistent than others. Later, I understood the reason for their yearning for foreign passport holders: higher tips. I was tired and hungry, having finished as breakfast the packed lunch handed out on the bus when we started from Kolkata.

The coolie seemed to guess.

'Do you want tea?'

I nodded vigorously.

'Rang chaa or doodh chaa?'

'Rang chaa.' Rang chaa must be the milkless variety, and safest, I reasoned.

He came back with a glass of sweet, reddish tea. I thanked him and handed him a hundred taka bill for his services. He seemed eager to stay till he put my luggage on the bus. He sat down across from me and started questioning me, but I could only answer with nods, head shakes, and monosyllables.

My first glass of tea from a tea stall in the land of my birth—I sipped it reverentially. It was strong and more fragrant than any roadside tea in India, and it was served in a glass, not a crumply plastic cup. I was getting sentimental, sipping the ruby-coloured liquid from the thick, not-so-clean glass. It was almost 2 p.m. I was hungry and we were still far from Dhaka, though the Sohag officials had promised to get us there by 8 p.m. I had stopped believing them long ago.

Around ten at night, the bus drove onto a ferry, where it sat parked among other trucks and buses. Tableeghi Jamaatis had resurfaced on this bus too! Why was I fated to share all my border crossings with them? Was there some hidden, mystical significance to these chance encounters with the Tableeghis? It was dark outside, and I thought of safety. What if the rickety ferry sank from the weight of so many vehicles sitting on its chest, burying us in the bosom of a murky river?

I asked the Tableeghis what they were going to Dhaka for.

They were standing in a group outside the bus, looking like distressed white ghosts in their flowing kurtas and caps. They were discussing safety of another kind in their Bihari-accented Urdu. The bus was late and nobody knew when it would arrive in Dhaka. 'We are not going to Dhaka,' they said. 'We have to go beyond Dhaka, much farther. We have to get to Tongi, near the Turag river.'

'What's happening in Tongi?'

'We're going to the largest gathering of Muslims in the world, after the Hajj,' one of the group explained with not a little pride. 'We are going to the Bishwa Ijtema.'[2]

I had never heard of the Bishwa Ijtema. But now I understood the reason for the preponderance of beards in the line for visas at the Bangladesh High Commission in Kolkata. There was no Bishwa Ijtimaa when I lived in Bangladesh but then there were no Muslim religious fundamentalists either.

---

[2]According to one estimate, the 2010 Bishwa Ijtema was attended by 5 million Muslims from more than 70 countries. Read more about the gathering at http://dhakadailyphoto.blogspot.com/2007/02/bishwa-ijtema-at-tongi-dhaka-begins-on.html

'A Muslim Kumbh Mela?' I almost blurted, remembering the tent city of pilgrims set up annually on the banks of the Ganges in Allahabad.

'But we won't reach Dhaka until after midnight,' the Tableeghis lamented. 'How will we get to Tongi? So late at night? Dhaka is not a safe city. Allah knows what we'll do. Where will we spend the night in the cold? Under open skies? What if it rains?'

'It might not rain. Allah is ever merciful,' I tried to console them.

I left the vexed Tableeghis and walked over to the edge of the ferry and leaned out. We were creeping across a wide, sluggish river. Later, I looked up a map and realized it must have been the Buriganga. I pondered the irony of running into Tableeghis on entering Bangladesh. Just as I had upon entering Pakistan! I imagined their reformist fury if I told them I was a Muslim and a Buddhist, married to a Hindu, and wavering in the shadowy no-religion land called agnosticism since I was fifteen.

There was a fullish, creamy moon out, squandering its silver on the swirling dark waters below. This air felt different, the smells here smelled different. Different from what? I couldn't say, but it was like coming once more upon the first just-before-rain smells of childhood we thought was our unique find. As a child I loved river crossings whenever my family travelled from Dhaka to Chittagong to visit my grandparents and we had to take a ferry. Dhaka and Chittagong were part of East Pakistan then, but now those cities of my childhood were cities in a new country with a new name. The moon seemed to sense my wistful longing for definiteness and unchanging definitions. It kept watch over me that night, bearing testimony to this oddness of the heart, this yearning to belong, and not belong.

The bus rolled off the ferry onto the road on the opposite bank. The man next to me went back to picking his nose and to talking on his phone. I turned and stared out into the darkness. The moon was now resting above the indistinct line of trees and bushes lining the highway. It travelled with me until the bus took a turn and I could no longer see it.

How many years had I waited to return to the land of my birth? Leaving as a child, soon after East Pakistan became Bangladesh, and returning when she was turning forty—I was returning to my birthplace, but my homeland? What is a homeland? For somebody always on the move across countries, what are motherlands and homes? For someone who hasn't lived at the same address for long, what could home be? India, Pakistan, Bangladesh. All three have been my homelands, at different times, for different reasons. I live with the joyous ambiguity of belonging to three nations that were at one time one. The indistinct longings for a definite homeland would remain real and unchanging, but to belong to a space beyond borders, beyond boundaries drawn with blood and war, is an abiding desire, a deep, strong, great desire. The heart aches for a return to a primordial state of life, a state of embryonic union, not the later life—a life divided and diminished between multiple identities and spaces. My journeys are my struggles to reconnect with the heartrending beauty of all my landscapes,

real and imagined, from the past and of the future. Peace—
that elusive, precious gift, how can it be our gift without us
first weaving a coverlet to receive it? A coverlet woven with
strands of love and acceptance. Love—and the price for
such abiding love—which among nations would be the first
to make an offering of patience and humility to others?
Who would have the courage to wash away blood to win
peace?

Why had I waited for so many years before returning? I
was hoping for a hamsafar, a fellow traveller. There were
other legitimate reasons: the children were young, I had no
contacts in Bangladesh; no place to stay. I had very little
money of my own—I was my husband's dependent. I didn't
speak enough Bengali. But when I changed my thinking,
when I made up my mind to travel, all these legitimate
reasons stopped being obstacles. They fell away because
they were barriers my thoughts had erected. This book
provided the most wonderful pretext to go off on unplanned,
impossible journeys I had always shelved to the back of my
mental priorities folder as impractical. Maybe I wasn't meant
to have a travelling companion after all? Some journeys are
best accomplished alone. The joys of being a solitary traveller
were continually unfolding for me. And I wasn't ever alone.
Wherever I looked, there was an eternal presence, a watcher
watched me, like the sacred moon on this river crossing, the
night I crossed the border into Bangladesh. The moon
accompanied me as the most reassuring hamsafar.

My Indian phone no longer worked so I requested the
somewhat friendly bus conductor to call my friend, Arif,

who was to meet me in Dhaka. 'Tell him when we'll get there, whenever you think we'll get there,' I said in Hindi.

A couple of months earlier I had met Arif, a young Bangladeshi sculptor at an art gallery in Karachi. We had exchanged numbers and emails.

'Don't worry. I'll help you find a place to stay in Bangladesh,' Arif had said. And his earnest eyes told me he would. I trusted him because it was the voice of intuition that told me I could. Arif had emailed me about a room he had arranged for me at the Working Women's Hostel in Dhaka.

We didn't get to Dhaka until half-past midnight—1 a.m. in Bangladesh. Bangladeshi time is a half hour ahead of India and I had forgotten to move my watch forward. Arif was waiting for me at the bus stop. I apologized.

'No problem. After your bus conductor called me, I stopped worrying. I knew you'd be late,' he said.

It was after we piled my bags into a green, cage-like auto rickshaw that he informed me of the bad news. The room at the Working Women's Hostel had fallen through. The warden wanted him to get approval from the ministry of something or the other because I was a foreigner. She didn't inform him of this essential formality till that morning. Obviously he couldn't get the approval at such short notice.

'Oh? So where do we go now?' I asked.

'I'll take you to my friend's sister's apartment. She lives with four other women. They have an extra bed. If you don't like it there, we'll look for something else.'

I wasn't worried, only glad to have a bed, and grateful we

didn't have to wander the city that night. The auto jounced and sputtered on the potholed streets of a cold, deserted Dhaka. Inhaling the foggy, particulate air, peering out of the green cage at the shuttered shops in the dusty glow of weak street lights, I knew I was coming back to a very different Dhaka than the one I had left as a child.

We pulled up beside an apartment building on an unpaved street crammed with more such buildings. Arif's friend's sister was waiting for us and undid the padlock on a thick iron-grilled door. We did hushed introductions and Arif left.

Tara was a thin, young woman. She looked too delicate to carry even one of my bags but refused to let me carry any of them. We kept going up and up. 'One more to go,' she whispered.

We were out of breath when we finally entered the flat. Mosquito nets were strung like giant spider webs in a dimly lit room. Bodies lay under those nets. Tara showed me the toilet, the wash basin in the kitchen, and my bed. The flat was small: two rooms, a bathroom and kitchen.

I washed and climbed inside the mosquito net and slid under the quilt, hungry and claustrophobic, but grateful for a bed to rest my sore back on. The body was too tired to fall asleep on an unaccustomed bed, and the mind too restless. There was one other bed in the room and somebody was asleep on the floor between the two beds. Tara had gone to sleep in the other room. As soon as it was quiet, I became hypersensitive to noises. I heard a rat. Lids dropped in the kitchen. Subtler creatures bustled right under my mattress, scrunching and scraping. All sounds were magnified. For a long time they kept me awake, but exhaustion from the sixteen-hour bus ride finally overcame me. By my tenth day in the apartment, I was sleeping through the night, particularly after the nonchalance with which Tara handled my concerns about rats and termites. 'Oh, *edur*? We've tried all kinds of traps. Oh, *pokah*? Yes, I know they eat the wood of cots.'

I awakened to the discordant blaring of azaan from several mosques simultaneously. Greyish light was seeping in from a narrow window next to my bed. I sat up, enjoying the shadowy dawn. The person who had slept on the floor between the two beds was not there. In a few minutes she entered and spread out her prayer mat on the floor.

I finally emerged from the canopy of the mosquito net. I took it down, folded it and put it away. How long would it take before I got used to sleeping under it, and in the company of rats and termites? I opened the window. A fuzzy disc of a blood-orange sun peered out from the space between two high rises in the distance. I listened to the birds and the plaintive singing of a faqir in the street below. I couldn't see him. He was hidden by the tops of dusty coconut palms. We must be on the fifth or sixth floor, I thought. As it got lighter, I stared wistfully at the coconut palms and the rooftops of rain-stained houses. A lone crow was cawing from the roof of the next building. The rain-darkened drabness of the buildings awakened memories of my first house in Chittagong. I had received my first dose of peace with the blurred sunrise, the singing faqir, the birds, and the woman in my room, sitting on the prayer mat.

'Why are you up so early? Go back to sleep,' the woman said softly, rolling up her prayer mat.

'*Apnar naam ki*?' I whispered, mindful of the other woman, still asleep.

'Shahida,' she replied. I followed her into the kitchen and sat on a low stool and felt drawn to her slow movements as she turned the tap on, and started filling a large pot with water. There was an intricate pattern of cracks in the red cement floor. She set the pot of water to boil, and got busy washing dishes and preparing breakfast and tea.

'Everybody calls me khala,' she said. Khala, the term for maternal aunt.

She cooked, cleaned, and washed dishes for the four women who shared this flat. And she did the same for some students who lived in a flat upstairs. 'I never saw my father and my son never saw his,' she said, slicing potatoes, the boti wedged between her toes. Her husband had killed himself. She was pregnant with her son when he died. I wasn't sure if she expected sympathy from me. She didn't look at me as she spoke. Her eyes were on the potatoes and the blade of the very sharp boti. She kept talking and slicing. She had come to Dhaka to work and support her son's education after her husband died. The son lived in the village with her sister and she saw him once a year. I was pleased with myself for following most of her Bangla. I told her the names of my daughters and showed her their wallet pictures. She seemed embarrassed when I asked if she had a photograph of her son. She didn't.

When everybody was up, we had breakfast. Khala served

us rotis, fried eggs, spiced potatoes, and cups of strong, sweet tea. And as a special treat, she placed a piece of last night's chicken on my plate. It was Friday, the start of the weekend. Tara introduced me to my other housemates. The beautiful woman with impossibly long hair was Champa. She worked in a real estate company. Tara's sister, Farah, was a telecom engineer, job hunting in Dhaka. The third woman was a graphic design student. Nobody was from Dhaka.

I couldn't believe how much I ate that morning. True to Bangladeshi hospitality, Tara apologized for not serving me a good enough breakfast!

The women got busy cleaning and dusting, washing clothes and bathing. By mid-morning water had run out. So everybody watched TV until the water supply came back. Tara and I stood among the just-washed clothes hanging in the balcony and talked. Tara said she didn't like her job. She wanted a more challenging, better-paying job but those were hard to find. Her father lived in a small town. Her mother had died of cancer some years back.

'My father wants me to get married and settle down, especially because Ma is no more.'

'And you're waiting for Mr Right?'

She smiled.

'There are no Mr Rights. So don't wait forever!'

'I know.' Tara smiled a lot, and her smile made her look lovelier and younger. Her girlish soul oozed out from the corners of her mouth, as did her uncorrupted, not yet hardened by the city self, the self she tried to keep concealed to survive in the city. 'I want a husband so I can have children and stay at home with them. I love children. Maybe I'll go away to Canada.'

'Why Canada?'

'Work here. Work there. What difference does it make? But I can make more money in Canada. Life is good there. People don't gossip the way they do here. Everybody is after my father because they think I'm too old and he should get me married. I love going home but I hate going out of the house. I don't like meeting any relatives.'

'How old are you?'

'Thirty.'

'No woman should get married before thirty,' I said. 'Only after thirty do women become sensible.'

Tara laughed. 'Nobody wants to marry women over thirty!'

'And love? Have you thought about love? Don't you want to fall in love?' I asked.

'I do, but I don't know how. Nobody's ever fallen in love with me. I don't have a boyfriend, so what can I say? There's probably no boyfriend in my fate.'

'So it's okay with you to get married without love?' I asked.

'If I can't fall in love, what can I do? I can try to fall in love after marriage?'

'With your husband, you mean?'

Tara laughed again. 'Yes, of course!'

Tara's pragmatism was beguiling! She seemed almost post-feminist in not treating love as a pre-requisite to marriage. Instead, her pragmatism made her consider marriage as a precursor to love, which may or may not develop later, if it developed at all. At least, she wasn't naively equating love with marriage. She, who hadn't traversed the prickly path of old-fashioned feminism like the women of my generation, she who knew nothing about feminism, and had never actively campaigned for equal rights, or egalitarian relationships or companionate marriages, was in some sense, wiser than me. She knew that an institution premised on inequality could not be expected to deliver equality. And she accepted this situation. Unlike her mother's generation, marriage for Tara's generation is not a career. It's more like a retirement plan.

'Maybe you won't need to fall in love at all, as long as you can marry, have kids and go to Canada!'

'Funny boro didi! I'll call you boro didi. I don't have an older sister.'

The most popular Bollywood number that season, *Sheela ki Jawani*, began blaring from the building opposite, a boy's hostel, forcing us to leave the balcony. There were several schools and colleges in this area. The other three women were sitting on the bed, watching TV. I joined them and had my first lesson in modern Bangladeshi culture.

A hijab-clad cosmetologist was explaining in a mixture of English and Bangla what she was doing to her client's face. She was using a bewildering variety of cosmetics on her makeover volunteer—a slightly obese, thirtyish woman with not fabulous skin, who was reclining in a salon chair, her hair pulled back, and her hopeful face upturned. The cosmetologist had on a fashionable headscarf and lots of makeup herself. Sporting a hijab was a modern woman's identity statement, that of a brash, elitist, urban, and consumerism-driven Muslim woman. But unlike other modern Bangladeshi women who had sold their souls to the West, and forsaken the rituals of Islam, and forgotten to cover their bodies and heads, she was using her headscarf to advertise her Muslim identity. Covering her hair with a scarf didn't mean she was oppressed, and it also didn't mean she was an advocate of a Western lifestyle. Peddling facial transformation to millions of women, having her own cosmetology show, was in no way in conflict with her Islamic values. I noted down at least ten items she used on her volunteer's face: blemish remover, foundation, eye brow pencil, eye shadow, eye liner, kohl, lip liner, lipstick, blush. 'We want to give her a very elegant but natural dinner party look!' the cosmetologist pronounced. How much would it cost to buy the blemish removers and blushes to get such a natural look? At the end of the show, we all agreed the multiple layers of foundation, the lipstick and eye shadow had not enhanced her victim's elegance or naturalness.

Later that morning, I went out with Tara for the weekly shopping and to check my mail at a cyber café. I also wanted a Bangladeshi SIM so I could start using my phone. At the market, I admired her bargaining skills with the fish and vegetable sellers. Lovingly I took in the plentiful piles of greens, the purple eggplants, the yellow pumpkins. I listened to the cheery banter between buyers and sellers. It was a cool January morning and though the sun was out, it was cool under the shaded lanes of the market. It felt good to be in the city of my childhood and in the market. By the time we had finished shopping, we needed a rickshaw, as Tara had filled two large sacks with pumpkins, beans, eggplants, cauliflower. And of course, fish.

'Do you know the name of our building?' she asked when we were settled with the two sacks in the rickshaw. 'Dollar Villa.'

'Dollar villa?'

'We live in Dollar Villa. Dollar is our landlady's grandson's name.'

'Her grandson's name is Dollar?'

'Yes. And she named Dollar Villa after him. She wanted Dollar to grow up and make them even richer, but Dollar's turned out to be hopeless. It's only the building that's made her rich. The landlady once asked me if I would like to marry Dollar.'

'And you refused, I hope?'

'Yes, but she found him a pretty wife anyhow. Now Dollar's wife is going to have a baby!'

'The great landlady will become a great-grandmother! What will she name her great-grandchild? Euro? Yen?'

We reached Dollar Villa and while Tara was fiddling with the heavy padlock, I stood back in the street and gazed up at Dollar Villa. It was a grotesque brown vision of its owners' naïve and naked ambitions. A narrow, six-storey high building, with cage-like grilled balconies. I recognized our flat from the clothes hanging in the balcony. It was on the fifth floor. As we climbed up the stairs with our loaded sacks of vegetables and fish, an irresponsibly expressed silent wish materialized. A shrivelled, wiry old lady accosted us on the first floor.

'Ayee, Tara! Coming from the market? Good fish?'

'Salaam nani, no, the fish today wasn't that good.' Tara turned to me and spoke in English: 'This is the owner of Dollar Villa and our landlady. We all call her nani.'

'So you're the new guest?' Nani eyed me, her mouth working the paan. Paan mulch was smeared around her lips. Her thin, rod-like body was wrapped in a dirty white sari. 'I'll come up and see you,' she said to me.

The red rim of betel leaf juice on her lips reminded me of a tired clown.

She was loath to let us go, but Tara said we had to take the vegetables up to khala to cook for lunch.

'Don't nani's legs hurt from climbing up to the fifth floor?' I asked, as we reached our flat, panting. 'She must be at least eighty.'

'Nani? No, no! She has the strength of an elephant. She gets all the repairs done in Dollar Villa. Even goes out to pay bills. She doesn't trust anybody else to do it. She works hard. She's even got a garden up on the roof. And she loves to talk.'

'I can only listen,' I said. 'She'll be disappointed in me.'

We bathed and sat down to eat a late lunch on the bed in front of the TV. Meals were always eaten in front of the TV. Glamorous shows with Bollywood stars were the programmes of choice. I ate and escaped quietly to my bed for a nap, the kind of nap that eating more rice than your stomach can hold necessitates.

The next day was Saturday, a working day, and the girls got up early. I sat drinking tea, while Tara brushed her teeth at the kitchen sink.

'We work six days at work, and on the seventh day we work at home! That's how our week is.'

'Take a day off. Let's go see your family,' I said.

'We can go, but I don't have a nice house,' she said. 'It's falling apart.'

Tara and the girls left. Khala went upstairs to cook for the students. I was finally alone. But not for long.

Nani knocked and came in, mulching paan, and without meandering much, went to the point. She informed me Dollar Villa was just one of several properties she owned. She had foreign connections: one of her daughters lived in Australia, one granddaughter lived in Korea.

'I'm not giving away my property to my daughter or grandson. If I give it to them, they might throw me out, and where will I go then? They'll get it all when I'm dead.'

I was impressed with her unsentimental shrewdness.

'This city is full of thieves and hijackers. You should be very careful,' she said. 'I'm used to it. I could live in Australia or Korea. But they're foreign lands. I'm not used to living anywhere else. I've lived here all my life.'

Then she moved on to interrogating me, the real reason for her visit: are you Muslim? Married? Kids? How many? No sons? What does your husband do? What's your book about? You were born in Bangladesh? How come you live in India?

She wanted to take me up to the terrace to show me her

roof-top garden but I wanted to be left alone. 'Not now. We'll go later,' I conveyed in broken Bengali.

My limited communication skills didn't daunt her enthusiasm for sounding me out. I managed to answer her with a combination of smiles, sign language, Hindi, English and Bangla. As she was leaving, she said: 'You understand a lot more Bangla than you speak.'

The following Thursday, Tara managed to take a day off without pay, and we boarded a bus for Tangail. Tara's father had called to ask what I wanted to eat.

'Fish and mishti,' I said.

It took the bus more than an hour just to weave its way out of Dhaka traffic and exit north on the highway leading to Tangail. On the way, we passed by the banks of the Turag river. That's where the Tableeghis I met on the bus would be. Crowds of cap-wearing men in long kurtas were milling about. The second phase of the Bishwa Ijtema was in full swing.

'We'll have a hard time getting back,' Tara prophesied. 'They'll have the akheri munajat, the concluding prayers when the Bishwa Ijetma ends on Saturday, around the time we're returning. Don't know what good so much religion does,' she muttered.

'The maulvis like to put on a show to promote themselves like everybody else,' I said.

'Religion is not about putting on a show,' she said.

'What is religion for you?'

'It's about love and respect, and doing good for others quietly,' she mused. 'That's how my mother practised. She didn't care much for the maulvis.'

We were passing fields of enticing shades of green, green like green is meant to be: the lime green of young paddy and bright yellow-green of mustard. Dust-coated banana fronds and spiky coconut palms leaned into the road. The narrow two-lane highway was intense and impatient with cars, trucks and buses.

A small-town movie theatre was advertising its current film. The title, *Love Me or Kill Me*, was painted in English on a bright billboard. I jabbed Tara, who was staring ahead, lost in some Indian TV serial on the bus' video screen.

'Is getting killed for love better or is living without love better?' I asked.

Tara shrugged and went back to spacing out with the TV serial.

Tangail was a cloister of a small green town ringed by sluggish green rivers. It was only eighty kilometres north-west of Dhaka but it took us more than three hours to get there. Tara's family home was a charming and old-fashioned house of bamboo and tin. Its quaintness tugged at my heart. The kitchen had a large, low window that opened onto the courtyard where there was a hand pump from where the family got its water supply. The hand pump reminded me of a similar one in my Chowk Bazar home in Chittagong, the house where I was born. Tara introduced me to her aunts, her little cousins, her father and her uncle. Everybody was friendly though our conversations were strained, and I had to use Tara as an interpreter.

Her father seemed glad to have me as a guest but didn't say much. He sat, like a man trying to get past loneliness, in the raised, covered verandah, and cleaned a pile of greens to be cooked for lunch. The older aunt, the one who was famed for her culinary skills, sat in the kitchen, supervising the cooking. Tara's little cousin frowned over his homework. One of her cousins worked the hand pump in the courtyard, filling a bucket for my bath. I understood why Tara loved to come home from the harshness of Dhaka. After we bathed, we went into the dining room. Her two aunts kept piling my plate with rice, fried fish and curried shrimp and pumpkin flower fritters. And there was mishti doi for that final, killing touch that only this thick sweet caramelized yogurt could give. After a lunch like that, what could we do except take a nap?

That evening after tea, we went out for a walk into town. Tangail carried the feel of something small and precious that reminded me of my Dhaka memories. It wore serenity like a soft silk shade. Though it had its share of raucous traffic and garishly-lit sari shops where you picked out what you liked from the racks and paid for it to an indifferent cashier, most of the streets were quiet, and most of the shops were dim, amiable tin and bamboo cabins. I wasn't in a mood to buy or carry much. It was more a wistful hunger for the sights and sounds of its narrow back lanes, the kind of shops and streets that I had seen in my childhood that were no longer to be seen in Dhaka. I was searching for the Dhaka of my yesteryears in Tangail: in its sweet shops with fat, fish-belly shaped cham-chams swimming sluggishly in vats brimming with syrup; in its flower shops with swaying braids of shocking orange-yellow marigolds.

Tara bought me yellow and red roses. 'Yellow's for friendship. Red's for love,' she said, presenting the bouquet.

I put the flowers in a vase on the mahogany dresser in our room. Tara and I slept in her room with pond-green walls, where her mother had slept during her illness. 'I came home from college to be with her. I slept next to her in her last weeks in this room,' Tara said.

Every morning in Dhaka, I'd seen her stand next to a framed photograph of her mother, eyes closed, hands folded, before she left for work. In her wallet, she carried a passport size photo of her mother. After lunch, we lay on the same bed her mother had lain in, and I felt a motherly concern for this young woman. The distant chatter of women washing dishes at the hand pump in a neighbouring house poured in with the light from the small window above the bed, tingeing the walls of the room a softer green.

'I worry about my father,' Tara said. 'He's very lonely after Ma. And he's worried about me and my sister. He's not forcing us into marriage. But our marriage is his main worry.'

I opened my sleep-heavy eyes and looked at her wan face. The tiredness in those words—marriage and worry—sank into me. Women have made great strides in Bangladesh. Tara and thousands of women like her, small-towners living and working in Dhaka, are the twenty-first century architects of a new Bangladesh. Though things still look hopeless when I see women like her wading in murky waters, striving for independence and giving it all up to conform to socially-sanctioned roles, there is an inchoate lamentation which is getting louder, and a rightful but guarded anger—songs of reassurance.

I wanted to tell Tara that marriage didn't remove worries, only placated parents who felt they had executed their responsibility towards daughters. I sensed in Tara's sadness an imposition of expectations. Whether she cared to or not, she would soon have to get married to make her father feel relieved of his responsibility. I wanted to hold her sadness for her, to make her see that she was not a burden, her worries were not borne of her failures, but society's failure to let her live the way she would like to. In my most pained moments, I often imagined myself being held in the safe womb of an immensely wise feminine soul. Could I offer such a womb for her to feel safe in? Could I become a tightly braided marigold garland with several strands of love—a mother's, a sister's, a friend and protector's—for her?

Two days of excessive eating and napping made me restless to get back to Dhaka, to less homey surroundings. But Tara wasn't ready to go back yet. She hated the idea of returning to Dhaka and to her work, but neither did she want to stay on in Tangail. And we had to take the bus back a day before the Bishwa Ijtema to avoid the exodus of millions that would hold up all traffic to Dhaka for hours. She was silent on the way back, as if trying to mollify her conflicted heart by forcefully watching another TV show on the bus.

'May a boyfriend come along soon to cheer you up,' I suggested as we waited for a rickshaw to get home after reaching Dhaka.

'Boyfriend? Boro di, I don't need a boyfriend! I need a better job,' she said. 'I've applied at a bank. Please pray they call me for an interview.'

~

The following week I went out exploring on my own. I got a taste of the trendy, new Dhaka. I gave a reading for a book club that called itself The Reading Circle, at an upscale café in Gulshan, far from the unseemly streets where Dollar Villa was located. Perhaps because I was somebody who wrote in English, I also got invited to a ladies' lunch hosted by one of the book club ladies. Almost all the guests present at the lunch spoke nothing but English, and wore nothing but silk saris. The ladies spoke of London and the US and Australia as if those were neighbourhoods they visited, not countries. Soundless waiters in black and white attire carried trays of beverages, including white wine. The entire flat was air-conditioned, the food was excellent, but the conversation exceedingly dull. The ladies chatted a great deal among themselves, but hardly anybody elicited much interest in me. I had violated the dress code by not swaddling myself in a silk sari, not styling my hair, and by not wearing any jewellery, so I couldn't complain.

I had lunch at Prabartana's adda, a women's only restaurant, with Dr Niaz Zaman, better known in the literary circles of Dhaka as Niaz Apa, a writer, teacher, and translator of Bengali literature into English, and valiant publisher of Bangladeshi women's writing. The cheap newness of post-liberation Dhaka failed to impress me. It was while reading

Niaz Zaman's introduction to *Fault Lines*,[3] an anthology of fiction by Pakistani and Bangladeshi writers on the trauma of the 1971 war that had resulted in Bangladesh's separation from Pakistan, that I understood my own disenchantment with the new Dhaka. For Bangladeshis, whose dream of a sovereign homeland materialized in 1971, it was a 'golden age,', she writes. But the golden age didn't dawn without dark stains of 'violence, rape, genocide. It was also promise: promise that when Bangladesh became independent people would not only be free, they would be equal, there would be no injustice, no class distinctions, no divisions between the haves and the have-nots. But the promise did not materialize.'

Parts of the new Dhaka, with its air-conditioned malls and cafés, sadly seemed like a Band-aid plastered over wounds that continued to ooze out from the edges. I invited Tara and Arif to my reading at the café, and they didn't refuse outright. But they didn't come. Later, as I was eating a perfectly cut, dainty white sandwich and sipping a full-bodied Americano after my reading, and conversing with the very suave and dapper former World Bank official who owned the café, I understood why Tara and Arif had chosen to be absent.

I went to see Munem Wasif's photographs at the Chobi Mela and stood quietly by each of his stark black and white portraits of water devastation in this river-rich land of seven hundred rivers. I went to the War Liberation museum and

---

[3] *Fault Lines: Stories of 1971*, Niaz Zaman and Asif Farrukhi (eds), University Press Ltd, Dhaka, 2008.

stared disinterestedly at war heroes posing with medal-inflated chests. The women's photos were few, and the most striking one was of a young girl, who had been repeatedly raped by the Pakistan army, and whose face was covered with her hair to hide her shame. The women were victims, the men were victors. I met Arif and he took me on a tour of Dhaka University Fine Arts campus and we had lunch in old Dhaka. The charming walks, and the old, magnificent trees on the university campus entranced me, but nearby, the traffic and pollution in old Dhaka was as scary an encounter as in any other South Asian city—narrow lanes bursting at the seams, and people and vehicles packed into them. Everywhere there were signs of promises that hadn't materialized. I gripped the flamboyantly painted rickshaw seat as the driver cavorted recklessly through hairline, airless lanes. I tried to imagine the Buddha returning to old Dhaka. How would he appear? Outwardly calm, inwardly agitated? The heaving sea of irate bodies, cars, buses, and grimy merchandise being sold in shops on the ground floors of buildings that yearned for a fresh coat of paint, shops huddled under a canopy of criss-crossing electricity cables—was this part of the answer to my disappointment? Are all of South Asia's cities fated to become like this? I wanted to get a pollution mask from a man at a traffic-choked street intersection in old Dhaka. Pink, blue and yellow masks on a bamboo frame, but the sellers themselves were maskless.

'Those who need it most don't wear them,' Arif remarked wryly.

After that afternoon spent in the old Dhaka, I felt tired and wanted to return to Dollar Villa and slump on my bed. This wasn't the Dhaka I had ached to see. Here the heart was constantly sending up fresh laments each time our spirited rickshawala came to a standstill in the jammed lanes. One afternoon, I set out in search of our old house in Dhanmondi, the house we had lived in at the time of Bangladesh's independence. The house was no longer there, having transmuted itself into a private school in an unrecognizable Dhanmondi. Later, those inchoate longings for houses and homelands would turn into an essay I would write for the Bangladeshi newspaper, *The Daily Star*.[4]

The Dhaka International Trade Fair was on and one afternoon my housemates dressed up in their best clothes and took me along. The fair turned out to be nothing more than a vast field filled with shops and eating joints, a makeshift mall, with hundreds of thousands of people. Few people were buying, most were just there for an outing. Prices were high, and people were walking mostly empty-handed. The noise level was several decibels past tolerable, and incessant announcements of incentives for shoppers over loudspeakers couldn't mask the disbelief in people's faces and chatter. People strolled in and out of stalls, watching how others were dressed or what they were buying. We posed for photos, ate phuchka from a food stall outside the fair, and

---

[4]For my essay, *Landscapes of the Heart*, see http://www.thedailystar.net/newDesign/news-details.php?nid=188490

exited the consumer chaos to wait in a long queue for an autorickshaw to get home.

I was looking for the DVD of an award-winning Bangla film, *Ontorjatra*, directed by Tareque Masud. The story of Bangladeshi diaspora, told through a divorced woman's return after many years to Dhaka, her hometown, had some resonance with my own return to Dhaka. One evening after work, Tara took me to Hollywood Videos.

We were crossing the street outside the mall, and I pointed out 'Magdonald's' to her, amused by the perfectly replicated red and gold sign. 'We live in Dollar Villa and we buy DVDs at Hollywood Videos, and we can eat at Magdonald's,' Tara commented. 'You don't need to go to America. America has come to Dhaka.'

~

My alarm went off at six-thirty every morning. Khala would be praying or reading the Quran when I would get out of bed. I would tiptoe past her, fumble in the semi-darkness for matches and put on water to boil. I would make tea and sit on the stool sipping it, and stare at the cracks in the kitchen floor. The cracks would begin to gleam as faint, tentative light from the kitchen window fell on the floor. Khala's praying in the next room would somehow calm me. I would place my bare feet on the wrinkled smoothness of the cracks, and think how they were symbolic of my life—cracks connected to other cracks, a chequered existence shaped by chance and choice; chaotic to the untrained eye, yet not quite so disconnected. In fact, becoming unfocused from myself, I would find the cracks were a map of human existence, not just mine. They symbolized a transcendent beauty. If I put my finger on any one point, I would find myself connected to the farthest crack, like the points in a maze.

Much later I thought the cracks were also an answer to my sadness. They had revealed what living was all about. Did I regret my unplanned, non-linear, zig-zag life? Marriage and motherhood messed me up, set me back by several years. Set me back from what? That became harder to answer, the more I thought. Later when I was writing this chapter, I remembered what the cracks had symbolized, and all my sadness seemed pointless. Life was relevant only as a continuously unfolding collage. Even entering Bangladesh with the expectation of reconnecting to my past life, hoping a thousand arms would encircle me, was like trying to re-enter the past. Was it even right to have such expectations? Remember the three words about life? It goes on. And it's never the same. My dislocation, not fitting in, feeling worthless for not meaning much to the world, was my looking for meaning in an inherently meaningless world.

The deep disappointment with Dhaka was also a facet of disappointment with my own life. Dhaka and I had started out around the same time with dreams of a new, happy, independent, achievement-filled existence. But like contradictions thriving side by side, there was in my disappointment with myself also a sense of awakening into a sacred knowing, into a deeper communion with disillusioned beings and disappointing places of the world. The cracks might look different, but how were my cracks so different from cracks of millions across the planet harbouring unfulfilled hopes? Our crackedness was precious, because it tied us together, made us human, made us pervious. Cracks hold a past, a history of fighting back, a culture of defiance, of civilization wriggling for room to express itself.

And cracks, unlike perfectly polished surfaces, also let in light.

~

A day before Valentine's Day, Tara came home looking devastated.

'Tomorrow is my test and interview at the bank,' she announced.

'So be happy! Why are you looking like you got hit by a bus?'

'I'm not worried about the written test,' she said. 'But the interview—I can't converse in English. I stammer.' Then she addressed khala. 'When you say namaz today, please pray for me.'

'What have you been speaking with me all these days? Japanese?' I asked. 'Don't worry. We'll do a mock interview tonight. If you really get stuck in English, switch to Bangla. Then switch back to English. You'll appear naturally bilingual.'

We drew up a list of anticipated interview questions: Five sentences to describe yourself. Where do you see yourself in five years? What makes you think you'll be suitable for this job? What is the history behind Valentine's Day? Write a few sentences about Mother Language Day.

I sat up with Tara as she rehearsed her answers. She recited her introduction to herself in English several times. Then she selected one of her mother's silk saris for the interview and ironed it. She seemed a little less nervous when we went to bed around midnight.

The next day Tara entered with a V-day rose for me, but her face looked ashen like the Dhaka skies.

'I made a mess! No job for me! I couldn't speak in English all the time. And this one man kept saying, speak in English, speak in English. Finally I said, I had studied in Bangla medium all my life. I can't speak good English. He frowned. He didn't look happy with me.'

'And the other candidates? How were they? What else did they ask you?'

'They asked me for an introduction to myself. That went off well.'

'Good! Did they ask about your goals? Why you wanted this job?'

'Yes. But the one who didn't like me, he asked me who discovered America.'

'Oh?' We had missed that one in our mock interview.

'I said it was Alexander. Then I said it was Vasco de Gama. He said it didn't seem like I had paid much attention to history or geography in high school.'

'They didn't ask about Valentine's Day on Valentine's Day?'

'No, they didn't ask me about Valentine's Day. Tell me, do customers at the bank need to know who discovered America?' Tara asked, genuinely puzzled.

'I think you are worrying too much. You might still get a call.'

'I don't know, but I've made up my mind,' she said irritably. 'I'll teach my children English only. They'll learn A, B, C, while they're still in my womb. English! English! English only! I'm not going to teach them a word of Bangla!'

'Don't be silly. You can't deprive your children of their mother tongue just because of some idiot who interviewed you. Let's go out tonight, it's Valentine's Day.'

I thought of the pink, heart-shaped balloons for Valentine's Day, globalization's sleek-footed entry into countries like Bangladesh, hanging at the newly inaugurated coffee bar at the street corner. I could see how tired Tara was. Cheated by an unjust education system: English for the privileged, Bangla for the rest. How tired she was of failing to meet expectations. Society's. Family's. The job market's. In one of the most culturally, linguistically and ethnically homogenous countries, it's the common language and not a common religion that was meant to unite. And it's the youth of Bangladesh—the largest proportion of its population—that was to define the new Bangladesh.

When I left Bangladesh this time, I left harbouring the most impractical vision. I felt poised for the birth of a global citizenship, transcending boundaries of race, class, ethnicity, and religion and the initiation of such a citizenship would begin from South Asia, which is in present times, the most iniquitous region on the earth along lines of class, ethnicity, race and religion. And the seed for such a flowering might germinate in the most fertile of soils for such a flowering: Bangladesh.

'I'm not going anywhere,' Tara said grumpily, folding and putting away her mother's now crumpled silk sari, and lying down for a nap. Her face resembled the creases in her sari. That night, to take her mind off her disappointing day, after she spent an hour bathing and washing clothes, I persuaded her to watch a film with me. We watched *The Japanese Wife*.

'See, even the Japanese wife can speak and write letters in English. Only I can't!' Tara said. Her voice lacked confidence and reminded me of shuttered shops.

The following week she enrolled herself in a spoken English course that met on Friday mornings—the only day she had off from work.

Bangladesh, my first homeland, a country unique among countries, for its freedom struggles were based on establishing its cultural identity, starting with the Language Movement of 1952, which aimed for the recognition of Bangla as the mother tongue of Bengalis. Hundreds of thousands died to get Bangla enshrined as the mother tongue of the new nation of Bangladesh, and to accord Bangladeshis the respect and recognition denied them by the Pakistani government. Where did this love of Bangla fit in with Tara's determination to teach her children nothing but English forty years after Bangladesh's birth? Was this a failure of a grand linguistic-nationalistic dream? Tara was right in her wry observations about Dhaka's employment scene. The well-paying jobs only went to those who spoke and wrote English fluently. A founding principle of this young democracy, its mother tongue, seems to have been sidelined by its globalizing economy, and love for Bangla is now rekindled annually in speeches and songs and cultural programmes, culminating in the Mother Language Day on 21 February.

Another constitutional pillar, secularism, also seems to be under threat. The clerics are now able to hold two, not one Biswa Ijtema, with special trains run to handle the influx of devotees, and the prime minister in attendance at the concluding prayers. The very fabric of a secular democracy seems to be coming apart. The Tableeghis were praying on the banks of the Turag, while in a village near Dhaka, Hena, a fifteen-year-old, was raped by a relative, and later flogged to death on the exhortation of village maulvis. She died from her injuries and the news channels shrieked and headlines appeared in newspapers for a few weeks. Fatwas still get issued by illiterate village clerics and are honoured by village folk, though declared illegal and unconstitutional by the Dhaka High Court in July 2010. The millions of Tableeghis, praying and meditating on the banks of the Turag in late January, hoping to get a ticket to heaven by shirking the Western model of consumerism, did not, to my knowledge, make any statement about Hena's heinous flogging at the behest of clerics. That would have been meddling with politics. And the Tableeghis supposedly don't meddle with politics.

~

My last day in Dhaka happened to be a Friday. Tara got up very early to make tea for me. She had often made her special brew for me, fragrant with cloves, cardamom and cinnamon. 'Your tea, not good. You make your tea in such a hurry,' she would say disapprovingly.

I told Tara I was going to Chittagong to find my first house.

'You are a *jajabor*,' Tara said.

'*Jajabor*?'

'A gypsy.'

'You mean one without a fixed home?'

'Yes.'

I saw something in her eyes that made me tearful, as if I had received the ultimate assurance from one who had come to know me well.

'You have many homes,' she said. 'This is one of them.'

I drank tea and waited for the singing faqir to appear once more in the lane. It was Friday, his day. This time I didn't want to miss him. As soon as I heard his faint voice, I flew down the five flights of stairs. In the time it took me to get down and undo the heavy padlock, he had moved on. I stepped out into the lane. He was walking away, his walking stick hitting the ground, and a little boy trailing behind him.

I ran after them. 'Wait. Wait,' I called out. They turned around. And I realized he couldn't see me. 'Can you sing for me?' I put together the request in halting Bangla. The little boy stared at me. He was holding a bowl with a few coins. The old man cleared his throat, leaned on his stick, and started singing a naa't I couldn't understand much, except the words Rasool and Mohammad, but I felt on the verge of tears. In some vague way his sightless eyes blessed my journeys. I placed some money in the bowl, and stood there as they departed, his singing getting lost in the noises of the gradually awakening lane, in the clamour of the vegetable sellers, honking cars, and the stridence of *Sheela ki jawani* from the boys' hostel.

10

152, Sirajudaula Road

The glass of tea I had, waiting for the train to Chittagong to depart

When you come
it rains in my heart
finger trembling like a blade of grass
long-closed doors open
in deep confidence.
when you come it rains
in my heart.[1]

—Vijaya Mukhopadhyay (1939-)

[1]From *The Unsevered Tongue: Modern Poetry by Bengali Women*. http://www.cse.iitk.ac.in/users/amit/other/ut-sample-gifs.html/

February 2011

Komalapur Railway Station, Dhaka

The CNG tears through Dhaka's cold streets and Arif and I arrive at Komalapur station an hour early for the 7.50 Chittagong Express. The high white arches of the station appear snowy in the morning mist. Arif leaves after helping me locate my seat in the right bogey and even goes in search of a newspaper but the hawkers haven't opened shop yet. How can I ever repay him for his time, his goodness? The compartment starts filling up. A woman and her son squeeze into the seat next to me. A cleaner enters swishing his broom and gets into a heated argument because a passenger doesn't move his legs out of his broom's path. It's clamourous, and nobody seems bothered that it's almost eight-thirty and the train hasn't stirred. Popcorn wala, tissue wala, beggars, chaclate-biscuit-chingam wala, have followed in the wake of the irate cleaner. I lean out of the window into the cool February morning. A man in a faded lungi is standing beside a huge tea kettle. I wave to him repeatedly to draw his attention. The passenger next to me yells: '*Ayee Chaa!*' And the tea seller immediately scampers up to our window. I smile gratefully. Reddish tea is poured into a lovely fluted glass, and as I sip and rest the glass on the window frame, sunlight glimmers through the thick greenish glass and lights up the ruby liquid within.

It's almost an hour and a half later that we do pull out of the station. By then, reaching Chittagong has receded to the back of my mind and I'm devouring the vanishing morning, letting the breeze blow into my face, my hair, and asking myself if the images flitting past reawaken long-buried memories. We've just passed the roadside squatter settlements, leaving Dhaka behind, and bright green fields under winter's lingering light are beginning to emerge. The parallel tracks racing alongside the train glint, and the rising-falling rhythmic prattle of the train pulls me into soft, dreamy longings. The desire for the safety and simplicity of childhood, a childhood spent in a house in Chowk Bazar; long spells of rain, taking shelter under the guava tree in my grandmother's half of the house, running to her across a courtyard filled with the fragrance of raat ki rani, beneath a silent sky. Arriving, feeling safe under her warmth, snuggling next to her in her bed. Will I still find that house? I'm not optimistic. And glad I don't have to carry on a conversation with the woman next to me, thanks to my linguistic limitations. I want to be alone with my thoughts on this mythical journey, the slow train returning me gently to my long-lost roots. I'm venturing out like the defenceless, love-torn women of Shah Abdul Latif's mystical tales, who set out in quest of union with their beloveds, but in truth, they were setting out in search for their true selves.

Tara calls from work. 'Where are you now? What did you eat?'

'We're not very far from Dhaka, we left an hour and a half late. I ate popcorn and biscuits and drank tea.'

'I miss you. I hope you find your house.' Before I can reply, I lose the network on my phone.

I get more tea from the clean and courteous dining service waiter and pull out the previous day's *Daily Star*. I feel duty-bound as an educated person to make sense of what's going on in the world by reading the papers, though the heart warns of repetition and tedium. The seemingly concrete world, the real world, exists outside of the fascinating, murky, past-future universe floating inside me. Which is more real, the realm inside or outside me? A thirteen-year-old rape victim in a village near Dhaka has died after giving birth to a dead baby. There's news of the Egyptian uprising, in the wake of the Tunisian uprising. Forty thousand have marched in Lahore to protest reforms in the draconian blasphemy laws. Thousands more are marching against government corruption in India. 2010 has been declared the hottest year on record after 2005. Unrest, disorder, protests, no matter where you turn for news. The silent spectator-listener inside me retreats into a place of seeming unconcern. When I, the doer, seem agitated and impatient, she, the silent one, simply throws up her hands. The novel has to be written, she says. Don't demand answers, don't get impatient, wait and see how the plot thickens. Enjoy the novel as it unfolds. Keep learning. Suffering is a good teacher.

During the day we kept pulling up at small, white-washed, sun-drenched stations. Little dark boys ran up, shouting, even before the train halted. They were selling mineral water bottles, chips, singharas, jhal muri. The countryside beyond the tiny stations was a collage of green paddy fields dotted with clumps of banana and coconut trees—the razor-blade fronds of the banana trees swaying like ecstatic singers in the breeze. The afternoon coalesced into evening, and I wanted to jump out and melt into one of those smoky villages, where fires were beginning to be lit, make myself at home in one of those tiny huts whose yards were holding the last of dappled light on muddy ground, where shadows were trembling under dark trees, and dreamy-eyed old men were sitting aimlessly by the tracks. I wanted to sit next to them and their cows whose heads were buried in feeding basins. Another day was departing from this part of the planet. There was an overwhelming sense of sadness and peace in the sinking sun behind the line of trees, in the play of light and shadows, in the once-again beginning to blow breeze, in the slow, unchanging pattern of existence. I wished I could preserve this evanescent loveliness somewhere in that dark, fluid womb of the mind to nourish myself with during more barren times.

I had told Niaz Apa when we met for lunch, 'I'm going to Chittagong.'

As if to forewarn me, she'd said: 'I hope you won't be too disappointed.'

'Disappointed?' Disappointed with my rainy birth-town, nestled among green hills?

'It's not as bad as Dhaka. But everything is deteriorating all round, you know.'

As the day grows dimmer, and the train slower, and rows

of plastic-covered bamboo huts barely a few feet high and a few feet away from the railway tracks roll by, and beyond them the high, gloomy, buildings with lights and garment factory workers inside the broken windows, I begin to repeat Niaz Apa's words: *I hope you won't be too disappointed*.

The train finally enters Chittagong station. The long-awaited moment is here and as I step down onto the dimly-lit platform, I'm filled with foreboding, but there's also some sort of unspeakable joy and hope fluttering behind the foreboding. I search the crowd for Ali. When he finally meets me, he tells me he's been waiting since 1 p.m. We wouldn't have recognized each other so I called him from my mobile to explain my location on the platform.

'The train kept stopping in all sorts of little places, but I enjoyed the journey. I messaged you about being late. You didn't get it? What did you do all these hours?'

'I leave before your message comes. No problem,' Ali says, taking my bags. 'I come to station. Eat, sleep, read paper.'

His mother, Fauzia, worked in our house when we lived in Dhaka. She was a widow but remarried around the time of Bangladesh's independence, to become the second wife of a man who already had a first wife in Chittagong. After a few years of keeping her in Dhaka, he took her to his village near Chittagong, and left her there to live with his first wife and returned to his peon's job in Dhaka. It is to this village that I am going with Ali. Fauzia has been calling me every day since I first told her I was coming to stay with her for a few days. The great advantage of having Ali as a guide is that he speaks passable Hindi, Urdu and English, in addition to his mother tongue. He picked up these languages from his South Asian co-workers in Saudi Arabia, and is now home, waiting to land another work contract in the Gulf. He's about thirty-five and stuffed with useless information, which he begins pouring into my unwilling ears the moment we settle into an auto.

'Apu Bangladesh people very poor. Only few rich, they very very rich. Rest very very poor. Bangladesh land enough for sixty million. But Bangladesh population over 160 million.'

As soon as we are out of the crowded area with well-lit shops near the station, the city becomes dark, quiet and cold. I want Ali to shut up so I can soak in the darkness, coldness and quietness, the first whiffs from the city of my birth. But he chatters incessantly and loudly. I lean back into the seat, resigned.

We cross a bridge over a wide, dark river. 'This is Karnafuli river,' Ali informs me. 'In the morning, we take boat.'

I lean out excitedly. 'Yes, in the morning we take boat!'

Beyond the river, the auto bumps and jolts over a narrow, unpaved path between fields flanked by dark, dense foliage. Thatched houses lit by faint lamps twinkle warmly behind the trees. There's the cold air and there's smoke and mist, and I inhale this delectable bouquet gratefully.

Ali unclenches the fist in which he's holding his mobile. 'We're reaching soon. Keep everything ready.'

A few minutes later, we stop outside a house where three women are waiting in the dark.

'You've come, you've come. I thought I'll never see you

before I die,' an elderly woman steps up to embrace me and smothers my face in her sari. I recognize her as Fuzi – my childhood nickname for Fauzia. I can't tell who the other two are in the dark. When we go inside the house, Fuzi introduces them. The two women are her youngest daughter and her middle daughter-in-law. The house is brick and tin and I'm relieved to see there's electricity. I'm shown my room. The middle daughter-in-law has vacated it for me. Her husband is in Saudi Arabia and it's understood she has no need for privacy in his absence. She'll sleep in Fuzi's room. Ali and his wife occupy the next room. Mine is a tiny, windowless room sandwiched between Ali's and Fuzi's, full of furniture brought as dowry by the middle daughter-in-law.

Fuzi's married daughters and her grandchildren have also arrived. The house fills with people whose names I can't remember. Dinner is served and there's mutton, chicken and fish. I have to eat first as the guest of honour.

Fuzi sits with me and the others sit and gawk unabashedly. I eat while being watched from the sofa, the bed and the floor. I try to ignore their unblinking scrutiny as the inevitable curiosity village folk have for foreigners and city-bred curios. Fuzi's daughter and daughter-in-law hover around me, ready to pour out water, spoon more rice. Fuzi has lost most of her teeth. The spaces between the intact ones are stained the colour of dried blood from tobacco and paan.

'Fuzi, why did you cook so much? Daal and rice would've been fine,' I protest in my own mix of Bangla-Hindi-Urdu, which she understands, thankfully.

'You hardly ate,' she says. 'You don't like this food?'

'I like it! But how much can I eat? From tomorrow, don't cook so much. Promise me.'

'Tell Fuzi what you want for breakfast?' she ignores me.

'Tea and roti.'

'And eggs?'

'Just tea and roti.'

'No eggs?' she looks crestfallen.

'I've come to see you, Fuzi! I want to spend time with you. If you worry about what I'll eat, when will we talk?'

She looks around proudly and repeats to her daughters and granddaughters and daughters-in-law seated on the sofa, bed, and floor: 'Did you hear that? She has come to see me, so she doesn't want me to worry about cooking! She'll eat daal and rice. And not even have eggs.'

'I want you to take me around the village,' I lay a hand on her shoulder. 'I want to hear how you've been all these years.'

'There's so much to tell,' Fuzi's paan-filled mouth twitches as my hand rests on her shoulder and she wipes her eyes with her sari. 'Nobody cares for Fuzi. She has become a widow. And you've come only for four days after forty years. Fuzi will feed you only daal and rice?'

The next morning, Fuzi awakens me with a cup of steaming tea. She slides the cup into my hands under the mosquito net. I turn on my phone light. Is it dark outside or is it dark in here because there are no windows?

'What time is it?' I mumble.

'It's almost six. Should I heat up water for your bath?'

'No, no, don't bother. I'll bathe when I come back.'

Fuzi leaves and I prop myself up against pillows in the dark, cold room, grateful for the sweet hot tea that trickles down my throat, and I remember with a heaving gut—today is the day! I feel like a school girl about to take off on an adventurous trip to some long-dreamt of place. I dress with slow, deliberate movements to steady my topsy-turvy heart.

Fuzi is sitting in the thatched shed attached to the house, rolling out rotis. There's a bright fire crackling in the clay stove. She reminds me of my grandmother cooking on a similar stove in the Chittagong house. I sit beside her and contentedly inhale the warm, smoky air mixed with the cold draft from the yard. Two dogs are curled up like kidney beans in the yard. Fuzi warms up date palm syrup for me and I dip my roti into its golden-brown thickness greedily.

'Hmmmm! I want to eat this every day!'

'One egg? I can fry it quickly.'

I smile and shake my head and rush to rinse my mouth at the hand pump.

Ali and I head out into the chilly morning. The village feels cold, still and dignified in the silent morning. More than the city can ever feel. Trees seem wrapped in gauzy cotton. The horizon is just beginning to lighten. We head for the river through the pot-holed path, going past shuttered shops. Dark purple pea plants are wrapped on trellised fences with their violet blossoms and there's the peach-pink sky to the east—a hushed, exquisite morning. Everything appears to be nodding off, breathing softly, at peace with itself, and right where it should be in the universe.

When we reach the river, workers are piling into boats that will ferry them across to the city for five rupees. Ali and I squeeze into the bench of one already filled to capacity. The Karnafuli's waters are a metallic grey-green in the early morning. And they're totally fishless too, Ali tells me. Dirty foam froths as the boat rips the river's dense surface. The motor grunts and smoke rankles my nostrils and burns my eyes. We arrive at the other bank, and most passengers prance off but I waver, needing Ali's hand to steady myself and jump off onto a muddy bank overlaid with jute bags. Two boys are washing clay-coloured saris in the clay-coloured water. I feel cheated, as if some gargantuan, dark machinery has made this great river murky, fouled it and robbed it of its riches, yet hasn't quenched the river's unceasing quest to merge itself with the ocean.

'152 Sirajudaula Road,' I tell Ali. 'It's close to Chittagong College. Near Parade Ground.'

He explains the directions to the rickshawala and turns to me: 'Apu, I think you not find your house.'

'What makes you say that?' I snap at him.

I have a feeling Ali doesn't want me to find the house because he knows how much I want to find it. There's an undercurrent of antagonism between us, and power tussles have already begun to foment. He's used to exerting control; I'm not used to being controlled. I can tell he's thrilled with his role as my guide, and loved it that I needed his hand to jump off the boat. I'm in need of his guidance, but I won't let him predict the conclusions of my desires.

Ali starts shooting trivia: 'Apu, Bangladesh need many

more megawatts of electricity but Bangladesh not generate enough. Arsenic in ground water in north. No safe drinking water. Only 50 percent people with tubewell water. 50 percent drink pond water. Water disease too much.' Then he shifts to girls' education when I mention that I would like to visit my first school, St Mary's, if we have time. He has a two-year old daughter, and at home, I've watched him teaching her body parts and animals' names in English. He has big plans for her. 'I make her aeronautical engineer!' He tells me he read a book in Saudi Arabia which said that girls' brains are smaller than boys' brains. But there's hope: if you work on them, they can grow as big as boys' brains, he tells me in all seriousness.

I want to ask him why, where from, and how he accumulates these factoids, but I don't have the heart to. I am desperate to meet 152 Sirajudaula Road. I wonder how the house will meet me. The house will have aged much in forty years. Will her front door still be green? What will it be like to walk through her, walk across the courtyard? Unrealistic though it is, I am thinking of the guava tree, and the raat ki rani near the front door. Would the present owners allow me to walk, pause, stare, touch? I check my attire. I am dressed respectably enough so as to not invite any objections. I had repeatedly seen myself, notebook and camera in hand, standing in the courtyard that divided our half of the house from my dadima's. I would be conversing with the residents, jotting down notes and anecdotes lovingly, taking photographs of the well, the hand pump, the peeling walls, the cooking shed; preserving in words and images what was fading fast in memory. I had been introducing my daughters to the house in my imagined slide shows: 'See that window? That's where I used to stand looking out at the street for hours, and that? That's a well, a real well, yes, there used to be wells inside houses! We bathed with its water. And that's the shed where dadima cooked. We got our drinking water from that hand pump! And that's the door to the most frightening part of the house—the bathroom! I used to be scared of going there. Dada-jaan, my grandfather, kept his chickens inside the bathroom!'

We cycle past Chittagong College and go past Parade Ground. We turn left into a divided street with scattered high-rise apartment buildings and low-ceilinged shops.

'Apu, Sirajudaula Road,' Ali announces.

'We have to find 152 Sirajudaula Road,' I answer distractedly, surveying the street for any recognizable traces of my childhood.

We cycle up and down the almost empty street. It's still early for traffic. Ali stops a few passers-by. We peer at walls of houses and scan shop signs for numbers. But there's no house numbered 152. And I find no lane adjoining the house, leading to Chittagong College's campus through the back. Finally, we do find 152 Sirajudaula Road, but it's not a house. It's a paint and welding shop. A battered-looking van is parked in front of it and a gawky youth is staring at me from one of its windows. Ali finds a bearded man dressed in a kurta and cap who owns or manages the shop. He approaches me, speaking to me in Bangla-laced Urdu. He can't recall a house ever being there.

'That can't be,' I say passionately. 'I lived in that house. I was born in that house. There was a well in the back. And I used to walk to school by cutting across the Chittagong College campus,' I point vaguely to the spaces behind his shop, to that shortcut which used to lead from the back of the house to the college campus. My mother and I walked that path every day but I can't show him what seems as clearly etched as lines on a map but only in my head.

'Did you bring any claim papers? Any photos?' I can sense the alarm in his voice. He thinks I have returned to reclaim my property.

'I haven't come to claim anything. We didn't own it. Our rent was 100 taka a month.' I blink away the tears. I'm disconcerted. His questions are perfectly reasonable. I never imagined I'd have to present any proof of residency other than my memories. I shake my head, stifling that something that had arisen as soon as I had stepped down at the station the previous evening. How idiotic! I don't want Ali to see me cry. But why should it matter? Why should I wait till I am alone to let my tears flow? What else would soothe my pain, this unnamed pain, except my tears? You took too long to come, the stifled something says. I'm new to this grief. Who will I speak of it with? I sit and sob silently in the rickshaw, holding my dupatta over my face to shield myself from Ali's questioning gaze.

~

Many months later, back in India, it would be almost winter again when I would start writing this chapter during a five-day retreat at a river-front cottage of the Krishnamurti Foundation, tucked away on the outskirts of unruly Varanasi. I would spend many mornings sitting at my desk, staring at the sluggish, slender-waisted Ganges, unable to pull together the thoughts beneath scratchy notes jotted in my spiral notebook. I would stare listlessly at the volumes of hard-bound spiritual tomes and then check out a slim unbound book on Kabir's life from the library. Leafing through it, I would enjoy the legends about Kabir's life, chuckle at the irreverence of the weaver-saint-poet for figures of authority. Kabir once went with a group of Raja Bir Sinha's friends to visit a brand new palace built by the raja. All the raja's guests admired the new palace, but when asked what he thought of it, Kabir expressed two objections. First, the palace won't last forever, he said, and second, it's owner would pass away even before the palace. Kabir's unabashed directness would wrap me in a soft embrace of acceptance. I would experience a strange and quiet peace that night. Nothing was meant to last—houses or people. Old houses get demolished. Decrepitude is replaced by freshness, only to fade into decrepitude, I would repeat to myself, sitting out on the covered verandah, listening to the living woods in the otherwise silent night. Inevitability. Cycles. Transience. Filled with a tranquil resignation, I would return to my desk and write the next hundred words of this chapter.

~

Ali hops in next to me and the rickshaw starts cycling. Where to now, he wants to know. I tell Ali I would like to walk through the Chittagong college campus. Maybe we'd still find the remains of the shortcut through the college to the other side. Maybe we'll find vestiges of the lane connecting the college to my house even though there's no house. The college gates are open and a few students are conversing lazily, leaning against fences. We walk across the college campus and reach the boundary wall that separates it from Sirajuddaula Road. There's nothing but an unbroken wall that stretches along the periphery of the campus. I stare at it in dismay. There are no breaks in this wall, no quick path leading to the other side.

I start to walk away, and the neglected college buildings reflect my disappointment. We too have withstood disrepair, lived long with broken, dust-clouded windows, coexisted with disappointingly dim rooms, and tables and chairs scattered about us as if nobody cared, they seem to say. I can stash my memories along with the memories of displaced millions—climate refugees, war and genocide refugees whose homes live only in their memories. Painful as the revelation is, it came as a question: can a bricks and mortar house ever be mine? And, can such a house be the abode where the spirit comes home to rest?

'Now, Apu?' Ali asks, impatient to execute the next item on my itinerary and get back home.

'Bayzid Bistami's dargah,' I find myself saying. This wasn't part of the plan. I'd heard of the famous Persian saint's shrine from my grandmother and though he probably never came to Chittagong, legend has it he travelled and lived and died here. I need a saint's shrine to close my eyes and hang my head low and savour my grief; and think about what to do next to stall Ali's dictatorial management of my day. What better place than a shrine to lose myself in the crowd of supplicants and petitioners? I want to taste the heart's heaviness amidst incense and rose petals and folded hands, and the silently moving lips of seekers.

Ali tells me he won't accompany me up to the mausoleum. He believes it's un-Islamic to pray to dead men as intermediaries and through them ask favours of Allah. There is a dog and a man with an amputated leg, both asleep near the entrance, and an alms bowl between them. I drop some coins into the bowl. Ali waits for me near the steps of the turtle pond at the bottom of the shrine. I climb up the steps, and sit on the bench running along the parapet, and close my eyes. When I open them, I sense the cool fading afternoon's shadows, and somehow I'm less restless, as if the losses have settled down, having percolated down into the very fabric of my being.

I return to the pond and find Ali in conversation with an elderly lady.

'Apu, she say she drink this dirty pond water,' he turns his face and shakes his head. 'For asthma! Illiterate people. Only Allah can cure, it says in Quran.'

I look at the woman and then at the green, lichen-coloured pond. I smile at her and she smiles back with her eyes and her puckered face. A few dead-looking, motionless turtles are floating, half-submerged under the pond's surface, and children and adults are trying to get them interested by waving pieces of bread and fruit impaled on bamboo sticks.

'Maybe she drank the water because she had only her faith to cure her,' I tell Ali. 'Anyway, I'm ready to go back.'

I buy a kilo of golden, plump cham-chams from Bhoj Bazar, which used to be my father's favourite sweet shop, to take back for Fuzi, and we head back for the Karnafuli. I say very little to Ali as he prattles on about his televangelist hero Dr Zakir Naik, and how Islam has been hijacked by superstitious practices such as the one I just indulged in. I don't answer, so he fiddles with his mobile. We pass large billboards with life-size photographs of the Bangladesh cricket team. The World Cup's due to start in a few days and Bangladesh is to host the Olympic-style, lavish opening ceremony.

'Apu, all beggars getting 150 taka per day from government to keep off streets,' Ali can't resist telling me.

'Really? Permanently?'

'No! For World Cup.'

'Oh! Where did you hear this?' I ask, not believing him, not sure how to respond to this tragic-comic info byte.

'I looking TV news.'

'I see.'

What I did see during rest of the ride is my own pain, pain I had no clue I was hoarding. At the same time I was hoping this pain would find release in liberation, and tear me away from my clinginess. What was I clinging to? Memories? Love of a house entwined with more memories, losses wrapped around more losses. The heart was stuck in grief— for the house, for memories, the loss of its looming presence. Our Dhaka house had turned into a school, but there were fewer happinesses attached to it. The Chittagong house was about dadima, my grandmother, the only one who loved me utterly selflessly. She passed away years ago, and now the house which I had cherished and thought of as her shrine, where I had lived with the constant awareness of her love, where she made guava jam, where I hid my face in her faded white saris—that house had perished. There's a finale to all memories, and all tales must wind up. The heart and mind would have to erect a shrine to her memory in memory.

As we approach the village, Ali calls home and shouts orders to keep coconut water and lunch ready for me. He has started organizing my afternoon at home already.

The many guests who had filled the house have left and the house is aloof and serene in the winter afternoon. Ali's cousin has brought fresh coconuts from his trees. I gulp down the cool, sweet water, and the cousin scrapes out its creamy flesh for me. Fuzi watches me for a while and then asks about the house.

'It's no longer there,' I tell her in a tone which conveys to her I don't want to talk about it. She doesn't ask more.

My mother calls from the US from my sister's house. My sister was only three when our father moved us from Chittagong to Dhaka for his work.

'Did you go to the Chowk Bazar house?'

I tell my mother what I told Fuzi.

'Is there a new building there? New buildings are always going up,' she says stoically, without a trace of grief or shock.

I tell her nothing about my grief and shock. There's very little sharing of my emotions with my mother.

The grief, the shock, the disappointment, the loss is all mine, all without a visible trace in the outer world. And it's all in the mind. My mother and I lived almost the same amount of time in that house. She had come to it as a bride. I came a year later as her child. She hated living there and sharing my father, his income and his attention with her in-laws. She was their detested daughter-in-law, I was their beloved grandchild. The house meant very different things to her and me: rejection versus unconditional acceptance; oppression versus affection.

I bathe in the windowless, lightless bathroom, whose door can't be shut. I stand a flashlight upright on a low stool. Fuzi's youngest daughter, Shumi, has filled a bucket from the hand pump for my bath, and now holds the door shut, though I tell her not to bother. The water from the hand pump is cool but not stingingly cold so I decide to wash my hair as well. During the four days I'm there, Shumi follows me around constantly, giving me shy, pained, approval-seeking smiles. She keeps barging into my room with cups of tea and toast, a broom and duster, or a tennis racket-like gadget for catching mosquitoes. After a whole day of repeated interruptions, I say irritably, the way the weak by displaying their weakness incite the strong to speak: 'Why are you following me everywhere?' She gets so flustered, she leaves. She's a frail-looking adolescent, a worker who hardly speaks. She looks frightened of adults, especially her brother Ali. And I've probably frightened her too.

'I want her body to mature a little more before giving her in marriage,' Fuzi confides in me after lunch.

'Mature for what?' I gasp.

'For having children!' Fuzi says as if this should be obvious.

'Has she finished with school?' I ask. Fuzi's talking about Shumi but Shumi could be a cow or a goat that had to mature before being hauled to the cattle market and sold to the highest bidder.

'She had to take care of her father. He moved here from Dhaka when he fell ill. He would shit and piss everywhere until the day of his death. She had to clean up after him. How could she go to school? I needed her to help out.'

'Why can't she go back to school now?' I ask. 'She has to mature mentally too. She's so quiet and shy.'

Fuzi thinks I'm admiring her daughter's shyness and quietness. She tells me about her daughter's unflagging capacity for housework—her qualifications to be an uncomplaining wife. It's just her slow body that's out of sync with her job description.

'Why are you in a hurry to marry her off? What did you get out of your marriage?'

'Nothing,' Fuzi muses. 'I got nothing out of my marriage. It was the worst thing I did.'

'But you married twice!'

'My first husband I was given to when I was a girl. Then he died. My parents were also dead by then. I had no brothers. How long could I live alone? I had to marry,' she says. 'Her father is dead. If I don't marry her off, and I die, there'll be nobody for her.'

'Won't her three brothers be there for her?'

'She has no brothers! What good are they? They care only about their wives and their own children.'

'You have four sons and you were feeling bad for me! Why did you want me to have sons?'

'You're right. What good are sons? I have one in Dhaka, two in Dubai. And one here. But look at him,' she says about Ali. 'He finds fault with me and his sister all the time. We can't do anything right. He only listens to what his wife says and she hates us.'

Fuzi makes me a paan and fills her mouth with a fresh one. She's got me hooked on after-lunch paans, stuffed with freshly chopped betel nut from her trees.

'You had eight children!' I say in genuine admiration. In this village where she arrived as a stranger, as a second wife and had nobody to turn to for comfort, and so little to live for, she had given birth to and raised eight children.

'It's Allah's blessings. You know he sent me to live in this village with Boro Ma . . .' and she recounts the story of her marriage. My family had moved out of Bangladesh when this part of her life happened. 'He' was not Allah, but her husband and Boro Ma was his first wife. 'I had to learn to get along with Boro Ma, I had to speak like village people do here. Sometimes Boro Ma and I would quarrel. Whenever he came to visit, if we fought, he would beat us both. He knew how to keep us under control. He taught us to get along with each other.'

I imagined her husband, an unfulfilled man, having worked at some low-paying job in the city, returning for respite, seeking peace in his old age, and frustrated by constant bickering between his two women, both begging for his absent attention, like two children. And he, his desire having shrivelled for both, resorts to beating them to shut them up.

I make Fuzi eat with me. I don't eat at the dining table that came with the middle daughter-in-law's dowry. We roll out bamboo mats and eat on the floor next to the kitchen, the way Fuzi's used to eating. Today's lunch was simpler fare: rice and fish curry with white beans. Fuzi whispers as Ali's wife walks in, serves food from a different set of pots into two plates, and walks out: 'She doesn't eat what I cook. She cooks separately. They eat in their room.'

Ali's daughter comes in, waving a stuffed toy. 'Eli-phent!' she shrieks. 'Eli-phent.'

'Oh, look, look, my Isha-muni is speaking to her dadu in English! But dadu doesn't know English,' Fuzi tries to feed her from her plate. 'Come and sit down and eat with us.'

'Eli-phent!' the little girl pushes away the food her grandmother holds out, and waddles off into her parents' room.

~

The next morning, after stuffing myself with more rotis and warm, golden date syrup, Fuzi and I set out for a walking tour of the village. We pause at the pond. It's full of fish, she says, but the boys need to get in with a net. She points out trees she had planted herself—coconut, jackfruit, and her pride and joy—her five betel nut trees that supply her yearly needs. The pond's surface is a grey-green mirror and her stately, silent trees are mirrored in it. Tranquillity is a palpable presence here. We wander into the adjoining fields. Thin, gauzy mist is lifting off the fields in the glare of the fast-climbing sun. Neat rows of beans, turnips, and tomatoes are planted over acres of openness. We tip-toe across the fields on narrow, raised paths. As soon as we enter a compound of mud houses, and the residents spy me, they start pouring out of their houses. A group of children follow us, and an elderly bent woman joins them.

'Who's she?' the old woman asks.

Other women look up with the same question in their eyes.

'Who does she look like?' Fuzi quips.

'Your sister?' the old woman ventures.

'My sister? My sister! My sister? Yes, she's my younger sister!'

Fuzi smiles with mischievous pride as we enter the house of one of her friends. I sit and smile at peering faces while Fuzi prattles on about me to women who have mysteriously appeared, and are thronging the doorway to the dark room with mud walls.

'She won't eat meat or chicken. Doesn't even want eggs. No, will eat only rice and vegetables. And will eat with me on the floor. Won't eat at the table.'

'Stay with us, eat with us, come to our house,' the women say.

'She can't stay. She's leaving in two days,' Fuzi says territorially. 'Now do you have a paan for me and a new mat to show her?' she addresses her friend.

The friend disappears into an inner room and comes back with a large, rolled up reed mat. She's a weaver. She's very thin and her voice is apologetic as she squats on the floor and rolls out the mat for me to see. 'I wouldn't ask you for any money, since you are her friend, but—'

'I'll pay you, don't worry.' I run my hand over the zig-zagging greens and purples in the mat. 'It's beautiful.'

And a little later when Fuzi has received two freshly made paans, we walk out, the lovely purple and green reed mat tucked under my arm. About two dozen children and the old woman follow us. I turn around suddenly.

'Photo?'

They shriek delightedly and pose. Then run up to stare in disbelief at the images on the screen and giggle some more.

'It's only the start of the day, and how many paans have you already had?' I tease Fuzi as we walk back to the house.

'Shumi's Abba, Allah bless his soul, introduced me to paan, tobacco and purdah,' Fuzi speaks despite her full mouth. 'I learnt to wear burqa after I married him. Ali says, don't eat tobacco, you'll get mouth cancer. But my teeth hurt and tobacco is the only thing that helps the pain,' she says, resorting to the circular defensiveness of addicts.

We return to the house to find Ali standing in the yard with his laptop perched on a chair. 'Apu, I try connect. Better connection here in open. You check mail?'

I shrug. I'm happy to be away from the world of constant connectivity, but he had to show off his laptop. I sit on the steps of the verandah, listening to the haunting koo-hu-koo-hu of koels in the fading afternoon. Fuzi brings out a glass of coconut water and Ali fiddles with the laptop. Isha pokes her fingers into his laptop and he scolds her. She bawls until Fuzi lifts her into her lap and rocks her. Finally, he comes up to me, looking crushed, cursing the slowness of all things Bangladeshi.

'Apu, not working. We try again tomorrow.'

'I'm not in a hurry,' I say. 'I can check mail when I get back to Dhaka.'

He changes the topic. 'Apu, which country capital Lesbian?'

'Lesbian? You mean Lisbon?'

'Lisbon. Yes, yes. Lisbon.'

'Portugal. Lisbon is the capital of Portugal.'

'Portugal still rule in Pune in India, Apu? People there not free.'

'No, the Portuguese were in Goa but that was a long time ago.'

That evening, when I am sitting in front of the TV, having taken control of the remote from Shumi and switched to *Al-Jazeera* to catch the latest about the revolution re-shaping the Arab world, I have a schizophrenic moment. Where am I? Trying to detach from reality and living in multiple realities simultaneously. I am in a village that is and isn't an isolated corner lopped off from modernity, I can connect to the internet, can watch a revolution unfolding thousands of miles away, but I can't go for a walk alone without being stared at. Women have started wearing burqas which they didn't forty years ago, and girls like Shumi are being pulled out of school, and their bodies groomed for marriage.

God, where stands this village in your universe? Where stand I? Which loop of space-time am I trapped in?

The next morning, following Fuzi's wish, she and I walk between fields from the back of her house to pay our respect to Boro Ma. She lives in a small mud and tin house. The front room is very small and its roof sloping and low. Boro Ma is old, much older than Fuzi, and very bent. She has to be escorted into the room. Her daughter-in-law seats her next to me. I say salaam, and wait for Fuzi to explain who I am. Boro Ma extends her bony hand criss-crossed with bulging veins and takes my hand. All the time we are there, she doesn't let go of my hand. She doesn't speak a word but from the varying pressure of her hand in mine, tries to convey her feelings about my coming to see her.

I hand the box of sweets we have brought to the daughter-in-law. I can tell our visit was expected because she soon disappears into the back room and when she returns, she is holding a tray with tea in dainty china cups which probably came with her dowry, and special snacks she has made.

'How old is this house?' I ask Fuzi.

'Very old. I don't know how old. Ali's grandfather built it.' She and Boro Ma had quarrelled and learned to get on with each other in this house before Fuzi was moved to the new pukka house built by her husband, with his retirement money and help from his sons working in the Gulf.

'Ali is lucky. His grandfather's house still stands,' I say enviously, recalling my demolished hopes at 152 Sirajuddaula Road.

'People don't like mud houses, they're a lot of work, and difficult to keep clean,' Boro Ma's educated, city-bred daughter-in-law says in a smooth-toned voice. 'These days people prefer pukka houses.'

I look with longing at the thick mud walls of the house which keep it cool in summers and warm in winters, its smoke-darkened wood, and the smooth bamboo rafters on which its tin roof rests. What could be wrong with such a house? But then I don't have to plaster it with fresh mud or place pots under its leaky roof in the monsoons. There are large colourful wall posters, probably bought from the city to conceal the brownness of the mud walls. One of them is a Dutch tulip garden inscribed with: *Imagination rules the world*; another, a close-up of Sydney's Opera House under crystalline skies: *God loveth the clean*. Another bewildering moment: in a mud house tucked away in a corner of a little country called Bangladesh, its walls reflecting, like love unrequited, a faraway world so spruce, so alien, so unattainable . . .

~

Fuzi has been filling a sack with goodies for me to take back: betel nuts and tamarind from her trees, coconuts, and freshly made gur. And even a bottle of date palm syrup. 'Take some fish with you,' she says. The village boys had dived in and caught some fresh tilapia in their nets.

'Fish? I'll get thrown out of the train!'

'When will you come again? I won't live forever.'

'Build me a small bamboo hut in your yard. I'll pay for the bamboo and the roof. Then I'll come.'

I don't think she believed me, but at that moment, I am certain I could spend a couple of months holed up in a bamboo cottage next to her house, reading and staring out at the pond and the fields and breaking the perfect stillness only with the morning call of koels. But I also know such mornings wouldn't be as perfect and as still as I imagined them. There'd be inevitable interruptions, irritations, and inconveniences.

The morning when I have to leave for Dhaka arrives. Fuzi is upset because I am not extending my stay. She tries to feed me more insistently to ward off her sorrow, and wakes me up early with a cup of tea. Ali has called his friend, an auto driver, to come at five-thirty. At six there is still no sign of him. Fuzi, Shimu and I stand outside the house, wrapped in our shawls, scouring the empty, fogged-up street for signs of an approaching auto. Ali curses the dishonesty of Bangladeshis and sets off on foot to find another auto. I try not to feel anxious about missing the train.

The sky is painted pale lavender and pink just above the fields to the east, and a gigantic electricity pylon is blocking the view. I cross over to get a closer look. Closed bean blossoms lie innocently curled up on the wire fence at the field's edge, and a dense mist hangs like white sheets above the stubble of harvested crops. I am in a freshly-created landscape, and I would never witness a quieter, more sublime dawn. I turn back and see the two waiting women huddled against the softly-glinting tin gate. Fuzi is curious at what is so special to have drawn me away, and Shumi is standing with folded arms and downcast eyes. She hasn't spoken to me at all since I told her I didn't like to be followed around the house.

I walk up to her and take off my earrings and press them into her palm. 'For you, so you won't forget me. Thanks for all you did to make me comfortable,' I say in Hindi. She says nothing, but I know she has understood, being from generation Bollywood.

Then she mumbles, 'Why are you giving away your earrings to me? Your ears mustn't remain empty.'

'I have others. But you go back to school. Marriage can wait.'

Just then we hear the whir of an autorickshaw and see its squat greenness emerge from the mist. The three of us hug and I climb in. Ali clicks on his mobile stopwatch to time our journey from home to station.

'Twenty-two minutes,' he announces when we finally reach. This time, the train isn't late and I am glad I don't have to put up with Ali much longer. Nobody pays attention to the prayer recitation on the speakers because most passengers are dozing off or making calls. During the six-hour journey back to Dhaka, I reckon my losses and gains. I hadn't found my house. Memories of dadima and her simmering pot of guava pulp would have to recede to some seldom-opened memory chest. But I had found another house where at least two women would welcome me with love if I returned. Fuzi and Shumi. Fuzi's carefully packed sack of goodies is resting snugly on the luggage rack. I want to put aside my cynicism and think of them as precious offerings of love. It isn't just because she had worked for my family, or because my family had continued to send her money over the years, or because she expected me to continue this relationship. Maybe there was some element of selfishness in her affection. But love could mingle and coexist with self-concern; in fact, it would be extremely naïve to expect it not to.

11

Love, War and Widows

Mahmuda with her first husband, a love killed by war

Before I left Dhaka, I got a call from a war widow. She said she had listened to me read from *Ghalib at Dusk*, my book of short stories, and wanted to meet me.

'I'll pick you up tomorrow afternoon,' she said. 'I've just finished reading all the stories in your book. "Mehru and Zainab"—their love story was so beautiful. And "Trains"— how do you know so much about men?'

'I watch men,' I said.

'Yes, yes!' she laughed. 'I can tell. My husband is that kind of man, like the man in your story "Trains". I also have to call him three times before he answers the phone. I wait between the second and third time, to give him time to answer. So he can't say he never heard it ring.'

I gave her directions to Dollar Villa but then remembered cars couldn't drive all the way up to the building. Two concrete pillars at the entrance to the lane allowed cycle-rickshaws in but not larger vehicles. The next afternoon, she called me to let me know she'd pick me up in ten minutes and we'd have tea at the Golf Club. I tied up my hair and checked my clothes. There was no time to change. She wouldn't mind crumpledness. She couldn't expect a writer to be dressed like her Golf Club friends.

I walked down in my kurta and khaki pants, both handed down to me by a friend, to the intersection with the concrete pillars. A few minutes later, a sleek grey sedan pulled up and her driver stepped out and held the door for me. I was standing next to the street corner garbage dump. A thin woman in a faded saffron sari was sifting through the garbage, looking for sellable recyclables, and she watched me as the driver got out and held the door. I felt pried open and laid bare before her eyes.

Over the phone I had mistaken Mahmuda for somebody else—I was confusing her with the tall, smokey-eyed, elegant, fifty-something, string-of-pearls woman I had met at the book reading, who asked me if the grey in my hair was age or if I was sporting the newest salt-n-pepper trend.

'I confess, the only thing real about me is Lóreal,' she had declared, charmed by her own witticism.

Mahmuda, seated in the backseat, was certainly not the demure Lóreal lady at the café. Her face was flushed and something seemed chaotic about her. Bright in a lemon outfit, lots of gold on her neck and wrists. Effusive and lively.

Mahmuda shook her head at the worsening traffic and changed her mind about going to the Golf Club that afternoon. 'But where should we go where we can talk without being disturbed?' she asked me, and before I could think of a reply, she was giving instructions to the driver to take us to Prabartana. During the drive, she continued to scold the driver though I didn't think he was doing a bad job. Speeding isn't a possibility on Dhaka's congested streets. All the car owners I met in Dhaka employed drivers. Driving in Dhaka is a speciality requiring nerves of steel, infinite patience and a sense of humour. When we reached Prabartna, we walked up to the women's adda on the fourth floor. I was craving Bangali sweets but at Prabartana they only had a baked pudding for dessert. Mahmuda called up the driver, and gave him detailed instructions for getting gur sandesh from a nearby sweet shop. I could see what a pro she was at organizing and handling subordinates. The driver returned several minutes later, a little out of breath, but carrying the wrong kind of sandesh. Mahmuda gave him a good scolding, repeated her instructions in even greater detail, and sent him back. Finally, he returned with the right sandesh: beige, velvet-soft, made-to-melt fragrant squares of sweetness. I felt sure he cursed us on each step of the four flights he'd had to climb twice. But putting myself in his shoes was a fleeting departure from more urgent tasks. We devoured the sandesh with tea and I got ready to listen to Mahmuda's story.

She talked as if she would never talk again.

'When you were telling us you were born in Chittagong at the café, after your reading, did you see my face? Did you see I was about to cry?'

I hadn't.

But I could now. A network of crimson veins criss-crossed under the skin of her cheeks. She was starting to cry softly now. 'Do you know how long I waited, how long I searched for my husband in Chittagong? I was like a crazy woman. The Pakistani army picked him up, and never returned him to us. Afterwards, I went searching for my husband in the mass graves. I thought I'd recognize him from the ring on his finger. But where was I to find his hand among all those rotting bodies? I never thought there would come a day when I would call myself a war widow. But I'm not a war widow. I'm a freedom fighter's widow. He died for his nation. If I ever meet that Pakistani brigadier I'd like to ask him what they did with my husband's body.'

'We had gone into hiding at my sister's house just before the military got my husband. We lived on top of a hill and my sister's house was across the hill from ours. The Pakistani army ransacked our house. We had left the house just that morning. They smashed all my flower pots. All ninety-one of them. All around the hill was strewn my household. I remember watching my things roll down the hill—the children's pram and their toys.

'I had to give up waiting for my husband. I didn't know when I could start calling myself a widow but I had to start living and working. I started learning to drive. People thought I was crazy to do such a thing when the situation was so unsafe. There were hardly any women drivers in those days. I had two daughters to bring up so I had to think like a man. I was wearing white saris like a widow and I was looking for a job.

'I had also started going to this holy man we called Pagla Pir. All the desperate women were going to him as if he could locate their husbands and sons. I thought he'd have a vision, or pass on some message about my husband's whereabouts. I still didn't believe my husband was dead. I started going regularly to Pagla Pir's evening sessions at his house. He used to comfort all the young women who came to him. They'd ask if he could "see" their husbands. He would tell them, "yes, yes, I can see him, he's going to return to you soon." One day I said to him, "please, just tell me the truth, don't give me false hopes." So he didn't say anything at all. I said to him, "why aren't you speaking? Why don't you say something?"

"'What do you want me to say?" he said. "Tell me if I'll find him," I said. "There's nothing to find," he said. "What do you think you'll find? All you'll ever find are his *sara gulla* bones, if you find anything." I felt so humiliated when he said that—*sara gulla*—rotten, decayed. I stopped going to him. But when I got an offer to teach at Dhaka college, I went back to ask him if I should accept it. "Go, go immediately, don't waste a minute, don't lose this opportunity," he said. "You're an educated woman. Do what you think best." Women cursed him later for lying and giving them false hopes. But I think he was doing what he could. What else could he do for all these weeping women who kept coming to him?'

Mahmuda looked away and wiped her eyes. She was light-skinned, and the little red veins under her skin made her face flush as if it were the map of her soul, carrying the pain and beauty of her like the cracks in the kitchen floor of Dollar Villa. She fell silent but this was the only break from talking she took that afternoon. I became distracted by the gentle movement of her gold chain. A tiny blue vein pulsed in her neck, making the gold chain heave with each intake of breath. Was it her fragmented, divided self, her loneliness, or the unceasing shock of lovelessness that made Mahmuda so garrulous that afternoon?

I am a kid and we are living in Dhaka around the time when the liberation war is swallowing Mahmuda's husband. Schools are closed for most months of 1971. One day my father comes home looking whiter than usual. The colour of his skin has won him the dubious privileges of a white man among brown men. Today his colour has saved his life. He has just escaped the clutches of the Mukti Bahini, thanks to his driver's ingenuity. Pretend to be a foreigner, sahib, just read your newspaper when they ask questions. I'll deal with them. The driver says my father is a foreign journalist. He speaks no Bangla. As soon as my father enters, he relates this incident to my mother. I can see he's afraid. He calls up relatives in a part of town that is deemed safer, and later that day, we leave our house and move to theirs.

I'm playing up on the terrace of that old house. We aren't allowed to step outside. The lane outside the house is deathly still during the curfewed days and nights. But inside the house joy and warmth and companionship reigns as if there is no war. It seems like most happy, ordinary households. We, the children, think of our confinement as an unending in-house picnic. At mealtimes, we eat at the long table before the adults sit down to their meal. There's an elderly grandmother who spreads out her paandaan and chops betel nuts and tells us stories with her mouth full of paan. But she only tells stories when we pester her too much. I watch her paan and spit-filled mouth move as she speaks. The adults seem tight-lipped and discuss the political situation at every meal, but we never stick around to listen. We prefer the raja-rani stories of the betel-leaf chewing grandma. Or we run up to play on the roof. I smoke my first bidi in a little attic-like room.

A nation is coming into being; my birthplace is going through renewed birth pangs. There are fighter jets, kidnapping and looting and raping, but I have no idea who's looting whom, who's bombing whom, whose men are raping whose women or why. I am a child. And my unseeing eyes and my unfettered heart finds joy in the house-house games we play up on the roof while real houses and real people are being pulled down and torn to pieces. My nine-year old heart has no room for harbouring hate. After the war ends, and it's safe enough to return, we come back to our house in Dhanmondi. I miss the stories the grandmother used to tell, I miss watching her red mouth, and hearing her paan-clogged voice, but most of all, I miss all those friends I made, and the hours of house-house we played on the roof. My playmates are gone and the month-long picnic has ended. I stand at the window of my room in the Dhanmondi house during long days of no school, and gaze out at the once-lively but now deserted street, wondering what has changed, since everything has changed. Somehow the square of world I can see outside my window seems sadder and quieter. But nobody's willing to explain anything to me in language my nine-year old mind can comprehend.

Around this time Mahmuda has stopped searching the mass graves and has given up hopes of identifying her husband's ringed finger among the sara-gulla corpses. His return is beginning to seem far-fetched, especially after Pagla Pir told her she's not even likely to find his sara-gulla bones.

'I wish I could put your story in my book,' I broke the silence.

'I was hoping you'd say that,' Mahmuda smiled from the corners of her still-moist eyes.

'Okay, let me ask you something. Tell me honestly how do you feel about what the Pakistanis did?' I asked a little uncertainly, not sure how she would treat this question coming from somebody whose family had migrated to Pakistan because they felt threatened in the newly-born Bangladesh.

'I don't hate the Pakistani people! No, no. I only hate what the Pakistani army did to this land, I hate what they did to the Bangladeshi people. My life has taken me to so many South Asian countries. My father was posted in Pakistan in the 50s. I attended a Bangla-medium school in Karachi in the 50s, can you believe that? A Bangla-medium school in Karachi! I'm a citizen of the subcontinent. I know one day this whole region will become united, it'll evolve into something like the European Union.'

'If we're to be united, why so much violence and bloodshed and rapes?' I asked her helplessly. 'Doesn't that make all the wars and hatred we've lived through totally meaningless?'

'Of course it does. Do you know it was my Jewish professor at Fletcher who made me read the Quran? He said read it again and again. And each time you read it, you'll understand more. When I read the Quran, Pickthall's translation, I understood that we have all the ethical principles of living peacefully and harmoniously. But we're just not following any of those principles. So of course, we have to suffer the violence and the ugliness.'

I loved her for what she had just said about the possibility of an eventual coming together of South Asian nations into a oneness, a foreseeable future of peace. It revealed a rare generosity of spirit. She, who lost all she loved to a mindless war, was more spiritual a being to me than the Pagla Pirs. More spiritual than those in-charge of disseminating spiritual blessings. I recalled Firdaus Hyder's unshaken belief: our turbulent times is the admission ticket to a new era of a peaceful, global consciousness, she had said. I recalled her exhorting me to think of myself as a citizen of the cosmos. 'You're not just a Muslim or a Pakistani or an Indian or a Bangladeshi,' she'd said. 'Stop defining yourself so narrowly.' Be a little more reckless, she meant. As I had done in that moment, I did in this one: I claimed Mahmuda, this strong, opinionated, generous, and forgiving woman as my mentor. She was one of the true twenty-first century prophets, carrying forth mazhab-e-ishq, the religion of love, of peace, of sisterhood and selfhood.

'Before I got married, I was a student of political science at Dhaka University,' Mahmuda continued. 'And later, I went to Fletcher on a government scholarship for my second Masters in international law and diplomacy. But you know, I was never a serious student at Dhaka University. All I wanted was to get married and be a good wife, and write cookbooks. But life had other plans for me. The crux of my story is that my life made me the first woman ambassador of Bangladesh. That's not what I had planned for myself. I just wanted to be a lovey-dovey housewife, the wife of a very, very loving husband. I didn't know I was going to end up as a war widow. And after the war, did I know I would represent my nation as a diplomat? Now my mother, she never wanted me to be just a housewife. She wanted me to get a PhD! She never got a chance to study because she was married off at fourteen. So the war made her dreams for me come true! There's one thing I learned from all those books I was forced to read,' Mahmuda mused. 'The history of humanity is painted with blood. Europe's so developed now, but look at what Europe had to go through. They lived through hundreds of years of bloodshed and wars. But do you know what's the saddest thing? We're capable of so much love but we've lost the capacity to love selflessly. That's what we're not paying much attention to. To love. I have tasted selfless love, even if very briefly. But I know it exists. You see, that's why I ask God, why did you give me a taste of such love, and take it away so cruelly? My first husband really loved me. He was very caring. We were married five years when the war broke out. We had two daughters. We were an ideal family. I'll show you photographs when you come to my house.'

We were lingering on beyond our second pot of tea. Mahmuda was unaware of time but I had noticed the puzzled glances from the staff. There weren't too many people in the café at that hour, so Mahmuda's loudness, her emotion-ridden voice, and her flushed face had only the staff's muted attention. Since most of our conversation was in English, they could only watch the mime.

'Everybody is dying for want of love, but there's no love to be found. Like water, it's disappearing from the planet. There's such an erosion of values everywhere,' she continued, shifting from political philosophy to the personally political. The liberation of Bangladesh may have made it possible for her to enter the foreign service, a privilege hitherto reserved exclusively for men, but it didn't make it any easier for women diplomats to be taken seriously as diplomats by the largely male establishment. 'I stayed a widow-in-waiting for so many years. I didn't know what to call myself. It was many years before I agreed to remarry, thirteen years after my husband's disappearance. But the second time I didn't marry for love. I married because a woman without a husband is a second-class citizen. In the diplomatic service my male colleagues would poke fun at me for being so uptight. "Madam, why do you put up such a barricade around yourself? You laugh and joke with us but you don't let us get close to you." Even my boss wanted my attention. Once I presented him with a volume of Tagore's stories. I've always loved Tagore since I was a child. He looked at the book, and smiled. "Everybody gifts me books. You have so much else to give, you can gift me something better," he said. I came home and flung myself on my bed and cried all night. This is what he thought of me! To him I was not an employee. I was just a woman. May be a little more thrilling to spend time with than a Tagore book.

'Even my own parents didn't respect me when I showed up at their doorstep as a widow. I came back to live with them after my husband disappeared, and they welcomed me. But my sister, who had a husband, was always more welcome. As a married woman her status was higher than mine. My father went out of his way to buy a bed for my sister because she had her husband to sleep with. He didn't mind if I slept on the floor with my kids.'

I looked at Mahmuda. I was sitting across from one of the first women in Bangladesh's foreign service, the first woman ambassador of her country, a diplomat who had represented her country in several countries, and hobnobbed with the world's top political leaders. Yet she seemed as disconsolate, insecure and lonely as a runaway teenager. Her hurt, astonished face reminded me of a young girl who'd just been dumped by her first love.

'I was in Selfridges once,' she went on. 'I live in London half the year and I spend the winters in Dhaka. So I was in Selfridge's and I suddenly burst out crying in the ladies' room. The women asked me why I was crying. Was I depressed? Was I lonely? No, no, I'm not depressed, I'm not lonely, I said. I have a family, I have daughters, I have a mother, I have brothers, I have a husband. But what I couldn't tell them was, I don't have love! I was crying for love! I could buy anything from Selfridges I wanted. But I wanted somebody to buy it for me as a gift of love.'

'You mean your second husband? You wanted him to buy gifts for you?'

'Yes, but such a thing would never occur to him. And yet we live together. So, you want to know why I live with him? Why do women live with their useless husbands? They either need the money or they have kids. Neither of those things is true in my case. So why do I keep my husband?'

She started listing the reasons. Initially she had hoped for love and companionship. But that was not to be, so he was best as a symbolic helmet for warding off undesirable male attention. He was charming. He was learned and lovable. He impressed her friends, her parents revered him, and he was good for taking to weddings and parties. She liked to talk, and he was somebody she could talk to, if not talk with.

She retired from the foreign service in 2000. After her children grew up and left home, she felt she would go out of her mind from loneliness. Besides, he himself was too old now, and completely dependent on her, so how could she ask an old, dependent man to move out?

'I can talk to you. You're a writer. You know men. You'll understand. He's like the man you wrote about in "Trains". I can't talk to my friends like this. They adore him. They call him dulha bhai. Should I tell you what made me cry in Selfridges? I was posted to Abu Dhabi, and he had to go off to London. I was to meet him in London after a few days. He asked me to bring his driver's licence with me. When I went to look in his desk, I found letters from his girlfriends, from before our marriage and even after our marriage. When I arrived in London, I was crying but I allowed him to make love to me, and as I was holding on to him, squeezing his body into mine, as if I wanted to squeeze the very life out of him, I hated myself for being so weak. I polluted my body with his touch but I vowed never to let him pollute my womb, so I never had children with him. He continued having relationships with many women. He was a good-looking man and women found him very charming. Women flirted with him and he treated them like kites. They came and fell into his aangan, his courtyard, and when he was done playing with them, he sent them flying off. I wasn't anybody special for him!'

'How would he feel if I write your story and all this is mentioned? How would you feel?'

'Oh, write it all! I don't care. I've retired from the foreign service and why should I be ashamed? Tell my story. May be some woman will learn something. Women are always getting fooled by men who pretend to love them. This man too pretended to love me, but he only loved my body, my glamour, my position as a diplomat. Did he care for my soul? No. He didn't even look for my soul. Now my first husband, he was the one who loved my soul. I say I hate this man, but you know, I also love him. How can I explain? My heart is like that. Love is not only about getting love. Love is about giving love.'

I couldn't understand her contrariness. Loving him and hating him. But in the language of love, in the incoherence of the heart, loving and hating the same person was perfectly possible.

For our next meeting, early one morning, before the traffic grew frenzied, Mahmuda picked me up and we drove to the Golf Club. We sat down at one of the tables under the covered verandah, looking out on to the golf course. The clipped, grassy course wore a soft sheen in the just warming day. A few men in uniform were working on it with garden hose and lawn mowers. In a few minutes the husband joined us. He looked like a pile of freshly laundered and ironed clothes after his morning swim. He was dignified yet boyish, white-haired, bushy eyebrows, and tall. I could tell from the way his lower lip hung out in a pout every time he smiled that he still coveted his reputation of unsettling female hearts.

Tea and sandwiches arrived while Mahmuda was chatting on about her Indian golf coach who coached her when she was the Bangladeshi ambassador in Bhutan.

'Tell me how the two of you met,' I said, tossing out the invitation to either one of them. But of course, the ball was caught by Mahmuda. She made it clear I was her guest that morning, and it was her story I would hear.

'Do you know how I got fooled into saying yes to him?' She was talking animatedly, almost flatteringly, consoling the charismatic old gentleman, who didn't quite know what to make of me, a writer, interested in his wife's life story. 'The first time I met him at his house, he was carrying a baby in his arms. It was his niece's baby. And he was holding the baby in such a caring way. I had never seen a man hold a baby like that! How can I describe it, it was a motherly way. I was nervous. This was our first meeting. So I just burst out laughing when I saw him with the baby, and he told me later that it was the way I laughed that made him propose to me. It sounds so romantic, doesn't it?'

I looked at the husband. He was shaking his head and smiling, his pouty lower lip taking years off him.

'It does sound romantic! Is that true? Did you decide to marry her for the way she laughed?' I asked him specifically.

'The baby part is true,' he said, chewing his sandwich, and avoiding me, gazing shyly at the golf course. 'The rest is her imagination.'

Mahmuda looked miffed.

We talked. He asked me about my Bangladesh connection. He told me he had always been a Leftist in his student days. 'I still am a Leftist at heart,' he said in a voice lacking conviction. 'But these days,' he said, 'I'm also turning to spiritualism, especially Sufism.' He was a member of the

Ibn Arabi society and he attended their symposia regularly when he was in London. 'Only Sufism or socialism has the power to save us,' he said.

'I am afraid of all kinds of fundamentalisms,' I said.

'Bengal has a very long history of intellectual and spiritual movements. Buddhism. Sufism. Hinduism. There's no room for growth of fundamentalism here,' he said.

'But you must have watched the Biswa Ijtema on TV? The Tableeghis held it this year in two phases, not one! You don't think the Tableeghi influence in Bangladesh is anything to worry about?'

'Fringe elements,' he pronounced. 'Not a serious threat. Very peripheral.'

I'm sitting there, looking out at the sun-speckled golf course, listening to the soft clanking of forks and knives, and the sophisticated, muted voices of upper-class men and women over their morning tea. I'm barely paying attention to the white-uniformed bearers bringing in trays of food, and carrying out used cups and plates, moving about as unobtrusively as if their bodies were powered by silent motors. Yes, it is possible to believe that religious fundamentalism or any kind of extremism thrives on the fringes of society. Especially if you're having breakfast at the Golf Club, seated at the rim of a soft, serene, dew-soaked golf course, it's easy to forget about the 'fringe elements'. You imagine yourself at the centre, and the millions on the fringes fade from your expansive consciousness.

Mahmuda asked me to stay for lunch and from the club the three of us drove to her lake-front apartment overlooking a placid lake in a noise-free, people-free, pollution-free neighbourhood. Seated by her long balcony windows we had more tea. Her husband left, tucking a book under his arm, to attend a meeting to discuss Ibn Arabi, the medieval mystic-philosopher, with his reading group. Before he left, he gave me a copy of a paper on Sufism he had presented at a conference in Delhi some years ago. I glanced at the title: 'Diversity of Religions from a Sufi Perspective.' It seemed interesting enough so I ran my eyes over the first page:

'According to Abdullah Yousuf Ali, before and after Mohammad's life on the earth, all who bowed to God were "Muslims" and their religion was Islam.' What? Really? I read a little more: 'In his commentary on verse 68:35[1] of the Quran, he (Abdullah Yousuf Ali) writes: 'Through this work I have translated the term "Muslim" and "Islam" in accordance with their original connotation, namely as "one who surrenders himself to God". It shall be understood that the use of the term to indicate its exclusive application to the followers of Mohammad represents a post-Quranic development.'

I read that sentence again and again—the one about not limiting the definition of Muslim to the followers of Mohammad. The sentence filled me with jubilation, and also something bordering on seismic shock. Muslim can be a non-specialized label, a label for any soul that submits

---

[1]Shall We then treat those who have surrendered as We treat the guilty? Quran, 68:35, Marmaduke Pickthall's translation, http://www.khayma.com/librarians/call2islaam/quran/pickthall/surah68.html.

itself to divine will? Relief at last! Islam could then be a purely spiritual state, a state of living in submission to Truth, to the One Intelligence, so any seeker of Truth could lay claim to being in a state of submission to the Truth? A Christian could be a Muslim, a Hindu could be a Muslim, and a Muslim could be a Christian or Hindu! It didn't matter as long as they were all seeking the same truth. He may not have been a faithful husband to Mahmuda, but on this one point, her husband and I connected, and we became ham-khayals, like-minded souls.

But, wait.

Hold the ecstasy! Mahmuda's sophisticated Leftist-Sufi husband and I could wash away differences in the ocean of oneness. But the teeming multitudes on the banks of Turag river, the Tableeghis I met on the bus from Kolkata, their hopes fettered by daily defeats, could they buy into such expansive, loose, liberal definitions of Islam? Where would they be, forgotten, superfluous beings, without recourse to religion for erecting demarcations and definiteness? Muslim and non-Muslim, believer and kafir, made a difference in their lives. They could be fringe elements, contemptible in the eyes of those in the centre, but they could stake their claims as God's chosen people. Segregated from the world's elite, the real evildoers, what could they turn to, except congregational prayers, rituals and rites for succour? The millions who were squirming on the fringes, why would they dole out Islam to all the world as a non-definite, non-separate, non-special, 'come one, come all' identity?

Mahmuda went into the kitchen to give instructions for lunch. Through the filigree of coconut fronds outside the window, the Gulshan-Banani lake sparkled like a green jewel tossed out forgetfully into the mayhem of Dhaka. It was hard to gauge how polluted the lake was from here. It seemed untouched, virginal. Birds were chirping, and a jogger or two traipsed past in expensive-looking sneakers on the path along the perimeter of the lake. Tea was brought in by a soundless maid, and poured out by Mahmuda from an ornate silver teapot into delicate china cups. As I sipped it, the noisy sewer rats that visited Dollar Villa nightly fought for attention with the lullaby-like space I was sitting in now, and the mystical cracks in the kitchen's red cement floor crackled as if they were begging to be etched afresh in my mind. The tea I made in the dark mornings, the pot I rinsed out assuming the rats must have traversed it in the night, were prodding the mind like giant question marks. I was resting my back against luxurious leather, I was surrounded by paintings and books and silence, but the giant question marks kept knocking for answers. They wanted to know if what my eyes saw was real? Or what the heart sensed was real? Was all the eye saw real? Was all well in this world, and all possible worlds?

Mahmuda came back. She had a folder full of old photographs. There was one of her as a captivating woman with large-kohl-lined eyes and thick long hair, posing with her first husband. I couldn't take my eyes off it. It was a black-and-white portrait of a good-looking young man and his wife. He looked as if he had found the answer to his soul's search in her, and she looked contented to be the answer.

'He was a very good-looking man!' I said.

'He's dashing, isn't he? But do you know how caring he was? He always showed it in little ways,' she said. 'When I first moved into his house, after the wedding, he emptied out all his closets for me. I had a lot of clothes and things, and they wouldn't fit into just one closet. He put his clothes in a cabinet in the study. There was a cook, but sometimes I liked to cook even though I didn't know how to cook well in those days. Once he invited his friend to dinner. I tried to make pulao and mutton curry. I had been adding water and simmering the mutton all day. But the meat was still tough. I was sitting on the verandah of our bungalow, and eating pine nuts someone from West Pakistan had gifted me, with his friend. And this friend, he started reciting a poem in praise of my long hair. My husband tried to appreciate the poem, but I could tell he was very jealous. He kept quiet. And when dinner was served, it was he who praised me like I had cooked the best curry in the world. And the curry was full of water! His friend ate very little of the mutton, but my husband ate the most, praising my cooking.'

I stared at the photo of her honest, loving police officer husband while she talked. His courage, his idealism, his innocence, his belief in a just, predictable world poured out of his eyes. But something else also seemed to be pouring out—a faraway look, a prescience, as if he knew his happiness would not last.

'But with this gentleman, my present husband, it's the opposite. It's all lies and lies with him.'

The maid came in to announce lunch was ready. We went into the dining room. Her husband joined us. He was just back from his reading group's meeting. He looked at me questioningly to gauge how much of him his wife had betrayed to me. I smiled back reassuringly and asked him something about Ibn Arabi's concept of divine love. The table was laid out for a banquet. Chicken curry, shrimp curry, fish curry, papaya salad, pulao, stir fried vegetables, and I can't even remember what else. I had to taste a little bit of everything as Mahmuda had gone to such lengths to cook it all herself. When I could eat no more, it was time to have dessert. Gur sandesh! But gur sandesh tastes very different depending on what degree of satiety you are attacking it with.

We moved back to the leather chairs by the balcony and tea was brought in. Mahmuda's husband pulled out a book from his collection and in answer to my question about love, recited these lines from Ibn Arabi:

My heart can take on many forms:
A meadow for gazelles,
A cloister for monks,
For idols, secured ground,
Kaa'ba for the circling pilgrim,
The tales of Torah,
The scrolls of the Quran,
My creed is love;

Wherever its caravan turns along the way,
That is my belief,
My faith.[2]

I made a note of the metaphor of a cloister and a meadow
for the heart, and gazelles as an infinitude of images that can
live wihin the human heart. I felt ready to shed a few tears
myself. If only Ibn Arabi could come back to this age of
ours, if only we could have tea together and discuss poetry.

'These people sit for hours in silence after they read one
line from Ibn Arabi,' Mahmuda said of his reading group,
laughing. She didn't want to lose me to a discussion on Ibn
Arabi with her husband, or let me lapse into a reverie at that
moment. 'I read a whole Ibn Arabi book in one night. And
what did he have to say? He said you can't understand God
with words. God is unknowable. So what's there to read and
understand if you can't ever really come to know God?' she
laughed again. 'I already knew that!'

Her husband sensed she didn't want him around, and
excused himself, smiling his pouty, boyish smile. He retired
for his afternoon nap.

'All he wants to do is discuss Sufism or politics with me.
Every night,' she said. 'And I'm not interested in those

---

[2]Muhyiddin Ibn Arabi (1165 -1240 AD): Mystic, philosopher, poet, sage,
Ibn Arabi is one of the world's great spiritual teachers. This translation is
from Poem 11 of his *Tarjuman al-Ashwaq* translated by Michael A. Sells,
Stations of Desire: Love Elegies from Ibn Arabi and New Poems (2000); Ibis
Edition. Also available at http://www.ibnarabisociety.org/poetry/ibn-arabi-
poetry-index.html.

things. Not just before going to bed. I told him I'll sleep in a separate room. But he's scared. He won't let me do that either. The other night we had an argument. And I sat up, watching TV till late. I didn't go to the bedroom. He kept calling me. But I didn't go. I said I'll come in only when my show is over.' She paused. And picked up the photo of herself and her first husband. 'He knows I've shared everything about him with you. That's why he got up and left us now. He's ashamed.'

'How do you know he knows?' I asked.

'I know. From his face. There was a pleading in his eyes when I was talking to you. He knows he can't be a hero like my first husband was for me. And a man always wants to be his woman's hero. But he knows he can never be mine. That's his curse. He has to live with it. I curse myself for being so harsh with him at times and I feel sorry for him at other times. I do love him in my own way. Why have I failed so miserably as far as love goes? I ask God why he made me so naïve? Why did I trust him and so many others so easily?'

'You are who you are may be because the universe needs you to be that way,' I said. 'Love is not just about getting love, it's about giving love, didn't you say that?'

'Yes. You must write about my courage. No disaster broke my back. I'm like a desert camel,' she laughed. 'I just keep going. I use laughter as my shock therapy to absorb all kinds of shocks to my system. This country has fought and established herself in the world arena, and I sacrificed my love, my home, my children's father for her sake.

'And, and, this is important. Don't forget to mention that

I removed the barricade for women in the foreign service. I took eighteen government officials' widows to Banga Bandhu's office and I said: what is to become of us? I fought and I made the Banga Bandhu sign the 10 percent quota for women into law. Before that, no women were allowed in the foreign service. War and widowhood turned me into a fighter. I hope I am making sense.'

'You are making perfect sense,' I said, reaching out a hand to hers.

~

After I return from Mahmuda's place, I make tea and go up to Dollar Villa's roof-top garden. Enterprising lady that she is, nani has planted a cornucopia of lemons, mango, pomegranate, guava in giant drums. I'm leaving Bangladesh to return to India and I'm not at all sure how I feel about the month spent here. I feel attached to this land, but like all nostalgic fools, am squinting at the changes and newness confronting me. The sadness is also perhaps due to hormonal changes, the coming on of menopause, or it's about my inability to define my place in the world, about confronting life's unseen challenges. The hot flashes are like an embarrassing interruption of functionality, but sometimes, when I'm sweating and sitting through one, like now, I feel I'm participating in a sacred sweat. I'm at the threshold of a new knowledge about my personal and biological life. My reproductive years are behind me, and the world can obliterate me as a middle-aged woman, but I feel very differently about myself: I'm reluctantly beginning to

celebrate myself, and celebrate the ending of my fears—
fears that plague most women, such as pregnancy, periods
and rape. But more profound fears too. The ones Mahmuda
is also struggling to free herself from. I'm freeing myself
from fears of failing to live up to expectations—my own and
those of others.

Fifty and finally free! I want to print this slogan on
everything I wear. The revolution of remaking me is mostly
invisible to the world and perhaps it should remain so. The
world can only see a greying, carelessly-dressed woman,
who shuns company and prefers staying in her room to
going out. My remaking may be accompanied by an
indefinable sadness at its fringes, the deep, deep sadness of
not belonging, and not having a space in the world to call
my own. But in the ever-expanding spaces within me, there's
no sadness, there's only spaciousness. Generous, and
brimming with self-acceptance.

The answer to the soul's question marks, mine or
Mahmuda's is this—there's a divine embrace unfolding for
us. Causes leading to causes. And the signs are in the ruby-
red sun sinking to my right, and the shy, glorious, almost
full moon rising to my left. It's a rare spectacle in Dhaka's
dusty skies, the sun and moon appearing together in the
evening sky, easily lost moments between night and day in
the dusky clamour of birds and mullahs and people who
hardly have the time or desire to look out for the sun and
the moon. I watch the sun drown, and the moon rise, each
moment lovelier than the one before it. In the growing
darkness, a soft, reassuring breeze begins to caress me.

There, there, the wise, eternal universe counsels—'I'm listening. I'm a witness to your restlessness.' Two sparrows come and perch on the branches of nani's dwarf mango tree. A young woman comes up to collect the washing on the neighbouring roof and leans out over the parapet, hoping to see someone special in the street below. The mullahs from all the mosques start shrieking, ostensibly calling the faithful to prayer, but making me want to ban loudspeakers and unmelodious prayer calls. I sit on the steps till the mosquitoes make it impossible to sit any longer.

As I'm writing this chapter, several months later, I remember a relevant story. In Lahore's Anarkali market, I had found a little book called *Heart-endearing Images of the Devil's Ardent Desires* (*Shaitan ki haseen arzuon ke dilfaraib manzar*). I had paid twenty rupees for it. I love buying populist literature, especially religious pamphlets from roadside stalls. They're inexpensive, unintentionally humorous, and their language is meant for the masses, and I read them as a useful indicator of what the populace is being fed. This booklet was filled with parables about antics used by the devil to entice and mislead people. There was one about an out-of-tune maulvi, whose azaan was an infliction from the devil, and served as an auditory insult for the villagers until the villagers collected enough money to get rid of the maulvi and sent him off on a pilgrimage to Mecca! That aesthetics matter, that being musical is a desirable attribute in one entrusted with calling the faithful to prayer, and lack of musicality is an affliction from the devil, even in a man of god, seemed a radically progressive view!

I was waiting for a revelation in Bangladesh, or at least some spiritual guidance to set my sails in the right direction for the future. But there was no miracle, no revelation, no future waiting to happen. There was only this, the right nowness, the unceasing unfolding of time, moment followed by the next moment. And some invisible force propping up my weak, flagging spirit—through the simultaneous appearance of the sun and moon in the evening sky, the writing that faltered but didn't stop, and the daily rituals of love my Dhaka housemates performed for me—making spiced tea, slicing carrots for my salad, begging me to stay a few more days. Divinity leaped out at me through the people and places and sights. They helped me give up the search for the extraordinary, for some divine disclosure to claim as my spiritual legacy.

Love is the simplest answer to all of life's conundrums and love is the ultimate goal of all creation. The only path to becoming one with the One. Ibn-e-Arabi was right: the human heart was the greatest repository of all the diverse strands of love in medieval times. And it still is. Love was the way to bring diverse peoples together. And still is. Love, simple and ordinary, and thankfully there is an infinite variety and quanitities of it to go around.

Mahmuda thinks of love as a fast-depleting, non-renewable resource. I don't agree.

I find myself becoming more fearless, and more assured that love's labours will never be lost after talking to the women who are in this book, and many more who I couldn't include. They're teaching me to pay less and less attention to my ego's exhortations. The ego still disapproves of my laziness, but it does so in spurts now, less insistently. I feel I'm finally turning to my writing with a sense of calm, crafting sentences as a means to self-revelation, rather than the immature goal of becoming a renowned writer. The travelling and dislocation, the reflections enroute, the returning to the land of my first origins, all carry seeds of self-knowledge, which ultimately affirm my everythingness and nothingness.

I have been rewarded through my peregrinations. I'm not leaving the land of the red sun empty-handed. I am carrying back the seeds of an inner quietude, and I see them sprouting in my face—in the changing expressions of my face. That's the real revolution—the spirit's inner revolution. Whether or not it is reflected in one's external visage is secondary.

12

Ocean of Possibilities

Stone screen at mausoleum of Sultan Ahmad Shah, the 15th century founder of city of Ahmedabad, Gujarat

Ahmedabad, March 2011

Marriage might be passé. Fast fading as a social custom, a hanger-on from the last century, but old-fashioned twentieth century marriage, the kind I got into, continues to confer many material benefits. If it didn't, society would have done away with the institution much earlier. If you happen to follow a non-productive vocation like writing, and don't make much money, you'll always be on the lookout for free-of-cost, quiet retreat-like spaces where you can hide from the world and write. Because I am my husband's legal spouse, I can request to have this space—his dad's apartment, for a few days of unfettered solitude. His father passed away, leaving this modest apartment to him. We came to Ahmedabad during the Holi break to settle some financial matters, but now my husband and daughters have left and I'm here alone.

I am alone!

My first solitary breakfast in Ahmedabad. Tea and chilled watermelon at my husband's father's kitchen table, accompanied by exultance in being the sole occupant of this flat. The most hard-to-get and harder to justify gift in married life is solitude. There's a koel singing outside the kitchen and I taste my freedom in her song, and drift into an even more unobstructed mindframe. I drift and drift. I'm shielded from the harshness of the March sun in this cool, dark kitchen. It's a place perfect for dreaminess. I lean back in my chair and prop my feet up on another, grateful for the koel, the silence, the aloneness, the watermelon. I play the music I want, savour the sweetness of watermelon on my tongue, and there's plenty of tea to last the whole morning. I can daydream the whole day away. Today and the next few days—all are mine to keep. Silence wraps me like a frayed quilt from childhood. Nobody calls, nobody rings the door bell, and if they do, I don't answer. I write out each element of this freedom for myself, broken down into its minutest components, and read out the list so I can begin to believe it.

I feel very free since I got back from Bangladesh. I can't describe the quality of this liberation—it's a purely imagined state, since not much in my material world can substantiate it. I have few material resources of my own for an independent existence. And yet, it is precisely in the absence of such material resources that I feel so free. I believe this freedom is the real thing, because it's there in and of itself—the freedom of the mind and soul. And it's independent of a job and savings and a place to live. Nothing, I feel, nothing can compare with this imaginal autonomy.

Slowly I start making other notes—about my meeting with Ayesha last night before the memories fade. These days, hormonal havoc and life changes have turned short- and long-term memory into an evanescent gift.

I bring my laptop to the kitchen table. And from my music folders select defiant music that pollutes the exclusively

Hindu, middle-class, incense-purified air of Naranpura.
The neighbourhood where my father-in-law's flat is located
is one of the oldest areas in the western part of the city,
predominantly filled with Hindus and Jains, most of them
Gujaratis.

Nusrat Fateh Ali Khan and Abida Parveen sing their Sufi
kalaam. I turn up the volume and hum with Abida:

Mai hun mashoor ishq bazi main
Khasa dard o gham majazi main

I am known for my love for the Beloved, for
worldly love only leads to pain and suffering

There are no Muslim households, no Muslims live here, no
nameplates outside houses in this locality bear a Muslim
name. I play my music all day, sometimes to block out the
bhajan singing and cymbal-clanging from the nearby temple.
Nobody told me this, but I need not be told that I have to be
silent about my Muslim-Hindu marriage in this locality.
I'm not to make my Muslimness known in this apartment
complex or this neighbourhood. When I meet my husband's
polite relatives, their assertion that life in Ahmedabad has
returned to 'normal' rings hollow. There are no communal
tensions between Hindus and Muslims anymore, they say.
Hindus are frequenting Muslim-owned restaurants and
businesses, and the Muslim community has even started
showing political support for Modi's government. So? So
what?

Slowly, I start jotting down random notes about my

meeting with Ayesha. I was put in touch with her through a common friend in Baroda. 'You must meet Ayesha,' my friend said. 'She's a young journalist working in Ahmedabad. Very outspoken, very passionate. And a poet too.'

Last night I came home close to midnight. Ayesha and I had gone out for dinner and afterwards I took an auto home. 'This is another paradox of Gujarat,' Ayesha said as we parted outside the restaurant. I asked if it was safe to take an auto so late. 'As a woman you can feel completely safe in Gujarat, but as a Muslim you can't.'

'But my in-laws say . . .' I stopped myself.

'I know, they're probably telling you everything is back to normal.' Ayesha smiled. 'And they are right. Except that the definition of normal has changed forever.'

I asked Ayesha if the Muslims of Gujarat were now supporting BJP.

'There isn't much difference between Hindu or Muslim Gujaratis. The trading community is very matter-of-fact when it comes to livelihoods. The Muslim businessman is trying to move on beyond 2002. So they're doing whatever it takes to ensure their survival.'

~

I'll understand what Ayesha meant by the changed definition of normality when Sarup Dhruv, a writer, peace activist, and cultural historian takes me out on a heritage walk in the old city. Sarup behn's passion is the architecture of the walled city of Ahmedabad. Through her eyes and words I'll come to witness another Ahmedabad—the city of stone mosques and exquisitely-carved Jain temples, not Ahmedabad the city of bloodshed, hatred, and communal violence. Sarup behn points out the 'border' on our return from Sarkhej. On one side of the 'border' live Muslims, and on the other side lives the non-Muslim population of Ahmedabad. The other side is where my father-in-law's apartment is located.

Ayesha is right about feeling safe as a woman in Gujarat. Gujarati men are very decent, at least in public. They don't stare at women. If you're lost, you can ask any policeman for directions and he'll help courteously. An auto driver never demands a rupee more than his meter reading just because you're a woman, or because it's the dead of night. In most North Indian cities, this isn't the case. Muslim or not, as a woman in a public space you're an object to be stared at, pursued, harassed in North India. I've never felt safe on the streets of Delhi or Allahabad the way I feel safe in Ahmedabad.

I watch a large white Holi moon rise from behind the funnel-shaped water reservoir. If it were without any blemishes would it be as entrancing? Across the street and beyond the railway tracks, it rises like a promise, floating up slowly above the water reservoir. I can see its milky aura around the concrete tank of the reservoir, much before I see the moon, and momentarily I mistake that milky light for street lights. Even the moon isn't perfect is my last thought. I fall asleep thinking not everything in nature appears perfect but then, perfection is a human delusion. If the perfect blue-white moon isn't without imperfections who am I to feel bad about mine? Later I am awakened by a sudden, intense heat wave starting from my forehead, and spreading down to my toes. I throw aside the quilt and sit up, wiping the sweat from my upper lip and forehead, and wait for the wave to pass. By now I've become used to these menopausal hot flashes. There's something forlorn in the way they happen, especially when I'm awakened in the night. They wake me up, and I wait for them to pass. They subside and I'm more or less the same as before, just more awake and enlarged of heart.

The nights of uninterrupted sleep are over. I get out of bed and move to the living room and open a window and lean against the grill to cool my face. I'm grateful for the breeze that rustles the newly-sprouted bronze-gold leaves of two solitary Ashok trees outside. The street looks beautiful and unused because it's so quiet. Somehow, these awakenings are not unwelcome. They are a part of the vast, spiritual-emotional mosaic that's evolving and emerging, the makings of the new me.

Two men are sitting on the railway tracks across the street. I see their Holi-stained shirts and the glint in their coloured hair in the sulphurous street lights. Another passes by on a bicycle. What are they awake for? Since when did Holi become a big festival for sedate, ledger-loving Gujaratis? I ask the same question a few nights later when I'm awakened by firecrackers and murderous shrieks and slogan-shouting. I peep out and see flags waved as young men whizz pass on motorcycles. I wonder with a loudly beating heart if another communal riot is breaking out. I stumble into the living room, turn on the TV and find hysterical men and women announcing India's winning of the world cup cricket against Pakistan. Sports is a war by other means—the adage never seemed more true.

It's perhaps not purely coincidental that the last chapter of this book coincides with other personal lasts. This feels like a last visit to Ahmedabad, the city I think of as my sasural, my in-laws's city. A city with which I have an association that has lasted as long as my marriage has. I may not come back, at least not to this locality, not if I drift out to some other kind of life. At this point I don't know what that life would look like. *Drifting* seems the right word to describe it. The most momentous personal upheavals have come quietly, sans fanfare or emotional fireworks. Like ivy, an inner resolution has grown, grown with an imprecise definiteness, and slowly transformed my entire existence. I say I'm drifting, but this inner drifting is not that aimless. I'm willing to let myself drift onto something elemental that will reveal the true me to me. Marriage was something I should have constantly been overwhelmed by, but how aware are we of the earth's circumambulation round the sun? The humdrumness, the sedateness of a more-or-less happy marriage dulls your senses to the magnitude of inequities required to keep it happy, rendering the drawn-out tragedy ordinary.

Recently Ayesha has moved from Baroda to the Ahmedabad office of her newspaper. She lives in a Hindu neighbourhood close to her office building. She gives me directions to her apartment. She is the only Muslim living in a Hindus-only apartment complex. She doesn't drive and she didn't want to spend time and energy commuting to work. So she looked for a place within walking distance of her office. That wasn't easy. Her employer had to step in to help her procure the apartment she now rents. She has to pay higher rent because she's a high-risk tenant, not because she's single and a woman and therefore a threat for respectable middle-class morality, but because she's a Muslim.

'But you know,' she smiles, 'I've become very stubborn and shameless. I stay here as a matter of principle. I know I'm not wanted here but I want to foist my presence on these people. Why should I be forced to fight battles like housing that are not of my choosing? I'd much rather work on issues other than discrimination against Muslims in housing and jobs. Issues that interest me far more. Such as land-grabbing by the land mafia. But I'm not given a choice. To be allowed to work on issues of my choice would be a great mental luxury for me.'

Two years after the 2002 communal riots, Ayesha went with her family to a mushaira, a gathering of poets in her hometown, Baroda. When some of the poets started reciting ghazals with the riots as the central theme, the Muslim organizers silenced them for fear of offending the Hindu sensibility of the mayor and high officials who were in the audience. This incident and the self-imposed silence of the mainstream Muslim literary community left a deep impact on Ayesha. Encouraged by her father's poet friends and her own desire to understand how ordinary Muslims were coping intellectually and emotionally with the scars left by the riots, she set out to travel throughout Gujarat to collect poetry from relatively unknown amateur Muslim poets or anyone who had penned a poem about their 2002 experiences and insights. This was an unusual step since the Muslim community has been mocked and maligned for its lack of literary sensibilities. The poems she culled from her travels over a two-year period surprised her. They were anthologized in a book called *Scattered Voices*.[1]

~

Sarup behn had given me a copy of *Scattered Voices* and before I went to meet Ayesha, I read some of the poems and the poets' profiles. One of the profiles seemed to fit the definition of the unacknowledged, out of the mainstream literateur. The English translation of Farooq Qureshi's ghazal wasn't as haunting or moving as the original Urdu which I would hear him recite later, but his profile fascinated me far more than his poetry at that moment:

'A butcher by profession, Ahmedabad-based Farooq Qureshi has begun to make his mark in mushairas. Having studied in Ahmedabad Municipal Corporation school up to Class Ten, Qureshi is a keen reader of Urdu literature. Prodded by uncle Shams Quershi, he carries on the literary tradition of his late grandfather, Ahmed Hussain Hazeen, who was a well-known poet of his time.'

---

[1]Ayesha Khan: *Scattered Voices: An Anthology of Poetry*; Books for Change, Delhi, 2008.

A butcher and a poet? A high school graduate from a Gujarati-medium municipal school, what did he know about nuanced Urdu poetry? An avid reader of Urdu literature? His grandfather a well-known Urdu poet? Ghalib, Mir, Sauda—the classical Urdu poets were the products of a highly stylized court culture that bred and patronized poets as professional poets. Their primary vocation was poetry. None followed any other profession, and certainly not something as unthinkable as butchery. I wanted to meet Farooq very much, and ask him what made him write poetry.

With directions from Ayesha, I set out to search for Farooq in the mutton and beef markets of Mirzapur in the old, predominantly Muslim part of Ahmedabad, in the mohallas on the other side of the Sabarmati river. It is 10 a.m., and still early for meat buyers when I arrive. The heavy stench of slaughtered meat greets me as soon as I enter the large hall. The hall is sectioned off into little stalls. A few butchers in blood-stained vests sit inside their stalls. Carcasses hang from hooks, hides are drying, and intestines lie in huge coiled masses on the floor. I am watched with great curiosity as I approach one of the butchers and ask if he knows Farooqbhai, the one who writes poetry, holding up my copy of *Scattered Voices*.

'Are you from one of the TV channels?' the butcher asks, pressing his mobile to his ear.

'No, I'm a writer, a friend of Ayesha Khan's, the one who did this book. And she told me about Farooqbhai. I would like to meet him.'

'He's not here yet. But his house is only five minutes away.'

The butcher transmits excitedly in very quick Gujarati into his mobile all that I have told him, and I get the sense that Farooqbhai has agreed to meet me. This is my first visit to a meat market in vegetarian Gujarat and the irony isn't lost on me. I stare at the various non-meat cattle body parts—hoofs, lungs and fat lying in tubs.

'Do you sell those things?' I ask, pointing at the tubs.

'Everything is sold.'

'Who buys them?'

'Poor people. It's cheaper than meat.'

'Poor Muslims?'

'Hindus. Muslims. Christians. Dalits.'

'Do Gujarati Hindus eat beef?' I ask in disbelief.

The butcher smiles at my ignorance.

I decide to wait near the entrance to the meat market to escape the solidity of that overpowering stench. In a few minutes a tall, thirtyish, heavy-set man in a blue T-shirt and white pajamas appears from the crowded streets filled with street vendors selling fruit, vegetables, plastics. There are no women other than me waiting at the entrance to the meat market, so he comes up to me unhesitatingly.

'*Asalamalaikum, aap Farooqbhai hain?*'

He smiles and nods. '*Jee.* Ayesha sent you? Why don't you come to my house? We can talk there.'

A few minutes' walk through the crowded bazaar, and we reach his house, a messy, cluttered one room and a courtyard kind of place, tucked away in the corner of a narrow, labyrinthine lane of the old city. Farooqbhai sits me down on a cot where his wife is tending their newborn son. His aunt brings me a glass of tea and sits down on the floor. He brings out his diary of poems. I sip my tea and ask if he can recite the Urdu original of the poem that appeared in Ayesha's anthology.

In his shy, plaintive voice, his verses turn into beads of pain, a rosary of recollections endowed with a tenderness totally absent from the bland English translation. That's what I have come to hear—his voice, his pain, his Urdu verse.

> *Gunjayeshon ka dil ko samandar bana liya*
> *La jitna de sakey tu mujhe iztiraab de*
> *Had se guzar chuki hain mazalim ki aandhiyan*
> *Mazlumiyat ko zehniyat-e-inqilaab de*
> *Farooq, jis ko parh ke bare aadmi banen*
> *Bacchon ke haath mein koi aisi kitab de*

> Turn the heart into an ocean of possibilities,
> Give me as much restlessness as you can
> The tyrant's excesses have crossed all limits,
> Give the oppressed a mind for revolution
> Farooq, so that wise they may become
> Gift some such books into children's hands

'Why do you write poetry?' I ask.

'Why?' Farooq looks at me as if I have asked the most inane question. 'Why does any poet write poetry?'

'When do you write?'

'I'm composing all the time. Especially when I'm at the shop, new verses come to me.'

I imagine him hacking meat and bone with his chopper in his meat stall; a butcher in the land of Gandhi! I imagine him weighing rhymes and cadences of newly-forming ghazals as he weighs out meat and mincemeat for his customers. Ghazals reflecting the dignity and indignity and hopes and hopelessness of an entire community float into his passively alert mind amid the stench and flies in the large hall. I watch his timid wife with their newborn son as he recites his ghazals, and my heart fills with tears at his quiet dignity. If songs of love and lamentation could be composed by butchers in squalid, forgotten mohallas of such a divided city, who could definitively conclude that the ultimate story of civilization would be written exclusively in the language of hate and violence?

As I am leaving, I ask Farooqbhai's aunt, who has been sitting quietly by the door: 'Don't any of the women write poetry in your family?'

'Do women have time for poetry?' the aunt replies with a wry smile. Yet she had sat and listened with respectful attention to her nephew's poems, as if his words were also expressing her own sentiments.

That is at least one answer to the question I later pose for Ayesha: why are there only two women poets in her anthology? Women refused to share their poems, Ayesha says. So she accepted poems from whoever was willing to share them with her. Perhaps women were still processing the hurt, the humiliation, the shame, and it may be years before they'll begin to share it in verse, she adds. And another reason might have been more practical: women have no time for poetry. Raped, robbed, destitute and displaced, women were nevertheless expected to put up a brave front, tend the sick, the elderly, the children, rebuild wrecked homes, and provide the social glue to hold together fragile communities. Poetry can seem a luxury when there's so much else to take care of.

But there was an atypical response from the Muslim community regarding their women's rape, which Ayesha talks about at length. It was something she was shocked to notice when she visited the homes of riot victims. 'The Muslim community's response to rape and molestation victims remains absolutely atypical,' she tells me. 'The community members recognized, unprodded by any outside agency, that rape victims were not raped because they were women, but because they were Muslims—and so for their families, community, neighbourhood, rape became a non-issue.'

This is joyous news. I hope Ayesha will do a story on the modernness of this atypical response. This fact, this change in entrenched male attitudes to the phenomenon of rape, and rape's decoupling with honour or izzat, is worth documenting. A silver lining in the darkness of war and genocide. With the whole community's supportive response towards their women, and the men's refusal to acknowledge that they had been shamed or their women dishonoured, it's the women who ultimately emerge victorious. They would perhaps heal faster than rape survivors who are made to feel tainted, impure, and honourless. The most scarring aspect of rape isn't physical. It's the emotional burden that makes rape survivors prefer death over life.

~

I am sitting in Ayesha's sparsely furnished apartment. It has the feel of a college dormitory or the room of someone who has been asked to move out at short notice frequently. Books are everywhere and shoes and sandals are piled on the floor. The living room has a mattress on the floor and a cot against the wall. The door to her balcony is open and I can see the tidy rows of clothes, held in place by pegs, flapping in the afternoon breeze in neatly-stacked balconies. I can imagine a maid, or a housewife who'll come out in an hour or so to collect them, iron, fold, and neatly put away this daily load of laundry. It's an ordinary picture of middle-class life, and entirely unremarkable. Except that I know for two Muslim women to be here, in this apartment complex isn't an ordinary feat. Ayesha's not a tidy housekeeper and as I sit on one of the mattresses in her living room, I understand that Ayesha has no motivation or energy to waste on feeling snug and settled. Settledness is non-essential baggage for a vagrant trying to find her place in the constantly shifting dunes of a culture where she's made to feel like an outsider.

She had to move out of her previous apartment because her lease couldn't be renewed. The real-estate agent wanted a higher commission or he threatened to reveal her Muslim identity to the landlord. Ayesha laughs as she recounts how she dealt with him, but I can hear the hurt. After the riots, while she was still living in Baroda with her parents and siblings, they were forced out of their family home, a house where they had lived peacefully among their Hindu neighbours for years. They had to find shelter in a newly-formed middle-class Muslim ghetto. Ayesha is an elegant woman, and her intelligent, articulate speech holds an aura, adding dignity to her tall, lean attractiveness. Somehow she seems wiser, older, and wearier than a young woman in her thirties ought to look.

'And I might have to vacate this place too, but until that happens, I'm here,' she says, smiling.

I tell her about my meeting with Farooqbhai, the poet, and how grateful I was to hear him recite.

'He looks like a typical Bollywood butcher, doesn't he, but unlike Bollywood butchers he loves Urdu poetry! He shattered my stereotypes about Gujarati Muslims,' Ayesha says. 'I used to think of them as unlettered and unsophisticated. But I found it's in this community which the mainstream of Gujarat dismisses as uncultured, violent, and conservative, it's in this maligned community that the healing is happening, quietly and creatively, without resorting to any sort of retaliatory violence. I came across so many poets like Farooqbhai. I'm not saddened that they aren't getting published or their verse isn't marketed for consumption. That's not the point of writing poetry. Who'll publish them, anyway? The middle-class and upper-class elite of Gujarat, whether Hindu or Muslim, doesn't care about poetry.'

Ayesha's family's roots are in neighbouring Maharashtra

but she has lived all her life in Gujarat. Something happened in the course of her travels, and in her meetings with ordinary Muslims post-2002 and in the gathering of their grief in poetry. The experience made her finally, and self-consciously adopt a Gujarati identity in addition to her Maharashtrian one. I sense the conflicts inherent in this new love: it's not a blind love. She's deeply critical of Gujaratis in general, including Gujarati Muslims. 'Why are they tying up their goats and cattle all over the place if they have sixty-four heritage monuments in the walled city? The Muslim community needs to wake up. They need to pay attention to their own state. What are they doing for the wider dissemination of Urdu and Gujarati literature produced by Muslims of this state?'

Underpinning this new-found, mature and critical love for Gujarat and its Gujarati Muslims is all that she's lived through in the past decade, what she calls the most trying decade of her life. Post-2002 survival struggles have snatched away her dreaminess, the luxury of meandering and drifting towards other life goals.

For her it was the riots, for me it was marriage and family. We're both starting out now to wade in unknown territory, just beginning to bask in this new kind of self-exploration.

'Now when I take stock of what I did in the past ten years—only one word describes it—surviving,' Ayesha shares in an email she sends a year after our meeting. 'Those daily small battles sapped my energy and all mental resources, at the work place, outside . . . I know not if mere surviving can be called an achievement . . . hopefully I survived with some semblance of dignity and on my terms, no matter what the cost.'

The costs of self-assertion are always high, and can even be fatal. It seems like she's willing to pay the price in death and even beyond. 'I don't want to be buried in Gujarat,' she states adamantly. Elsewhere, in *Scattered Voices*, she explains: 'Like a dream home, I have a thousand times dreamt of a possible grave site for myself, and am yet to make up my mind if there ought to be a red champa tree, palash or cassia fistula nearby. While the Ides of Summer 2002 hammered in the determination to stay put in Gujarat for some years, I was equally determined that I will never ever be buried anywhere in Gujarat, inshallah.'

I am taken aback by the intensity of her feelings. Her acrid determination to have her remains not remain on Gujarati soil became stronger after she visited the site of Wali's tomb in Ahmedabad. 'The people of this state couldn't even offer the respect due to a great poet's grave. I mean the man's been dead for 300 years! Why would you want to desecrate his grave? Why would I want to be buried here?' she says.

Wali Dakhani, also known as Wali Gujarati, the father of modern Urdu poetry died in Ahmedabad in 1707. During the 2002 riots, his tomb was demolished, and a new road built overnight to conceal the spot where his mausoleum had stood for three hundred years. The tomb's site is now part of a busy street, as if it had never existed. 'I mean, look at the ironies of this place. Wali Dakhani, the father of modern Urdu poetry, chooses to come and live in

Ahmedabad and die here. Couldn't he choose some other city?' Ayesha says in dismay.

The same Wali, who like all true Sufis worshipped beauty, found no distinction between loving God's beauty and loving God's people:

Shughal behtar hai ishqbazi ka
Kya haqeeqi, kya majazi ka

Love is the most agreeable of diversions
Who cares if it be divine or worldly love?

What about Ayesha's Muslim identity which she had never so self-consciously needed to assert before the riots, but does so now. Eloquently she sums up the crisis-driven evolution of this new identity as a cultural-political identity more than a religious identity. In her austere and moving prose she writes:

'Godhra and Gujarat 2002 not only ushered in the realization of being Muslim, but also that of being a Muslim woman and what it means to be so in free India . . . strangely speaking, it is those Muslim voices (collected in *Scattered Voices*) and their poetry which made me claim Gujarat as my own after thirty-two years of living here . . . in a couple of years during the compilation (of the anthology) . . . I discovered a Gujarat in its unheard poetry, true in its love and passion for the land and its cultural milieu . . . a discovery that help[ed] an angry, tired, occasionally frightened woman realize that *she is Muslim, more in political or social terms than religious*. And as she discovers Gujarat, she comes to peace with herself . . .' [italics mine]

'It's really the love for this land, a kind of maturity I sensed in their writing that did it for me,' she says about the poets she met during her travels in Gujarat. 'Theirs is the poetry of betrayal—now where does a sense of betrayal come from? It can only come from having loved something deeply, having made a life-long commitment to it. Theirs is a love that is in many ways much, much deeper than what a Hindu feels for this place, because as a Muslim you pay such a heavy price for being here.'

~

We've been chatting during her lunch break, and it's time for her to get back to work. I ask if I can stay and read some of her books. Ayesha shows me the kitchen and all the different kinds of tea on the shelves. After she leaves, I make myself a big mug of green tea, and settle down on the mattress with the pile of books she leaves for me to look at. Achyut Yagnik and Suchitra Sheth's *The Shaping of Modern Gujarat: Plurality, Hindutva and Beyond,* makes me pull out my notebook.

Ayesha had mentioned the 'mercantile ethos' of Gujarat, which was partly responsible for the riots, and also for the pragmatism of most Gujaratis. All cultures are shaped by other cultures. But this book opens my eyes to how Gujarat's culture in particular was shaped by its geography. Gujarat owes to its coastline the development of its composite culture. The presence of a long coastline ('One quarter of India's coastline is in Gujarat') led to growth of early maritime trade with neighbouring regions, and made Gujarat's traders rich. It also brought them into close contact with Turks, Afghans, Iranians, and Arab traders, and this continued interaction over the last millennium left indelible marks on all aspects of Gujarati culture. Look at what it did to Gujarati cuisine and the Gujarati language:

> New food preparations like *jalebi*, *biranj* and *halwa* became popular . . . Persian words for dry fruits such as *badam*, *pista* and *jardalu* are so commonly used by Gujaratis that their Persian origin comes as a surprise to them. Similarly, among common fruits, *khadjur* and *tadbuj* (watermelon), *narangi* and *ananas* are local adaptations of Persian words.[2]

A few pages later, the authors reiterate the role of prolonged exchanges with other cultures that originated with Gujarat's unique geographical location within Asia and its role in the evolution of the Gujarati language:

> . . . Gujarati acquired its distinct character in the Sultanate era [starting in the late 13th century]. During the Mughal period it was further cultivated by saint poets and merchants on the other. As the court language of both the Gujarat Sultanate and the Mughals was Persian and because merchant communities had extensive linkages with Arabic-speaking West Asia, the influence of Persian and Arabic

---

[2]See Achyut Yagnik and Suchitra Sheth's *The Shaping of Modern Gujarat: Plurality, Hindutva and Beyond*, p. 13. Penguin India, 2005.

is immense and pervasive. It would not be an exaggeration to say that is is impossible to write good Gujarati without using Persian or Arabic words.

So what seems to be tearing apart the millennia-old hybridity of Gujarati culture? I wish the answer was something other than colonialism. But it isn't! According to the authors, the split is multi-factorial, but the role of British policies and their penchant for classifying Indians according to their religious backgrounds was instrumental in ultimately cleaving the Hindus and Muslims of Gujarat into mutually hostile communities, and in dismantling Gujarat's cultural compositeness. Religion that had hitherto mattered little as a social signifier, through the implementation of 'British policies—the census, elections in local self-government and separate electorates for Hindus and Muslims' write Yagnik and Sheth, 'contributed to hardening communal identities'.[3]

Surely millennia-old cultures are more resilient than that? The English colonized India for only a couple of hundred years. Could the colonial legacy of divide and rule be held entirely responsible for the virulent Muslim and Hindu communalism that thrives in Gujarat today? I explore this puzzling phenomenon through a simple and yet indirect question about that adhesive called love that cements diverse social groups.

'What's happening to love in these times?' I ask Ayesha when she gets back from work that evening.

---

[3]*The Shaping of Modern Gujarat: Plurality, Hindutva and Beyond*, p. 198.

'Love? Love has become a casualty of pragmatism,' she says regretfully. 'As Faiz said, *mujh se pehli si mohabbat mere mehboob na maang.*[4]

'It's all about survival now. There's education, careers, and marriage. So if love happens, it's almost like another career move. Even when people fall in love, they do so in a very calculated way.'

'Young people don't risk everything for love anymore?' I ask, thinking of Wali Dakhani who taught love of God or humankind as the best of all diversions to devote one's life to. What kind of an imbecile was I to forsake the luxury and guaranteed security of a marriage my family would have arranged for me, and hop on a plane with no clue to what I was rushing into? All for the sake of love? I related my elopement story in brief and asked how Hindu-Muslim romances were faring in post-2002 Gujarat. It wasn't that long ago that I had eloped, though *elopement* does sound quaint, too twentieth-century in twenty-first-century glitzy, development-crazed Gujarat. What room is there for archaic romanticism in such prosaic times?

'Hindu-Muslim romances are just not practical anymore,' Ayesha says, confirming my fears. 'Many young people say the 2002 riots took away from them a sense of innocence. When you're in college, you get into relationships, you fall in love madly, impulsively, even if you know it's not

---

[4]Faiz Ahmed Faiz, Urdu poet of the subcontinent (1911-89): Translation of above lines is roughly: My love, do not ask me to love you the way I loved you once.

necessarily going to lead to anything. You have your flings. That's what being young is all about. But there's a wariness now. Young people don't want to get into relationships if it's not going to lead anywhere. Why waste time? I had a Hindu colleague who fell in love with a Muslim man. After a while, he told her there'll be too many problems if they marry, and they won't be able to handle the pressure. So let's end it, he said, and let's just be friends. She was heart-broken but they both went on to get married to other people from their respective communities. And you know, it's not just about Hindu-Muslim relationships. This down-to-earthness now affects all kinds of relationships. People just don't talk about it.'

Why don't they talk about it?

'Whom will they talk about it with?' she says with deep pain. 'There's no space left in the culture for that sort of debate. They don't want their decisions dissected, or their inter-religious love affairs made public. They're worried about security. That's it. Security. Our neighbour's son was going around with a Hindu woman. His father found out, and without his knowledge, went to see his girlfriend's parents and informed them that his son and their daughter were in a relationship, which was not practical at all under present circumstances. They'll both get into a lot of trouble, their lives would be at risk if they married, he told them. The woman's parents thanked this Muslim man for being so understanding. And they amicably and lovingly made their daughter end her relationship with his son. She was soon married off to somebody and in time, he also got married. It was all very genteel and quiet. There was no drama of life and death played out in their break-up. But that's what's so tragic. People are now afraid to take risks for the sake of love. This is the tragedy, this is the demise that nobody is talking about. When you're young, you should be willing to explore, fall in love, doesn't matter with whom, but that instinct is dead in Gujarati youth now. It's been replaced by a cruel pragmatism.

'Why go far, look at what I did. I wasn't willing to compromise on my values. I ended my decade-old relationship after 2002.'

Ayesha's decade-old relationship started when she was still in college. He was a Gujarati Brahmin. When the riots broke out, he was abroad. He returned and suggested they get married and leave India. Ayesha refused.

'I'm not unhappy that I walked away from his offer. I don't regret it. But if you were to look at it from an absolutely romantic point of view, it's sad. I don't know if it was right or wrong. Now that ten years have passed, I can look back at that break-up dispassionately. I had so many other things to worry about then that I couldn't think of just saving my relationship. Post-2002, identity issues and politics consumed me. There was hardly any breathing space for other dimensions of life. When we started talking about getting married, he suggested moving abroad but I wasn't very comfortable with the idea of leaving. I had a young sister and a brother and their education had to be financed. I had to help my family. My parents had given me so much space and so much freedom to explore my choices. You know after graduation, I told them I wanted to do a Masters in physics, and they said, fine. Go ahead. But after one semester of physics, I said, I was bored with the subject. They said fine. What is it that you want to do? I said I don't know. I want to explore other careers. Then I somehow stumbled upon journalism. And the only thing my mother said was: "it doesn't matter which field you choose, I simply want you to excel. I don't ever want you to be number two." I couldn't betray such wonderful parents by leaving just when they needed me most. My father was getting old, he was about to retire from his job, and I couldn't expect my mother to work as hard as she always had. I wanted to buy a comfortable home for them. And this idea that let's just get away from this place, I couldn't go along with it. May be I could've married and gone abroad, or applied for asylum in some European country. But if everybody leaves, who'll stay? This is my turf. I have the advantage of familiarity, so I know how to fight my battles here, I mean in terms of strategy.'

I want to know if she would have reacted differently if there was no 2002? Listening to her, I think, love can't be sustained in toxic cultural environments. How can something as tender, as fleeting as love flower without the time, space, and cultural spaciousness needed to nurture it? 'What kind of love would grow in cramped, box-like cultural spaces marked Hindu love, Muslim love?'

'I don't know.'

Doubt is always a good response to complex questions. 'I don't know' is a good thing to say sometimes. Ayesha must've asked herself the same question countless times—what if there was no 2002? What if? What if?

'Since I made this choice in the post-2002 world, I can only talk of it in that context. And also, something else happened. We had never discussed this earlier, but we started talking about children. What will our children be? Hindus or Muslims? I said we'll keep options open. But I sensed that he was not comfortable with that idea. I don't blame him. The circumstances were such. He belongs to a very conservative Brahmin family. And I felt my identity was completely at stake. I said I'm not going to change anything about myself if we marry. Like the most fundamental things about me, my name, my religion, my politics. If there was no 2002, I might have handled the situation differently. But 2002 changed everything. He said, at least let's be friends. I said No, I don't want to be friends. I deliberately and consciously said, no, no more relationship. My mother cried more than I did. I think she felt I lost out, gave up something precious.'

'Your mother is not opposed to the idea of love?'

'No, no. Not at all. My mother narrates an old story from her Marathi textbook that she read in her school days. It's a famous story. She used to say when you grow up and fall in love, remember this story about love. My sister and I used to giggle but we only understood what she was trying to convey when we were much older. *What is love?* That was the title of the story. A young boy and a girl were in love with each other and they were also best friends. This girl is to be married off to somebody, and she has never seen her husband so she asks her best friend to go and see her husband-to-be and come back and tell her what he looks like. And this boy, because he loves her so much, agrees to go and see the man whom she's going to get married to, and comes back and gives her a description of what he saw. Now, this is love, my mother says. Whatever relationship you get into, there should always be this level of purity and total trust. So I can understand why my mother cried more when I broke up. She knew it was I who decided to walk away. And she was sad because she knew I had to muster up a lot of strength to do it. She always said love can be platonic, non-platonic, nebulous or just a vague sense. My sister and I found it very amazing that she, who was married off at sixteen herself, had such clarity about what love is and what it isn't.'

Ayesha's mother's marriage was arranged by her parents. Ayesha's father was much older than her mother. Her mother, a creative, artistic, hard-working woman, took sewing lessons and worked as a seamstress to supplement her husband's income while sending her three children to the best schools. I thought a lot about the young girl her mother was, and the young girl whose story her mother had narrated for Ayesha and her sister as an allegory of true love.

I meet Ayesha's mother when I visit Baroda, and find her charming manners infectious. There is something humble and youthful and honest about her, a quality of speech that defies age. She looks like Ayesha's older sister and as she is showing me some of the elaborate outfits she has designed and sewn for her daughters and daughter-in-law, I can see who she could've been—a fashion designer, a boutique owner, an entrepreneur, an artist. She is an eloquent and articulate woman. So this is where Ayesha gets her boundless faith and confidence from, her inexhaustible reserve of hope in the saddest of times.

~

We are sitting at a restaurant a couple of days after our first meeting. I'm thinking what is it that makes Ayesha so sure about her opinions, so rooted in the logic and material reality of her environment and the reality of losses and dislocations? And so wary of multiple interpretations of truth? Her losses have left little wriggle room for doubts or complex, multi-layered interpretations or the in-betweeness of existence. Still, I feel daunted by her unyielding certitude, having always been a somewhat tentative, doubting person myself, always cautious about reaching definite, non-negotiable conclusions about life.

Dinner is over and we are sharing a slice of cheesecake. It's quite late, past ten on a week night, and we're the only customers in the restaurant. But there seems to be no anxiety in Ayesha regarding the late hour so I too relax and we continue talking. I ask Ayesha if the fallout of pragmatism is lovelessness.

'Yes. People don't believe in devoting their lives to love anymore. In some ways there's a lot of liberalism that's replaced old-fashioned, impractical notions of love. It's all about personal freedoms now. There's a lot of talk about choices and personal rights. Everybody wants to exercise their rights. But I find that it's all very matter-of-fact and self-centred. There is no idealism left because we're living in such stressful times. Everybody is insecure about their future. I would want an element of dreaminess or impulsiveness in young people. When they're sixteen or seventeen, they're already stressing out about what they're going to do the rest of their life. I was clueless about my future at that age. I just had some vague ideas about changing the world. It's only when I got out of college that I tried to confront the practical reality of getting a job and so on. We're much more ambitious now. The drive to acquire a certain kind of lifestyle, to want to be this or that, to study at a particular college, to work for the right organization. Then marry so and so. It's the whole pressure of achieving. I don't know where we want to get by achieving so much.'

'So have you put the idea of love, companionship and marriage behind you?'

'No, not exactly shelved it. But I am very matter-of-fact about it. I'm thirty-eight. At this stage I'm not going to be a cradle-snatcher and fall for somebody in their twenties. And most of the guys who are in my age group are already married. And I don't believe in messing up a married man's life. I might fall in love at some point. I'm not ruling out love or marriage, but I'm also not actively searching. Motherhood is beautiful, to watch your children grow up. The way our mother made sacrifices for us—I find that very beautiful. That's my only regret, not having children. If I could get married to somebody who said he'll provide for me and said I didn't need to work, that would be great. I'll stay home and keep house for him.'

I smile inwardly at this charming contradiction in Ayesha's hard-nosed, sensible stance—so assertive about her politics and identity in the public sphere, and yet so compliant and willing to sacrifice it all for the romance of idealized domesticity. Was this a sort of naiveté, or a laying down of arms, a woman seeking refuge from a battlefield not of her own making, a weary soldier trekking home, hoping to find at least the homefront unchanged. As passionate, committed, and opinionated as she is, unable to compromise her values or her politics, I couldn't imagine her taking to traditions and domestic life like a water-parched fish. The passivity and self-effacing adjustments required of a stay-at-home wife and mother, the stifling monotony of married life, the suppression of passions closest to one's soul, I couldn't see Ayesha giving in to any of it. I couldn't see her living the life her mother had lived.

'The Hindu right seems as opposed to the idea of freedom to love as much as the Muslim right,' I say. 'I've paid a heavy price, really suffered emotionally for marrying whom I married. But I was clear about one thing—I wasn't going to compromise on my principles. I never judge a person by his or her religion. I went ahead with my marriage because I was clear on this one point. I was branded a kafir by my parents, told that my children will be kafir and go to hell. My in-laws had a much better attitude towards our marriage. They just wanted me not to openly assert my Muslimness when I visited Ahmedabad, but that was mostly for safety reasons.'

Ayesha and I, both of us, very principled people, had

exercised our principled stands under vastly different circumstances. Our social and politicial contexts were also different. Who knows if I were a victim of the Islamophobia, the kind she had to survive post-2002, if my loyalty as a citizen and a Muslim had been tested daily like hers is, if my being Muslim was pitted against my competence as a journalist, and my professional integrity checked repeatedly as hers had been, who knows how hard-nosed my stand in all matters including matters of the heart might have become. What would living in a place that first labelled me, and then doubted me for wearing those labels feel like? I might have hardened my identity, and refused to budge, refused to conceal or morph anything about myself.

But for me, growing up in very different times than hers, membership in an organized religion had never held much sway. At the age of fifteen, after reading the chapter on evolution in my biology textbook, I had become an atheist. Later on, I became attracted to non-theistic Buddhism. I was a Muslim Buddhist, or at other times an agnostic who sometimes thought of herself as an atheist, but most of the time I believed in God's existence, though the more I thought about God, the idea of what God is, the more undefinable and beyond perception God became for me.

Pretending to be a Hindu for a few days when I visited Ahmedabad, or taking on a Hindu name to deflect gossiping neighbours in my in-laws' apartment complex didn't cause much of an identity crisis for me. Going from Nighat to Nisha temporarily is the price you pay for living in a world full of mediocre minds, I reasoned. I was quite blasé about this whole name-switching and religion-switching business. How could these time-bound labels exclusively define something as limitless as one's faith? My parents addressed my husband as Rehman on the few occasions they met him, the Muslim name my father had chosen for him, so why did I expect my in-laws not to address me as Nisha?

What's in a name? What's in a religion? A state? A nation? A language?

Ayesha agrees with me, but times are very different now, is how she explains her attitude. 'There were so many Hindu-Muslim marriages that took place in earlier times, but well, all that was in the past, before 2002,' she says. 'People were not as frightened about such marriages. Maybe things will change again in the course of the next generation,' she adds wistfully, and I don't miss the longing in her voice for the dawning of a softer, gentler, more embracing era.

'When I read the Quran, I feel as if its ethos is one of love and justice and mutual interdependence. And above all it's about resisting oppression. The Quran advocates the sort of love that's not self-aggrandizing but involves giving up ownership, and surrendering your ego or a sense of a separate self.'

'Yes, you're right. I know we all need to loosen up. *Ham log bohot sehem gaye hain.*' And then she is silent as if re-tasting that paralysis brought on by fear. 'As a community, we've become weighed down by all kinds of fears. But maybe things will change in a decade. Every generation has to find its way out of its dilemmas.'

Her silence in that moment of reweighing is akin to her recognition that she and others had perhaps taken this identity struggle too far, and had paid dearly with their emotional lives to defend that which should need no defence in the first place. Defensiveness was a shield from those traumatic years following 2002, but it needn't be carried at all times.

When I tell her the ethos of Quran is love, she doesn't deny it. I prefer to think that the tender shoots of doubt poking their heads out of the hardness of self-preservation is a nudge in the direction of this nascent admission—*ham log bohot sehem gaye hain*. We need to loosen up, she'd said. It's only now, when I'm writing about her in an involved but detached way that I can see how hurt she still was a decade later, how hard the struggle to survive had been, and how that hurt had shaped her attitudes.

To understand everything is to forgive everything.

But I want to test how trustworthy, if at all, are the promising shoots of doubt that ultimately lead to rejection of fixedness. I ask: 'Have you thought of going beyond religion to the evolution of a global spirituality? I was thinking of the twelfth-century monk who said the perfect man is he to whom the whole world is as a foreign place. Could we think of transcending all of these divisive religious identities?'

'No, I don't think the question of identity is divisive in the first place,' Ayesha responds emphatically. 'You can't blame a religion if wars are fought in its name. You can rebel against that view, find it claustrophobic or whatever. But for me, religion means support structures. Religion gives you a framework for social norms. Any religion for that matter. I'm very sorted out as far as my religion goes because I can make a distinction between two things: culture and religion. Many of us don't understand the difference. I might curse the North Indian Muslim clerics but I'm only cursing the North Indian culture. Not Islam. To me the behaviour of North Indian men in general is insane. It makes very little difference whether they are Sikhs or Muslims or Hindus. In Gujarat, Muslim clerics are not issuing fatwas, nor are Gujarati Muslim men practising polygamy, nor are Muslim women being forced into purdah. So the Muslims of Gujarat bear little resemblance to the Muslims of North India and that's because of the cultural differences between these two regions. If culture didn't play such an important role, Muslims of Indonesia wouldn't be so different culturally from Muslims of India. Or for that matter Bangladesh, a poor Muslim country, wouldn't have such a successful family planning programme if they were not also part of a Bengali culture with a very different way of thinking about contraception than say, Pakistani Muslims. When we talk of Muslim countries, we forget that there's also a deep-rooted cultural aspect to these places which makes all of them different. It's local culture that makes each Muslim society different. We can't equate all Muslim cultures with Arab culture. When I am in Gujarat, I'm not just a Gujarati, I'm also Maharashtrian. And when I'm outside India, I represent myself as an Indian who happens to be a Muslim. So there's a plurality to my identity, and it's not an identity shaped only by my religion. I was taught to say my prayers like a Muslim so I pray in the Muslim way. That's all. In daily life, I go by what my parents taught me: they said, don't compromise on your basic values, and the rest of the world will fall into place. It's going to take time, but I don't ever give up. The moment you give up, you let somebody who wants to defeat you win. The poor-me syndrome doesn't make me a better human being. It just kills the human within me. Okay, the riots happened. But we have to move on.

'The last decade's been a painful journey. You learn the hard way. But what other way is there? I could've run away too, married the man I loved. I could've applied for political asylum in some European country. But how could I live in a country where I'd always be treated as a second-class citizen? I didn't want to do that. India is my country. I have the room to fight here. I have the tools. I have wonderful friends. My rakhi brother is a self-professed Modi fan. I don't have an older brother but this brother of mine, if he comes to know I'm in any kind of trouble, will be here in no time to help me. It would be very simple to see things as black and white, but life isn't like that. I know a little girl in my neighbourhood in Baroda who who was born during the 2002 riots, and she asked me, are all Hindus bad? But then my rakhi brother comes over and plays with her, and she doesn't even remember that he's a Hindu.'

Ayesha is friendly, she seems to enjoy my company and my probing questions. It's never difficult to keep a conversation going with her, but somehow she senses I'm not quite comfortable with her worldview, and feels I am urging her on to go beyond her fixedness, to give up hanging on to the limitations of a particular identity, hemmed in by religious, ethnic, linguistic, nationalistic boundaries.

'I'm tired of explaining myself and my religion and my allegiances to the world,' she tells me, as if I'm part of that brigade of liberals, the ones who've had it relatively easy, who haven't lived in the aftermath of communal riots, and therefore can talk about ending differences that separate and segregate groups of humans. 'There are so many other issues worth working for—land, water, the environment, issues of governance, issues of Dalits, tribals, irresponsible industrialization, domestic violence. Even saving sparrows is an important project because if there are no sparrows left, it means there'll be no trees left. The passing of fatwas by some North Indian clerics or the business of polygamy or burqa make sensational news, but they're non-issues. Farmland is being usurped through corporate expansion. That's a far more serious issue. That a few Muslim women are wearing burqas is not an issue because there aren't that many Muslim women wearing burqas to begin with. Women may wear head scarves but they're going to college, getting PhDs, becoming doctors and lawyers, working at call centres. The Muslim community is moving on with their lives. We would like to set our own agenda and not have it dictated to us.'

~

As I was adding finishing touches to this chapter, almost a year after that conversation I had with her in her Ahmedabad,

I emailed Ayesha to ask if she was finally finding the space and time to work on agendas of her own choice. I received a reply immediately. She had just returned from a poetry festival in Hyderabad, having resigned from her editorial position at the English language daily:

'I am jobless for now—having resigned against all good advice, and with no job in hand and needing one. But I am taking it easy, indulging my thoughts and am hopeful I will start a second innings in a way that I would want to, and not be dictated by circumstances as I was post 2002 in the last decade.'

I wished her well. Her survival struggles have been valiant as is her decision to opt out of the world of work to rethink and reevaluate what kind of work she would truly want to do, how she would want to live the rest of her life. The greatest jihad is the jihad one wages with one's soul. I guess we'd call it self-knowledge or self-realization in our post-modern times.

But as an aside, I must mention this. Before I left Gujarat, I met another Muslim woman whom I'd met a year earlier. After the riots, she started working for an NGO and was part of the travelling caravan of activists and civil society organizations that travelled to Allahabad, my hometown, for a day of campaigning for 33 percent reservation for women in Parliament. Saminabehn's home was looted in the riots, her husband lost his job, and they had to relocate to a Muslim slum that cropped up after 2002 in an already crowded area of old Ahmedabad. In her rented, one-room home, where she invited me to lunch, women kept dropping in, asking about their voter ID cards, their compensation cheques from the state government which many had yet to receive. When the women left, and we had a chance to sit down and eat, I asked her about Hindu-Muslim marriages.

'*Haan hoti hain na abhi bhi, kyun nahi?*' she said matter-of-factly. And related a recent case where she was asked to intervene. A Hindu woman married a Muslim man, and Saminabehn had to go bring the bride back safely after the registration ceremony took place in court. Before the media, and the woman's parents and relatives could swoop down on her to make her change her mind, she had brought the new bride safely to her new home.

'And Muslim girls, are they marrying Hindu boys?' I asked.

'*Woh bhi ho raha hai,*' she said. 'That's happening too. Now how long are people going to live with the memory of 2002? This is the tenth year after the riots.'

This is the best thing I've heard in Gujarat, I thought. Time's role as a healer. Love is an even better healer. Time and Love win against all odds!

The middle class may have become more hardheaded, more pragmatic in the stridence of globalizing economies and the ensuing identity and economic struggles and insecurities it has had to contend with. But poor Muslims of Gujarat, that doubly marginalized minority that toils and shimmers at the imprecise fringes of society, and accepts an insecure present and an equally insecure future with equal élan—for them uncertainty is something too familiar to get cowered by it. To give up the ecstasy of present love for a future predicated on pragmatism? Pragmatism is the killer of love. So they keep falling in love, keep taking risks with the wrong kind of people belonging to wrong religions, and keep the tradition of reckless love and impulsive performances of love-rites alive. Living and dying for love.

Who better than Ghalib could write of the heedless ecstasy of love?

> *Likhte rahe junon ki hikayat-e-khunchukan*
> *Harchand is mein haath hamaare qalam huey*[5]

I dared to write the blood-drenched tales of love
Even though the hand [that held the pen] was severed

---

[5]Ralph Russel: *Ghalib: The Poet and His Age*, p. 123. London: George Allen and Unwin Ltd, (1972).